SIX OF THE BEST

**Being an affectionate tribute to six of the most significant
school story writers of the 20th century**

by

David Bathurst

[signature] With very best wishes 1994

First published in 1994 by Romansmead Publications,
46 Mosse Gardens, Fishbourne, Chichester, West Sussex PO19 3PQ

ACKNOWLEDGEMENTS

I would like to extend my sincere thanks to a number of people:

All those who have kindly given permission for extracts of their works to be included. Those authors or publishers who have given me permission to quote from their commentaries are indicated by a star against the relevant book title in the bibliography at the end of this book. I would also like to thank Penguin Books who have given their permission for me to quote from the work of Angela Brazil; Anthony Buckeridge who permitted me to quote liberally from the Jennings books; Harper Collins who have permitted me to quote the extracts from the work of Elinor Brent-Dyer, Helen McClelland and Phil Redmond; and Hawk Books, who have permitted me to quote from the work of Charles Hamilton.

All those who have assisted in the preparation and publication of this book, particularly David Schutte and LR Printers. And most of all, my wife Lizzie, who has been so patient and encouraging during its preparation.

ISBN 0-9523936-0-3

British Library Cataloguing-in-Publication Data.
A catalogue record for this book is available from the British Library.

Printed in England by:
L R PRINTING SERVICES LTD
Edward Way
Burgess Hill
West Sussex RH15 9UA

CONTENTS

INTRODUCTION

Jan Mark, a contemporary writer for teenagers, claims that she had a fascination for school stories, as opposed to stories about outer space or the high seas, because she found she could relate to the characters and situations in stories of school life.

Her fascination is shared by millions around the world. While many children revel in the escapism of science fiction and adventure on the high seas, there is, and has been for over a century, a fascination for the world of school - a world with which every child, except the chronically disabled or habitual truant, can identify. The fictional classroom is your classroom. The fictional dragon of a headmistress is your headmistress. The field where the fictional First Eleven beat a neighbouring school by three goals to nil might be the field just behind your own classroom. Consequently, the demand for stories about school life has been enormous, and there has been no shortage of writers anxious to satisfy it. Some have produced immortal prose and immortal characters. Others have produced a single volume with one modest print run and have never been heard of again. Some had their names emblazoned on the spines of a seemingly endless succession of volumes; others might just merit a cursory mention at the head of a short story in a boys' paper. So much has been written, and is still being written, that a definitive overview, incorporating every known author of school stories, could never be achieved. It is hardly surprising that studies of the school story, either academic or nostalgic, have had to be selective in their analysis and specific in their objectives.

This book is no exception. To begin with, the aim was to be a kind of literary Star Trek; to boldly go where no man had gone before, and produce a definitive history of the school story. A glance, however, at the formidable lists of authors who would require study and analysis was enough to convince me that such an aim was, to take another cult sci-fi title, Mission Impossible. A more cool-headed appraisal of the situation and a careful consideration of my resources led me to a more modest and manageable objective, namely, to take a nostalgic look at the life and work of six of the most significant contributors to the school story in the twentieth century. This would enable me to study the six authors in greater depth than would be permitted by attempting to cover everybody, while still giving readers an overview of the history of the school story in my introduction to each author.

It follows, therefore, that my selection of six authors has had to be governed not only by their popularity but also by the style typified by their work. I begin with

Harold Avery, the much-loved writer of boys' public school stories in the Boys' Own Paper tradition. Next comes Charles Hamilton, master of the so-called "pop" school story, the creator of Billy Bunter, and most prolific school story writer of all time. Then it is the turn of the ladies. Firstly I take Angela Brazil, who was the pioneer of the girls' school story written from the girls' angle and portraying young women as achievers in their own right. After this I examine Elinor Brent-Dyer who created the Chalet School, famous for its location, its longevity and its progressiveness; in modern parlance, she created the girls' school soap opera. The last two writers are both male; Anthony Buckeridge, who wrote what I consider to be the funniest and best-written school stories of the century, and lastly Phil Redmond, who created Grange Hill with its realistic portrayal of life at a contemporary urban comprehensive school.

My choice is, of course, a personal one. Few would argue that Charles Hamilton and Angela Brazil, whose names are synonymous with stories of school life, deserve to be there; other choices may be the cause of rather sterner debate. My aim, however, has not been to choose the writers demonstrating the highest quality; while popularity is of course a pre-requisite to their inclusion, it is the style that they demonstrate which has dictated the selection. Their style has also, to a great extent, dictated the format of each chapter. The books of Anthony Buckeridge and Elinor Brent-Dyer, for example, have formed neat closed series, and therefore it is appropriate to provide brief synopses and quotations in the chapters devoted to them. Charles Hamilton's output was so vast as to render such an exercise absurdly impractical, and because Angela Brazil and Harold Avery wrote about so many different schools, the exercise would in their case be unrewarding.

Before embarking on this journey, two "why's" may spring to the lips of the reader -"why this book?" and "why me?" I hope that this book will bring back happy memories for those who enjoyed reading the original stories when they first appeared; that it may inspire a re-acquaintance with the stories, many of which are still available in second-hand shops; that it will provide information and enlightenment for those who are curious about the origins of those stories; that it will provide literary and social historians with more detail about this fascinating area of children's literature; and that it will assist collectors and dealers. It is not an academic study; although I have quoted from the work of academics, it is very much a book for the enthusiastic layman.

That last point leads me to deal with the second question, namely, "why me?" To answer that question, I need to go back to Christmas Day 1966, when I was just seven years old. My grandfather's Christmas present to me was a copy of Anthony Buckeridge's *Just Like Jennings*. My love affair with the work of Anthony Buckeridge began then, and enthusiasm for the work of other schools authors followed. It is this enthusiasm of almost thirty years' standing which has motivated me to go one step beyond the colourful covers and reassuring musty smell of the old books, and share with my own readers the delights that lie inside. This book will have achieved its aim if those who read it feel that even just a part of this enthusiasm and interest has been conveyed to them, and that they feel enriched and entertained by what they have read.

Please note that when discussing the authors in the text, I have used the past tense. When discussing the content of books, I have used the present tense in order to reflect the fact that the books continue to give pleasure long after being written. I have used the full names of my sources on my first referral to them in each chapter, thereafter by surnames only.

A bibliography may be found at the end of the book.

David Bathurst 1994

WHAT AN ABSOLUTE CAD!

"I've been thinking that during the summer term, and while the weather's warm, our two rooms might form a supper club. We'd hold it, say, once a week, when pocket money is given out, and have a feed together; one time in your room, and the next in ours, after every one's gone to bed. You know I saved some money at the beginning of the term to buy an engagement ring with; but I don't want it now, so I'm going to spend the tin in grub, and if you like I'll stand the first feed."

(The Triple Alliance)

What is love compared with a dormitory feast?

The first question which the reader might be forgiven for asking when commencing this chapter on Harold Avery, is "why Harold Avery?" His work is now largely forgotten, and it never achieved the phenomenal output of Charles Hamilton, the new ground broken by Angela Brazil, the longevity of Elinor Brent-Dyer, the irresistible style of Anthony Buckeridge or the down-to-earth common touch of Phil Redmond. Yet his robust tales of public school life could be said to typify an art form which was flourishing during the early part of this century.

Although tales of public school life had been published spasmodically from the end of the eighteenth century onwards, it was only in the last quarter of the nineteenth century that public school stories for teenage boys began to appear in large numbers. It was the publication of two famous works in the late 1850's which provided the first significant step towards the revolution that was to come. These were *Tom Brown's Schooldays* by Thomas Hughes in 1857, and *Eric Or Little By Little*, by F.W.Farrar, in 1858. Both books, which became best sellers, were of a "didactic" nature, that is to say, they were underpinned with strong moral messages, exposing many of the evils of boarding-school life. Humphrey Carpenter and Mari Prichard described *Tom Brown's Schooldays* as portraying "English public school life realistically, with all its unpleasantness, and at the same time (driving) the narrative along with moral fervour and Christian idealism." Ian Ousby described *Eric* as "heavily moralistic." During the 1860's and 1870's more school stories in similar vein were published in book form, although none of them caught the public imagination in quite the same way as *Tom Brown* or *Eric*, and almost all of them were turgid and heavy. Published in unappetising hardback, they had little obvious entertainment value for the children at whom they were supposedly aimed.

Alongside the didactic work that followed *Tom Brown* and *Eric*, there was through the middle of the nineteenth century a growth in the publication of cheap periodicals known as Penny Dreadfuls. These were so called because of the far-fetched and often rather tasteless material they contained. They frequently used schools and their excesses as subjects. At first they were not exclusively aimed for the juvenile market, but from the beginning they had young readers, and it was a recognised editorial technique to try them out on the publisher's office boy! An example of the material available to youngsters at the time was *The Wild Boys of London*. This was certainly not ideal juvenile reading; set in the London sewers, the adventures involved body-snatching doctors, ravishings, corpses and a bare-breasted woman being flogged. A reprint was stopped by the police. However, it could not be disputed that these periodicals were being enjoyed by youngsters, and the publishers therefore set out to create a more respectable type of Penny Dreadful for children. As a result, there evolved from the traditional Penny Dreadful a long string of magazines designed ostensibly to wean the young from "unhealthy" reading. The first issue of such a periodical was proud to proclaim that "our aim is to enthral you by wild and wonderful *but healthy* fiction" (my italics). In 1866 Edwin J.Brett, who had already established himself as a Penny Dreadful entrepreneur, launched *Boys of England* which promised to be "a hearty, free and trusty companion." In 1867 W.L.Emmett, who had also published full-blooded Penny Dreadfuls, founded *Young Gentlemen's Journal*, again apparently more healthy and edifying than those periodicals for which he had been known before. School serials became a popular feature, although the influence of the traditional Penny Dreadful was still quite evident; one of the first to appear in this new generation of watered-down Penny Dreadfuls was George Emmett's *The Boys of Bircham School*. In 1875 Charles Fox joined the circulation war between Emmett and Brett, with his *Boys' Standard*. A fierce battle for customers continued to rage between the three publishers for most of the last quarter of the century. Indication of the keenness of the desire to attract custom from rival magazines was clear. Brett offered competition prizes for purchasers, and although those prizes were hardly glamorous - they included 50 spaniels and 50 pairs of ducks - they lured to the magazine racks and shelves even youngsters who had not previously been captivated by the adventures of Ned Nimble, or the Pupils of Pickleton Priory, or Peeping Tom and Knowall Dick.

The overall content was scarcely less racy than that of the definitive Penny Dreadfuls. Indeed, those who over one hundred years later were calling for a return to Victorian ideals seemed to be overlooking frequent references in the stories to harsh physical punishment, and the existence of characters in the stories who rejoiced in such names as Scarum, Stingboys, Bircham and even Hackchild. When the boys were not bending over for yet another flogging, they were undergoing intrepid adventures at which current comprehensive pupils could only marvel. One of the most celebrated heroes, who appeared in *Boys of England*, was Jack Harkaway. When not taking on the school bully at boxing, or confusing schoolmasters by ventriloquism, he might be at sea or, even better, watching a man being eaten by cannibals. Carpenter and Prichard identified "hags and desperadoes, foreign villains, heirs cheated of their inheritance, sadistic drunken schoolmasters, torture, sex (up to a point) and cliché."

Between 1867 and 1900, eighty weekly or monthly boys' periodicals, in the same vein as *Boys of England*, were launched. Robert J Kirkpatrick was in no doubt as to their influence: "The school story genre perhaps owes more to them, as being the true progenitors of the popular school story, than has previously been recognised." As we shall see in a moment, the Penny Dreadfuls and the papers they spawned did have their critics, but it was indeed as an indirect result of them that the boys' public school story emerged as popularised by Harold Avery and his contemporaries, with many themes common to these "new generation" Penny Dreadfuls. Charles Hamilton and several of *his* followers were to turn out literature which bore an even closer similarity to their infamous predecessors.

Unfortunately, as has been said, not everybody welcomed their advent. The *Quarterly Review* deplored the Penny Dreadfuls, describing the material as "....foul and filthy trash (which) circulates by thousands and tens of thousands amongst lads who are at their most impressionable period of their lives, and whom the modern system of purely secular education has left without ballast or guidance." More significantly for us, there was another body which was most concerned about the harmful influence of these periodicals. That body was the Religious Tract Society, which had a long history of publications for children. In 1871 it began to issue a shilling volume for the "younger members of Christian families" to offset the effect of Penny Dreadfuls. The volume was not entirely successful in winning back the Penny Dreadful readers, and so towards the end of the same decade it was decided to begin a weekly paper for boys containing stories and articles of all types without pushing the religious aspect too hard.

The paper was, of course, the *Boys' Own Paper*, or the *BOP* as it was popularly known. It was entirely natural that school stories would appear in it; the popularity of the school stories in the Penny Dreadfuls, which had in turn been inspired by the popularity of *Tom Brown* and *Eric*, was ample evidence that youngsters liked to read about school life. The task of the *BOP* writers was to produce more edifying and uplifting school stories devoid of the excesses which were such a feature of the existing material, but at the same time not so heavy and moralistic that they became uninteresting to the young reader.

It is easy to see why public schools became the almost exclusive setting for such stories, even though many of the *BOP* readers would never be able to afford to darken the doors of such establishments. The ethos of public schools, which had increased in number quite considerably during the era of Dr Arnold, embraced many virtues, eminently compatible with muscular Christianity, which the *BOP* writers were only too keen to encourage in their readers. Indeed, by presenting in its school stories such a code of values at a time when jingoism was rife and the British Empire was at its height, and stressing the moral values which had helped to make Britain great, the *BOP* captured well the buoyant patriotic national spirit and thereby showed a high degree of entrepreneurial shrewdness. The fact that boys who did not attend a public school would also enjoy the material was, in the words of Kirkpatrick, "a testament to the power of their imagery and the attractiveness of their... idealised world." The very first issue of the *BOP* actually began with a school story, entitled "My First Football Match, by an Old Boy." The author was one Talbot Baines Reed, who developed the serial school story within the paper, and who had a number of his stories published in book form, the most famous being *The Fifth Form at St Dominics*. Leaving aside the satirical *Vice Versa* by F Anstey which had appeared in 1882, and which does not fit easily into the genre which forms the basis of this chapter, *St Dominics* proved to be the first real attempt to entertain schoolboy readers in book form with fiction about everyday school life.

A study of Harold Avery could not be undertaken without understanding the philosophy behind the works of Reed. Significantly, Reed, while anxious to combat the damaging effect of the Penny Dreadfuls,

The illustration leading into the first chapter of another Harold Avery yarn.

also reacted strongly against the sentiments of Hughes and Farrar. Instead he expressed the positive qualities of public school life, in full sympathy with the ethos of the *BOP* which was to promote a sympathetic understanding towards boyhood and its concomitant pursuits and pleasures. It was thus that out went the condemnatory outrage of Thomas Hughes (to be revived to a certain extent by Rudyard Kipling in his *Stalky & Co* in 1899) and in came, in novel form, a highly idealised and romanticised vision of the English public school. As John Rowe Townsend wrote of Reed: "he was content to produce solid, readable and not oppressively didactic stories on acceptable themes." P.W.Musgrave wrote that *The Fifth Form at St Dominics* as well as other school stories written by Reed, "very soon defined readers' expectations of what a school story should be." In his book *From Brown To Bunter*, a number of distinctive characteristics were identified. These will be discussed at length later in the chapter, but it is as well to allude to them in outline at this point. First, the stories were told and read from the viewpoint of boys. Secondly, they were about hierarchically organised public schools incorporating widely accepted values with a strong Christian ethos, with the character of the hero or heroes being developed for the good. Thirdly, boyish pursuits such as japes, pranks and games (including sporting activity) were prominent throughout. The direct, active Christianity which Reed advocated in his *BOP* stories had far greater appeal for boys from every social background, and the type of character depicted by Reed as admirable, with his high-spirited enthusiasm, lively mind and sporting instincts, was willingly accepted by his readers. It was suggested by Frank Eyre that Reed had brought the school story to a perfection of unreality that subsequent writers could only imitate. It would, as we shall see, be left to Charles Hamilton to develop the school story in another, less conventional direction. His type of story, described as the "pop" school story, will be considered in the next chapter.

There was no shortage of writers, many of them schoolmasters, who were willing to attempt to copy Reed, and this perfection of unreality, themselves. All the commentators seemed to agree that Reed was responsible for the blossoming of the school story for boys, establishing for it a conventional framework within which virtual indefinite repetition by other writers was possible. Eric Quayle, a keen connoisseur of schoolboy literature, recalled looking along his own shelves and reminding himself of a diversity of talent amongst a wide variety of titles and authors which almost without exception had long since sunk without trace, their only monument being the names gold-blocked on the spines of the stories the authors had hopefully penned.

Some authors, in fairness, wrote stories which, in the same vein as *Tom Brown* and *Eric*, set out to make a serious point or put across a serious message rather than primarily to entertain. Rudyard Kipling's *Stalky & Co* has already been referred to; described by Carpenter and Prichard as a "sympathetic portrayal of schoolboy sins and pranks" it set out to highlight many of the more unacceptable aspects of school life and demonstrate that "wily and even virtually criminal behaviour in a schoolboy can develop his ingenuity and strength of character, and these can be put to a worthy use later in life." This book, which appeared in 1899, was followed by Desmond Coke's *The Bending of a Twig* in 1906, and Alec Waugh's *The Loom of Youth*, both aiming to show what school was "really" like; H.A.Va-chell's *The Hill* in 1905 was the first major attempt to explore love between schoolboys.

It is difficult to know where to begin when considering those who wrote popular schoolboy fiction in the style of Reed. One might start and finish with P.G.Wodehouse; although he is best known for Jeeves and Blandings, his school stories for boys showed a future genius at work. The more devoted student, however, must inevitably turn to the many authors whose entire lifetime's output was given over to writing school stories for boys which embodied the ideals of Reed. The combined output of such authors was vast; Robert Arthur Hanson Goodyear, John Edward Gunby Hadath, Hylton Cleaver and Charles Harold Avery all produced more than thirty full-length school stories during the first half of the twentieth century. It is Charles Harold Avery, always known as simply Harold Avery, and acknowledged by commentators as one of the foremost disciples of Reed, to whom it is now appropriate to turn.

It is true that Avery was one of a multitude, and a commentator on the early twentieth century literary scene would argue that any one of the writers alluded to above might have been acceptable in the context of this chapter. Avery, however, stood out as a major contributor. He was particularly prolific as a school story writer, writing almost fifty full-length school stories, producing more work of this nature than almost all of his contemporaries. Whilst no work of Goodyear or Hadath appeared during the Victorian or Edwardian eras, Avery's first book appeared in 1895 and his last in 1938. He thus brought this genre into the twentieth century, beginning at a time when it was flourishing, and indeed still growing, but ending at a time when it was on the decline and the generation of so-called "pop" school stories pioneered by Charles Hamilton was more prevalent. It can thus be said that Avery guided the traditional boys' school story through its peak years of popularity. What was also significant was that he managed to combine the spirit, enthusiasm and morals of Reed with an ethos that was not specifically Christian, thereby proving himself more than acceptable to children who wished to be entertained in preference to being morally enriched. Moreover, his stories were recognised as entertaining, lively, cheerful, warm-hearted, reasonably true to life, well written, and reflecting the exhilarating side of boarding-school life. For these reasons, Avery could be said to give the perfect insight into the "respectable" popular school story for boys, as it was at the start of the twentieth century - the school story steeped in conventions given to it by Talbot Baines Reed.

Harold Avery was born in 1867, in Headless Cross, near Redditch, Worcestershire. His father was William Avery, a local justice of the peace. His early education took place at Dunheved College, Launceston, and the Midland Collegiate School, Birmingham. Like Anthony Buckeridge, who a century later was still writing school stories which were classics of their time, he continued his education in Sussex, at New College, Eastbourne. His education was completed at a large day-school in Dresden, Germany. From early in his life, he decided he wanted to be a writer. He began writing stories as a small boy, and for a time during his early schooldays, he organised and edited a handwritten "magazine" which circulated among his friends and relatives. He wrote his first story for boys in 1884, but it was not until the early 1890s that his short stories began to be published regularly. The periodical in which they appeared was *Young England*, a boys' paper. His first book was entitled *The School's Honour*, published in 1895 by the Sunday School Union, a collection of short stories and a modest 192 pages in length. In the same year he wrote a book of 279 pages en-

"Hullo, Denston - just the man I've been looking for."

titled *An Old Boy's Yarns* published by Cassell. However, it was a serial that he wrote for the *BOP* in 1896 which established him as a first-class writer of boys' schools fiction. It was entitled *The Triple Alliance* and was so well received that it was published in book form by T.Nelson & Sons. It ran to several editions, proving very popular as a school and Sunday school prize. According to Brian Doyle, the book really established him as one of the foremost authors of the Reed-inspired boys' school story. Although Avery wrote many adventure stories and also adult novels, it was at school story writing that he excelled, and it was this that constituted the majority of his output over the next forty years. A list of all his school stories in book form is given at the end of the chapter. Some were very lengthy - *Heads or Tails*, for instance, was an incredible 496 pages. T.Nelson & Sons published just under half of them, with Collins and S.W.Partridge securing the majority of those that remained. One of his books, *A Fifth Form Mystery*, was published by the *BOP*.

During the editorship of Arthur Haydon on the *BOP* between 1912 and 1924, he was a regular and much loved contributor to that paper, and indeed wrote for the *BOP* over a period of roughly a quarter of a century. He also wrote for *The Captain*, *Chums* and many other juvenile papers and annuals. He did not stay with one fictional school but invented new ones all the time. Although writing occupied him on a full-time basis, he found time to get married (to a rector's daughter) and was a keen sportsman and good hockey player. Despite having attained the age of 47 he joined the Army at the outbreak of the First World War, and served throughout the war with the Worcestershire Regiment. He died in September 1943 having spent most of his life in Evesham - also in Worcestershire - and achieved the distinction of an appearance in *Who's Who* for his contribution to the world of boys' fiction.

It is now appropriate to examine the aspects of Avery's writing which demonstrated his conformity to the conventions of the boys' public school story for boys. It will be noted, as the reader continues through this book, that several of these aspects will be reflected in the work of other writers.

Firstly one should consider Avery's determination to tell the story from the pupils' angle, empathising with them through the ups and downs of their school life. Where better to begin than in the language used by them. There is a goodly helping of schoolboy slang throughout, and there are numerous conversational snatches which have become the butt of many satirists in the past hundred years. Even if one has no interest in the plot or the welfare of the characters, one can at least enjoy the speaking parts. Re-reading the books almost a century later, it is hard to believe that there was no satirical or tongue-in-cheek element in the following pieces of dialogue.

"But seriously, I should think Roost must have been a bit off his onion."

(The Cock-House Cup)

"Matter," he moaned. *"Feels as if I'd sat on a hedgehog. All right, Tiber; I'll give you fizz-balls, see if I don't."*

(The Cock-House Cup)

"Oh, Diggy, she is a trump!"

(The Triple Alliance)

"Saved!" whispered Jack Vance, in an ecstasy of delight as the Philistines trooped back through the double doors. *"That was old Phillips. I hope he gives Noaks a jolly good 'impot....' The wonder is he hasn't killed some one before now. I don't see how it's possible for the Philistines to show up well when they've got a chap like him bossing the show."*

(The Triple Alliance)

"I say, Diggy," exclaimed Jack Vance, "you are a corker!" and the bell now commencing to ring for evening preparation, the meeting terminated.

(The Triple Alliance)

The stranger vanished in the darkness, and Diggory dropped down from the wall. "Here's a pretty go!" he remarked.

(The Triple Alliance)

"Pshaw!" returned the other. "Look here, I've half a mind to give you two a jolly good 'impot' to keep you out of mischief."

(The Triple Alliance)

There, sure enough, at the back desk of all, sat the late leader of the Philistines, with a rather sheepish expression on his face, somewhat similar to the one it had worn when the marauders from Horace House had been ushered into Mr Welsby's study. Jack Vance looked at Mugford, and Mugford looked at Diggory. "Well, I'm jiggered!" whispered the latter, and once more returned to his examination paper.

(The Triple Alliance)

"Oh, good business!" cried Gerald, flushing. "Thanks awfully, John. You're a brick!"

(Head of the School)

"I say," began the ex-chairman of the meeting breathlessly, "what a rotten idea this is of Vlair's! I've always said he was cracked. You two fellows be sure and turn up to-morrow night. It'll be a rare old lark, though don't you go telling him I said so."

(Head of the School)

"Look here, Eggy, it's rot that the whole place should be humbugged about by Pasnett. It's going too far."

(Head of the School)

"Then you know who did it? Faugh! what a stink! What on earth have they been up to?"

(The Dormitory Flag)

"Rather a cute dodge, isn't it?" he answered, forcing a laugh. "We've been gulling lots of chaps that way. Awful spree; but don't say anything."

(The Dormitory Flag)

"Pooh!" exclaimed Fisher, when the deserter had gone out of earshot. "Let him go if he wants to; the thing is, he's too big to have anything to do with us now that he's in Remove. Beastly shabby I call it."

(The Dormitory Flag)

"You talk about winning the flag," shouted Boxer; "you might win a duck in a raffle, but that's all you're good for, you old jam-roll!"

(The Dormitory Flag)

"Oh, kick and frizzle me!" cried 'Candles', and with this strange exclamation of

disgust he sat down to his uncongenial task.

(The Dormitory Flag)

"No, you won't!" answered the other. "I'd settle your hash any day, you moon-faced cuckoo!"

(A Toast Fag)

"Liar," he muttered. "Beastly cad; I'll pay him out if I get the chance, see if I don't."

(Day Boy Colours)

"You blazing fool! Did you prig anything?"

(Day Boy Colours)

"Leave him alone," said Martin. "Ludmoor's down and out. He knows he's been shown up as an absolute rotter, and you may be sure he'll sing small in future."

(Day Boy Colours)

"I should like, some day, to play against Tenderton, and make a hundred, not out. What a squasher it would be for Sands Major. Heigho! I'll stroll over to the pav. and find out what's the score."

(The Enchanted Bat)

"I say, 'Sappy', I haven't got a bat."

"Holmes - bowled Chapman," came back the monotonous croak.

"Look sharp, 'Crockery,' you're in next."

(The Enchanted Bat)

Avery's keenness to tell the story from the point of view of the boys means that not only is there plenty of choice schoolboy language and terminology to enjoy, but also there is no shortage of what might be regarded by adult

Were strolling across the quad.

- 17 -

readers as inconsequential and rather childish incident. Although this is of no direct relevance to the plot, it is tremendously important and exciting to the boys Sporting activity will be dealt with in more detail below, but worthy of consideration at this point is what might be called jolly schoolboy japing or ragging, including pranks, daredevilry, games and contests, as well as both strong friendship and intense rivalry between groups of boys. Angela Brazil, as we shall see, regarded a girls' school as a "state in miniature", and Avery, like many other authors, was supremely skilful at providing a new world for its readers where pupil power was everything, and where seemingly insignificant things took on almost a cosmic importance. As he wrote in *The Dormitory Flag*:

People may laugh at the smallness of a schoolboy kingdom, and the triviality of its affairs; yet it has its duties and responsibilities which have been the means of preparing British schoolboys as nothing else could for the positions of trust which they were destined to occupy in after years, either at home or maybe in that larger England beyond the seas.

The Triple Alliance, published in 1899, has barely started before we read of the first schoolboy frolic, this one in the snow:

Acton, however, had decreed that "some one had got to go down that slide on skates," and it seemed only meet and right that if a victim had to be sacrificed it should be a new boy rather than an old stager.
"Bravo!" cried the dux; "here's one chap at least who's no funk. Put 'em on sharp; the bell'll ring in a minute." Several willing hands were stretched out to assist in arming Diggory for the enterprise, and in a few moments he was assisted to the top of the slide.
"All right!" he said; "let go!"
The spectators held their breath, hardly daring to watch what would happen. But fortune favours the brave. The adventurous juvenile rushed down the path, shot like an arrow through the doorway, and the next instant was seen ploughing up the snow in the playground, and eventually disappearing head first into the middle of a big drift. His companions all rushed down in a body to haul him out of the snow. Acton smacked him on the back, and called him a trump; while Jack Vance presented him on the spot with a mince-pie, which had been slightly damaged in one of the donor's many tumbles, but was, as he remarked, "just as good as new for eating."

A further example of classroom capers from the same book involves a scenario upon which local education authorities today would cast a baleful eye:

One young gentleman sitting close to the blackboard cried, "Powder, sir!" and straightway scrubbed his neighbour's face with a very chalky duster. The latter, by way of retaliation, smote the former's pile of books from the desk on to the ground - a little attention which was immediately returned by boy number one; while as they bent down to pick up their scattered possessions, a third party, sitting on the form behind, made playful attempts to tread upon their fingers. Two rival factions in the rear of the room were waging war with paper darts; while a small, sandy-haired boy, whose tangled hair and disordered attire gave him the appearance, as the saying goes, of having been dragged through a furze-bush backwards, rapped vigorously with his knuckles upon the master's table.

(The Triple Alliance)

If it is not blackboard dusters, it is jets of water:

The fact was that Maxton, ever a reckless young villain, had discovered a hose fixed to one of the mains close to the building, and had immediately seized upon it as an instrument wherewith to wreak vengeance on his companions for having turned him out of the meeting. Words cannot describe the uproar and confusion which followed. As one man the whole assembly made for the door, but only to find it fastened on the outside. The water flew all over the small building, drenching every one in turn. Some howled, some laughed, and only Bibbs had sufficient presence of mind to creep under the sink....

(The Triple Alliance)

Nothing is sacred - whether it is waistcoat buttons or seances:

With a violent effort he shook off the restraining hands, and plunged into the aisle between the blocks of desks, minus two buttons torn from his waistcoat. An instant later he trod on a round ebony ruler which had fallen on the floor, his feet flew from under him, and down he came as if playing the classic game of 'Musical Bumps.'

(The Cock-House Cup)

Boxer had been admitted to one of their private seances, but had behaved so irreverently that he had aroused the wrath of his entertainers, who turned him out, neck and crop, into the passage, and never allowed him to witness another performance.

(The Dormitory Flag)

It seems that japing is Boxer's speciality:

"Well, we've had too many of your larks lately. Only the other day you were kicking up a beastly row riding a bicycle in one of the classrooms."

(The Dormitory Flag)

The foe, however, were prepared and waiting, and at the first glimpse of the advancing host the staircase was swept with a heavy fire of pillows, brushes, slippers and other missiles. For a moment the forlorn hope wavered; then Boxer, ducking his head, and armed with a tennis shoe which he brandished as though it were a short Roman sword, charged gallantly up the stairs with his comrades at his heels.

(The Dormitory Flag)

The centre of a jovial scrummage.

Not a term goes by without some midnight feasting:

"I wonder," said Morris... "how it is that it's always much jollier having a feed when you ought not to than at the proper time. For instance, eating this pork pie at a table, with knife and fork and a plate, wouldn't be a quarter the fun it is like we're doing now - cutting it with a razor out of Acton's dressing-case, and knowing that if we were cobbed we should get into a jolly row."

(The Triple Alliance)

Practical joking can take on sophisticated forms, as this extract from *The Fall of Jericho* shows. We are told of...

...A stag's head tie-pin, to which was attached a thin rubber tube with a ball at the end. The last-named portion of the apparatus having been concealed beneath the waistcoat, it was possible, with a sudden pressure of the arm, to cause a thin stream of water to squirt out of a small hole in the centre of the head, the result being rather startling, not to say unpleasant, for the unsuspecting victim...

Then there is the good old-fashioned catapult:

"Why, I took it into class one morning, and fired a preserved cherry at Gunberry's head. It bounced off and hit the blackboard, and burst in the middle of a big algebra sum old Trummel was working out - and he gave me about four million lines."

(Told in the Train)

The following sounds a most painful fate for the victim:

"What's up!" spluttered Gulpin. "Why, some silly ass has filled my box chock-full of dumb-bells!"

(The Dormitory Flag)

Life is not made easy for the new recruits; although they may be spared the bullying excesses of Flashman in Tom Brown's Schooldays they may be made the victim of the japer's perennial standby, the apple-pie bed:

He kicked and struggled, but try as he would he could not find his way down between the sheets, and his knees remained doubled up in the neighbourhood of his chin.

(A Toast Fag)

Bang! Bang! Bang!

They may be sent on fools' errands:

"I say," he began hurriedly, *"don't bother any more about those 'Greenem'*
Examples.'"
"Why not?"
"Why, because there isn't such a thing. They send every new kid after them, but it'.
all a hoax."

(A Toast Fag

Or they may just be made to look a complete idiot:

"What do you mean by calling me 'Sawdust', you cheeky young imp?"
"I was told it was your name."
"Well, it isn't!" shouted the red-haired boy. *"My name's Thomson. Now just hoo*
it!"

(A Toast Fag,

In *Head of the School* japing includes exploits with catapults, dormitory high-
jinks involving an allegedly sleepwalking dummy, and others:

"I don't know who invented it, but it had quite a rage once. You chucked an old
tennis ball on to the roof of the laundry, and when it came down the fellow who was
in whacked it with a straw hat."
And:
In a few moments the two combatants were blindfolded and placed at opposite
ends of the open space which ran down the centre of the room between the two rows
of beds. Gerald stood with his back to the window, and Upridge within two feet of
the door, each armed with his pillow, and awaiting the signal to advance until, as they
came within striking distance, the fray would begin.

An ability to improvise and to work off surplus energy imaginatively can be useful
in a crisis. Heroism, sparkling initiative and derring-do are commonplace:

"I said, 'look here, Joe Crump, you let me out, there's a good chap.' But he wouldn't,
he was afraid of what young Noaks would do to him. At last I gave him a shilling
through the crack of the boards, and vowed I wouldn't say who'd done it, and then
he undid the door. I fastened the padlock again, and threw the key into the hedge...
after that I got round through two other fields into the lane, and here I am."

(The Triple Alliance)

(Inexplicably, there is no subsequent mention of boxes of Cadbury's Milk Tray!)

Heroic acts of rescue receive full recognition:

"Oh, Egerson, 'twas good of you!" gasped Mabel. "And I never knew you'd gone until Shad ran in just now and said Patch had been found. How can I thank you enough!"

(Head of the School)

Games and contests as well as initiatives and projects can take on elaborate forms as the boys attempt to imitate the workings of the adult world. One delicious extract from *The Dormitory Flag* recounts how some boys write a magazine which contains its very own gossip column:

An Evening Breeze Whispers -
That Fisher minor has washed below high-water mark.
That this unusual proceeding was done by order of Fisher major.
That Aymes has no intention of entering for the Ramsay Scholarship.
That certain gentlemen always carry match-boxes.
That they have been known to come to class eating cachous.
That the contents of Duncan's birthday hamper were not confined to jam and cake.

Subsequent costly libel actions are not related!
Imitating adult behaviour extends to boys forming alliances and friendships to consolidate their position, and placing a show of solidarity against those who would threaten it, even to the extent of dispensing justice in hastily-arranged court sittings. Hence the frequent bonds of strong friendship and loyalty between boys, the rivalry and infighting, and mock court hearings.

"It's awfully jolly," retorted Boxer. "We're going to have fine larks here when we've started our society. We'll call it the 'Free Companions.' And now I vote we sit down and drink to its success in a flowing bowl." As already stated, the 'flowing bowl' took the form of three empty jam-pots. The weather was too warm for a hot drink; so in accordance with Tom Webster's suggestion, the cocoa was mixed in cold water procured from the stream, with a half tea-spoonful of sherbet added to give it a 'sparkle.'

(The Dormitory Flag)

"And now we three must swear to be friends, and stand by each other against all the world, and whatever happens."

(The Triple Alliance)

He turned, and taking something out of the biscuit-tin, said solemnly, "I, Diggory Trevanock, do hereby declare that the association known as the Triple Alliance is now dissolved; in token of which I break this bit of flat ruler, used by us as a sugar-spoon, into three parts, one of which I present to each of the members as a keepsake, to remind them of all our great deeds and many adventures."

(The Triple Alliance)

"Anyone who wishes to join 'The Raiders' can meet me in the cellar after dinner, and sign the roll in his own blood. There will be a small charge of sixpence entrance-fee to cover the secretary's out-of-pocket expenses."

(Head of the School)

With friendship as solid as this, feuding and fierce rivalry can never be far behind

Grundy was nearly a head taller than Vance; but the latter's blood was up, and in another moment the dogs of war would have assuredly broken loose had not the flutter of a gown at the end of the passage announced the advent of Mr Greyling.

(The Triple Alliance)

The feud continues a few pages later:

Once more the combatants approached each other, this time with a little more feinting and dodging, which showed a certain amount of respect for the weight of each other's fists. At length, urged on to further feats of arms by impatient ejaculations of "Now, then, go into it!" and "Keep the game alive!" from Fletcher and Anderson, they closed again, and after a sharp interchange of rather random pounding, Jack smote his opponent on the nose....

Things are no more peaceful at the King's School:

A dozen members of the Upper Fourth were drawn into the fray; day-boys and boarders formed themselves into a sort of blind scrummage, a joyful rough-and-tumble in the course of which two fountain pens and the glass of Page's watch were broken. Both sides claimed a victory; there was no bad blood, though Hampson declared that someone had bitten his ear - a complaint which was received with shouts of laughter.

(Day Boy Colours)

Loss of friendship can be painful:

His behaviour during the past five or six weeks had caused him to lose caste with the great men of Bridgewood.

(Head of the School)

Rivalry with other schools is of course also particularly intense:

"My eye," cried the dux, "won't the Philistines be wild! Fancy upsetting them in the mud, and knocking Bernard's wind out! They won't be in a hurry to meddle with us again. Well done, Diggy!"

"It wasn't I alone," said the author of the enterprise; "we did it between us - the Triple Alliance."

"Then three cheers for the Triple Alliance!" cried Acton.

The company shouted themselves hoarse, for everyone felt that the honour of the Birches had been retrieved, and the day was still far distant when they would be crushed beneath the iron heel of young Noaks, or be exposed as an unresisting prey to the ravages of the wild hordes of Horace House.

(The Triple Alliance)

But when it comes to resolving the disputes that arise, justice will take its own majestic and impartial course:

"I know what we'll do - have a trial. I'll be judge. Make that chap prisoner, and bring him before the court. The charge against him is that he's just told a blooming lie." The idea caught the fancy of the assembly, and the leading role of the judge having been secured by Pollard, there was a rush to claim minor parts. A sprightly youth named Searl proclaimed himself counsel for the prosecution, while Reeves asserted that he had been briefed to appear for the defence. Seven fellows crowded on to a front desk, and announced that they were the jury, while three stalwarts volunteered to act as warders, and took the prisoner in charge.

(Day Boy Colours)

The mock trial leads us neatly to the second major trait in the Avery-type school story, which is the unwritten code of conduct which governs the behaviour of the characters. Avery made this code very evident to his readers through slipping some acts of caddishness, bullying or beastliness into the action, either as his main plot or a sub-plot. Sneaking is the ultimate sin; fair play, sportsmanship and honour the ultimate virtues; the happy endings that the stories inevitably produce represent a triumph of virtue over evil, and honour over dishonour; younger boys look up to older boys; and authority is there to be respected, with misdemeanours leading to both the expectation and acceptance of punishment, the innocent often suffering for the guilty. It is small wonder that Avery's books were regarded as eminently suitable to be given as school or Sunday school prizes, or merely presents for children; second-hand copies of his books will often have a colourful plate in the front bearing the name of the lucky (and quite possibly now deceased)

recipient. This writer's copy of *The Dormitory Flag* contains a plate dated Decem
ber 1929 indicating that the Rayleigh Corps of the Salvation Army presented the
book to Ronald Cole who "for good conduct, diligence and regular attendance
obtained 104 Marks out of a possible 104."

Avery would have been delighted to know that a book of his was to be reward
for Ronald Cole's devotion to duty, for evidence of a similarly rigorous code o
conduct, with rewards for adherence and punishment for disobedience, abound:
right through his books. Beginning with sin, nothing is more unattractive in a boy
than a propensity for "telling on" others:

*He was a horrid fellow; every one longed to kick and punch him, but refrained from
doing so, knowing that he would have at once sneaked to the headmaster.*

(Robinson's Conquest,

"Then, in the first place, why didn't you tell me all this before?"

*"We were afraid to, sir," faltered Jack Vance, "and we thought it would be
sneaking."*

*"Dear, dear," exclaimed the headmaster impatiently, "when will you boys see things
in a proper light? You think it wrong to tell tales, and yet quite right that innocent
people should suffer for things done by miserable cowards!"*

(The Triple Alliance)

*"I'd have made the beast own up, jolly quick, if I'd been in your place. However,
you're a bit of a sportsman, I must say, to hold your tongue." (Head of the School)*

*Then Fisher turned, and picking up his watch, departed, growling out a number of
fresh threats as to what he would do if Sims 'sneaked.'*

(The Dormitory Flag)

The more positive aspects of observance of the code include respect for fair play:

*It was not fair that the reputation of a whole community of good fellows should be
lowered when one person had it in his power to show that they were in no way to
blame.*

(Day Boy Colours)

*"Gentlemen, however low Ronleigh may have sunk, there is still, I believe, left
among us a certain amount of love of fair play, and therefore I ask you to give me a
hearing...."*

(The Triple Alliance)

*When a boy was 'hauled,' the proceedings always followed a long-established
custom; the culprit was tried, then ordered to leave the room and wait in the passage
while the seniors deliberated before returning their verdict. In case the sentence was
the extreme penalty of law, namely a thrashing, the accused had the option of*

appealing to the head master.

(Head of the School)

Avery went on to point out that "the English schoolboy is sometimes misled in his ideas as to what the term (fair play) really implies." In his books, fair play prevails in a number of respects. Examples include giving an alleged wrongdoer a fair hearing, refraining from cheating or dishonesty, confessing to wrongdoing in order to avoid the dreaded collective punishment and/or sneaking, and holding proper elections in order to decide who the prefects are going to be. The honour of the school is paramount, and those whose behaviour is incompatible with the smooth running of the school must expect to relinquish their responsibilities, such as their prefectships, and to be punished by their peers as well as the authorities. Avery did not shy away from descriptions of beatings either:

It was a good thing for Thurston and Fletcher that they had their studies... in which to find shelter, or they would have been compelled to run the gauntlet.

(The Triple Alliance)

Never before had he received a thrashing at the hands of the senior prefect, and he winced under the first cut, which seemed to sting him like a scorpion.

(Head of the School)

Thurston and Fletcher One went home to return no more; practically expelled, though the doctor, in this instance, did not make a public example of their departure.

(The Triple Alliance)

The fact that a beating may be by a relative seems to be of no great consequence to a boy, if he realises that the honour of the School must come first. A female relative of both beater and beaten in that situation makes her views known, but the response is simply:

"She hasn't got the sense to see that it's the senior prefect's place to cane fellows who get hauled."

(Head of the School)

At the same time the rewards of virtuous behaviour are clearly set out:

The removal of young Noaks and Hodgson from the rival school caused a great change for the better among the ranks of Horace House. The old feud died out, giving place to a far better spirit, which was manifested each term in the friendly manner in which the teams met for matches at cricket or football.

(The Triple Alliance)

Finally on the subject of the unwritten code of conduct, the hierarchical structure of the schools is an important aspect of the stories:

Vanity prevented their thinking of themselves as ordinary school-boys; and not having as yet attained the honourable position of the highest form, they voted the 'Sixths' a lot of stuck-up noodles.

(*The Dormitory Flag*)

It was an awful thing to beard the lion in his den - for a new boy to face so great a personage as the football captain, and refuse point-blank to do as he was told.

(*The Triple Alliance*)

Prefects and captains are given an important role in the running of the school, and regarded as being a cut above the rest. One of Avery's short stories, *A Toast Fag*, concerns the relationship between the great Calvert, and James Pascoe, who is ordered to "fag" for him to the extent of preparing his toast:

Calvert was a great man - a member of the Upper Sixth, and captain of the house fifteen. Hitherto, Jim had only viewed him from a respectable distance, and now the thought of being brought into close personal relationship with such an important personage caused the small boy no little uneasiness of mind.

(*A Toast Fag*)

It is not difficult to blame young Jim when we are later told that Calvert's...

...manner of correcting the erring small fry of his house was usually more like what might be expected of a good-natured mastiff keeping in order an unruly family of fox-terrier pups.

(*A Toast Fag*)

Yet young James, at the end of the story, seems more than happily resigned to his menial position:

"Please, there's one thing I should like," he said, *"and that is, until I get into the Upper School I always want to be your toast fag."*

(*A Toast Fag*)

It is worth reading this story if only to read Avery's description of the group of fellow toast-fags all crowding round the fireplace in order to make toast for their elders. Perhaps surprisingly, this is a chore which none of them appear to resent. Throughout Avery's writing, prefect power is stressed:

"In any large school it is eminently satisfactory to find that a certain amount of the government and discipline can be trusted to the boys themselves."

(The Triple Alliance)

To be called upon to perform the duties of a prefect was to be singled out as worthy of trust and responsibility, and any one who filled the office was rightly entitled to a certain amount of self-respect.

(The Dormitory Flag)

"I should cane the beggar," said Pearson, "and lay it on thick."

"I shouldn't whack him," said Westwood. "I know the chap; there's some good in him. He's no coward, anyway, and caning'll only make him worse. Gate him for a week, and give him two hundred lines, and say that next time he'll be reported to the doctor."

(The Dormitory Flag)

Not that referral to the doctor, as the headmaster is called, will be any more palatable to the boys. Appearing before the headmaster is an experience to be feared, even when the party is innocent:

"My eye," remarked Diggory an hour later, "I wouldn't go through that again for something! I swear that by the time I'd finished the perspiration was running down my back in a regular stream."

(The Triple Alliance)

In stern, even tones the head master finished his recital of what had taken place in the reception room; his closing words were pregnant with meaning.

(Head of the School)

There are always a few tough cookies amongst the masters:

His rule was founded on the fear of punishment, and the sceptre which he wielded was a small black notebook, in which he entered the names of all offenders with an accompanying "Hundred lines, Brown!" or "Write the lesson out after school, Smith."

(Head of the School)

As we have seen, Avery's own voice would sometimes be heard through the narrative, and although his main mission was to entertain rather than to preach or teach, it is hard to discount an element of the latter in the speech of the headmaster in *The Dormitory Flag* after a shooting accident:

"What is true in school life is equally true in the world beyond, and undisciplined

men who will not be governed find that breaches of the wise laws, either of God or man, become, in a sense, their own punishment."

Thus have two traits been covered so far. Firstly we have seen examples of the portrayal of the schoolboys' own angle on school life, with colourful descriptions of high-spiritedness, japing, feasting, daring, bonding and feuding. Secondly we have become acquainted with the code of ethics, with the emphasis on honour, justice, triumph for virtue, respect for elders and punishment for misdeeds. The third trait can be set out very simply; Avery's fondness for staging, and graphically describing, sports fixtures in his stories. This could be said to fill a dual purpose.

"Well hit, sir!"

Not only could sporting contests portray boys at their most boyish, and demonstrate the rewards of a plucky, honest performance, but they could also depict the immediacy of the battle, and provide potential for stimulating, robust writing. The easy way in which readers could identify with and share in its dramas

and passions made it a natural choice of topic for a school story writer. A bracing walk on the clifftops, or nature ramble, would not provide the requisite excitement with which Avery wished to captivate his readers; high adventure in cannibal-infested mangrove swamps was however too far-fetched and escapist for Avery and indeed many of the followers of Reed, although not for Charles Hamilton as we shall see in the next chapter.

As far as plots were concerned, the outcome of the games played often mattered little. They were, like much of the schoolboy behaviour already discussed, often inconsequential sub-plots which a modern editor faced with unacceptably high production costs might invite his author to abandon in favour of a more streamlined and unfussy narrative. Cynics might ask "what does it matter who won?" Pragmatists might say "you can go and watch a real match for yourself, why do you want to read about a made-up one?" However, those already absorbed in the activities and antics of their fictional heroes would not dispute that a competent sporting performance on their part is an integral part of their appeal, and sadly real life rarely sees the good guy hitting a winning goal in the last second.

So important is coverage of sports fixtures to Avery that whole chapters would be devoted to them and familiar patterns would be established. Firstly the sporting scene is graphically set: (NB the extracts below are all taken from books referred to above).

Every day after morning school the thud, thud of the leather might be heard as fellows practised pace and drop kicks; while each afternoon players of all ages passed through the gates with mufflers and coats hiding their war-paint, and white knickers which began already to show the mud-stains of active service.

Then comes the build-up to the big match:

"Why? because they've beaten us now three times running; and the last time when our chaps went over to Wraxby and got licked at footer their captain asked Ally if in future we should like to play a master! Such rot! As if we couldn't smash them without! Look here, I'd give - I'd give sixpence if we could win!"

It was.... the sort of day when the thud-thud of a "punt-about" sounds like music, and makes every player long to get to business.

Even inanimate objects are supposed to take an interest:

The tall trees, bare enough now except for a few straggling yellow leaves, which still lingered among the branches, had witnessed many a gallant struggle upon that ground... but any passer-by who chanced to stop in the road and watch the finish of this memorable contest could have told that the game was one of exceptional interest.

The double line of flags fluttered in the gentle breeze, as though they shared in the general excitement.

The weather is of course relevant:

It is an ideal day for cricket, with a fresh breeze blowing, just sufficient to temper the hot afternoon sunshine....

There are the early disasters:

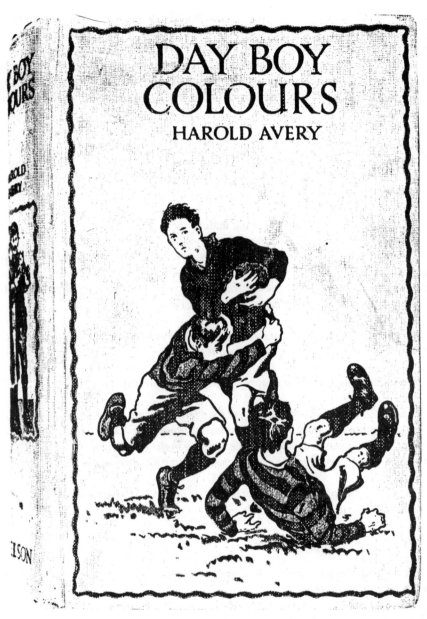

The cover of one of Avery's later works. The large stiff-backed volumes must have seemed quite formidable in comparison with the Thomson and Amalgamated Press papers!

Redfern, the next man, had hardly taken his place at the wicket when a sharp click, the glitter of bails in the air, and a Wraxby shout of "Well bowled!" announced his fate.

Then comes the turnaround, and subsequent reaction of the crowd:

Allingford shouted, the crowd roared, while the 'Happy Family' gambolled about on one another's chests and stomachs, and squealed with delight. "Played, Egerson!" roared the crowd, and one piping voice rising clear and shrill as the cheer subsided, "Played, 'Eggy!'"

"There he goes again! - Well held, sir! 'Pon my soul, I wish I was playing on your side myself!"

Then comes the build-up of tension:

Hobb replied with a grunt. Even his iron nerves were beginning to feel the strain of watching the finish of a match which was to be long remembered as one of the most exciting ever witnessed on the Senior Ground at Carsdale College.

The closing scene of the game caused an amount of excitement unparalleled in the history of Ronleigh cricket.

The incident, coming as it did at such a critical moment, seemed to rouse either side to make one last desperate effort, and an indescribable wave of excitement passed alike over players and spectators.

Victory for the School is sweet indeed:

With a splendid onehanded catch Thurston had brought the well-fought contest to a close, and secured a victory for Ronleigh College.
The memories of the heroics will last for ever:

And perhaps in after years, when in turning out the contents of a drawer they came across a faded cap or a frayed old jersey for which they no longer had any use, the scene may come back to them with a pang of regret.

Since sporting success may, among other things, mean exoneration from evening preparation, individual sporting prowess is a guarantee of popularity:

Borne aloft on the shoulders of half a dozen great men, with whom up to the present moment he could hardly have claimed to be on speaking terms, 'Crockery' was carried into the pavilion, while the crowd outside indulged in a fresh outburst of cheering.

Avery was applauded by commentators for writing stories which, in contrast to the Penny Dreadfuls and "pop" school stories, were entertaining, yet well-written and conformist. Alongside Reed, he was identified as a specialist in portraying cheerful manliness - a combination of hearty high-spirited behaviour that might be expected of any young male, and fearless impeccable morals.

However, to those considering Avery's most celebrated works as their centenary is reached, the quality of the content is questionable. Some might say he fell between two stools, failing to provide the charismatic escapist prose of Charles Hamilton, the definitive "pop" school writer, and yet failing to address the problems and injustices in the same way that Rudyard Kipling did in *Stalky & Co.* Some might be put off by the smugness, the cliqueyness, the exclusivity and the cosiness of life at a good school. They might be merely irritated by the propensity of even the most virtuous characters to indulge in silly reckless behaviour, and disturbed at the apparently uncritical way in which the less savoury aspects of public school life, such as the high-handed behaviour of prefects, are portrayed. Others might rail against the rather patronising way in which the advantages of good behaviour and the less pleasant consequences of misbehaviour are put over.

However, one should not dismiss Avery's contribution to the twentieth century school story lightly. He continued, almost to the halfway point in the century, to produce a certain type of school story which had been initiated by Reed, providing what was to many people an eminently acceptable middle ground between the Penny Dreadful and the didactic. Through him many youngsters would have learnt a code of behaviour which would enhance considerably their standing in society and their ability to interact satisfactorily with their peers. His stories opened up the fascinating world of the public school to many youngsters who would never be educated at such an establishment themselves. Perhaps even more significantly, the settings and the concepts used by him would be reflected in the work of two other writers described in this book, although there were a number of important differences between his writing and that of Charles Hamilton and Angela Brazil. Vast numbers of writers, some of which have been mentioned, were to follow in the tradition of Reed and Avery. Of particular interest in the context of this chapter would be Richard Bird, Athol Harcourt Burrage, Kent Carr, Sidney George Hedges, St John Pearce and Michael Poole, because many of their titles concentrated on sporting prowess and achievement, as so much of Harold Avery's work did. Although team games such as rugby, cricket and soccer were the favoured sports, others were included too - Sidney Hedges specialised in stories about swimming, for instance.

The traditional boys' school story as written by Avery and his contemporaries largely died out towards the Second World War. There were two major reasons for this. The first was that attitudes had changed. The unquestioning loyalty of many young men to a certain set of ideals and pattern of behaviour had been called seriously into question by the changing national and international scene. There was the appalling loss of life during the First World War, where those very same men that had trumpeted the British cause and sworn fierce allegiance to king and country lay dying in the mud and the sweat of the Flanders fields. There was the industrial gloom which followed the war, and the realisation that victory in 1918 had brought no real benefits to the country as a whole. Additionally, with the Depression and the rise of Nazism in the 1930's, there was a feeling of dread that the unstable inter- national scene might trigger an even more devastating conflict. Suddenly, the senti- ments of insularity, cheerfulness, ac- ceptance, self-con- fidence, enthusiasm, conformity to estab- lishment, obedience to orders, team spirit, "playing the game" and of course the thrill of combat and taking on the enemy, all stressed so dynami- cally by Avery,

THE MERCILESS PARO- DYING OF THE TRADI- TIONAL BOYS' STORY INCLUDED THE DEVISING OF WITTY CAPTIONS TO GO WITH ORIGINAL DRAWINGS. THIS IS TAKEN FROM A COLLEC- TION CALLED THE UNCEN- SORED BOYS' OWN.

Some of the masters at St Fred's were a bit queer. There was Hogson, for instance, who charged us half-a-crown a lesson.

seemed to ring rather hollow. Unquestioning ideals were no longer appropriate for a world that was questioning everything.

The second reason was the rise of other types of writing for boys. Even for those who still clung to the old ideals, the competition for their pocket money provided by the "pop" school stories was considerable. Throughout the 1920's, Charles Hamilton was at the height of his powers and his popularity, especially as his best-loved character, Billy Bunter, had even by that time become an institution. Not only were the periodicals in which they appeared cheaper, but they were less daunting than the large stiff backed books in which Avery and his contemporaries specialised. The ideals which were embodied in Avery's work were present in Hamilton's work, but Hamilton's work contained a greater degree of escapism which readers enjoyed. The D C Thomson papers which included *Wizard* and *Hotspur* and which rode confidently on the back of Hamilton's success, stressed the escapist concept and again were more 'user-friendly' than Avery's books or even the *BOP*. In their 1970 guide to boys' fiction, W.O.G.Lofts and D.J.Adley identified in the Thomson papers a more easy-going, exuberant and friendly relationship between editors and readers. They contrasted the ethos of these papers with the hearty morals that characterised such journals as the *BOP* or even, to a certain extent, the *Magnet* and other Amalgamated Press papers, which will be considered at greater length in the next chapter. The combination of these popular story-papers with the radio and cinema meant that the sturdy hardbound book (the paperback book was still in its infancy) was only one of several means of communicating a story to an audience.

The traditional boys' story, despite its virtual demise by the outbreak of the Second World War, can be said to have played a much-loved and important part in the development of English children's literature. Like many forms of literature, it has had its critics and those who would parody it. An example of parody was the 1975 *Ripping Yarns* episode entitled *Tomkinson's Schooldays*. In the story, Tomkinson arrives at Graybridge, a boys' public school, in 1913 as a new boy. He has to suffer all the normal privations of a newcomer, such as fighting a grizzly bear, being nailed to the school walls on St Tadger's Day, and beating the headmaster. Boys are woken from sleep at 3.30am by alsatians, and attempts at escape are foiled by the school leopard. Miscreants are summarily shot or left to rot in a heap of maggots, then are made to participate in the 30 mile hop which after the contenders have been "palfreyed" - hit over the head with a wooden stick - only the fittest can hope to survive. Even sports spectators are shown no mercy, being chained to a post while watching the school rugger match. There is also Grayson, the School Bully, to contend with; being waited upon by Filippino girls, being carried everywhere by junior boys, taking saunas instead of prayers, smoking opium, and having access to a private telephone, he has a mystique which is the envy of the Head himself. Eventually Grayson is displaced and after a majestic performance in the 30 mile hop, Tomkinson himself becomes the hero of the hour, and is elevated to the rank of School Bully himself. Although the programme was conceived as a spoof and not meant to be taken seriously, some of the themes - the clear hierarchical structure amongst boys, harsh retribution for misbehaviour, the disruptive influence of a bullying or otherwise beastly type, the adulation of fellow pupils for heroic and adventurous acts, and the obsession with team games and physical activity (organised or disorganised) - would be very familiar to the student of Harold Avery.

Unlike other authors covered in this book, Avery was not one of the immortals. His contribution to the school story in the twentieth century lies in his successfully bringing into that century a type of school story which was to keep many writers busy, and large numbers of readers enthralled throughout their childhood, with no parental misgivings. In due course, however, he and his contemporaries were to be overshadowed by a colossus who revolutionised schools fiction in this country. It is to him that we turn in the next chapter.

SCHOOL STORIES BY HAROLD AVERY

(All published by Thomas Nelson & Sons unless stated)

The School's Honour (1895)
Sunday School Union
An Old Boy's Yarn (1895) [Cassell & Co]
Frank's First Term (1896)
A Boy All Over (1896) [Sampson Low & Co]
Soldiers of the Queen, or Jack Fenleigh's Luck (1898)
The Triple Alliance (1899)
The Dormitory Flag (1899)
Mobsley's Mohicans (1900)
A Toast Fag and other Stories (1900)
Heads or Tails (1900)
Gunpowder, Treason and Plot* (1901)
All Play and No Work (1901) [S W Partridge & Co]
The House on the Moor (1903)
Out of the Running (1904) [Collins]
Play the Game (1906)
True to his Nickname (1907)
The Wizard's Wand (1908)
Off the Wicket (1910)
Head of the School (1912) [S W Partridge & Co]
Talford's Last Term (1912) [S W Partridge & Co]
Not Cricket! (1912) [S W Partridge & Co]
The Chartered Company (1915)
Line Up! (1918) [Collins]
Caught Out (1919) [Collins]
The Runaway (1920) [Collins]
Schoolboy Pluck (1921) [Nisbet & Co]
The Prefect's Patrol (1922)
A Choice of Chums (1922)
Between Two Schools (1923)
The Spoil-Sport (1923)
A Fifth Form Mystery (1923) [Boys' Own Paper Office]
A Sixth Form Feud (1926) [Ward Lock & Co]
Pocket Thunder* (1926)
Won for the School (1927) [Collins]
Day Boy Colours (1928)
Cock-House of Claverill (1929) [Collins]
A Term on Trial (1930) [S W Partridge & Co]
The Cock-House Cup (1933)
A Close Finish (1934) [S W Partridge & Co]
Chums at Charlhurst (1936)
Through Thick and Thin (1938)

* Contains short stories by Avery and other authors

I SAY, YOU FELLOWS!

"Bend over that chair, Bunter!"
"I-I-I say, sir...."
"Bend over that chair!" rapped Mr Quelch, in a voice like unto that of a Great Huge Bear.
"Oh, crikey!"
Billy Bunter, in the lowest spirits, bent over the chair. He gave an anticipatory wriggle as he waited for the descending cane. But he did not have to wait long.
Swipe!
"Yarooooooh!" roared Bunter.

(Billy Bunter's Benefit)

The start of one of a multitude of canings received by the best loved, most incorrigible and undoubtedly the chubbiest fictional schoolboy of them all - Billy Bunter of Greyfriars School.

In the previous chapter, a distinction was made between the "respectable" school story as conceived by Talbot Baines Reed, and the stories contained in periodicals of Brett, Emmett and Fox, which had had their roots in the Penny Dreadfuls. The man regarded as responsible for carrying the latter type of story right through to the Second World War and beyond, albeit in slightly less incredible form, was Charles Harold St John Hamilton. However, Hamilton did far more than develop a particular school story genre in his own inimitable style. Not only did he become the definitive writer of what Isabel Quigly called the "pop" school story; his genius was in the creation of a schoolboy, Billy Bunter, whose excesses and idiosyncrasies have enthralled, outraged and delighted not only his own generation but every generation since. Yet Hamilton at thirty years of age would have been amazed had he thought that almost a century thence he would be known principally for his invention of a single character.

Hamilton was born in August, 1876, in Ealing, West London. He attended a succession of private schools, and emerged with a strong taste for the classics. From his early childhood, writing was his major interest. He was seven years old when he started to write, and in his eighteenth year was put in touch with Dowling Maitland, a kind of literary agent who bought stories from writers and found markets for them. Having submitted his first manuscript to Maitland, and having been asked for more, he decided he wanted to earn his living as a writer. During his twenties he concentrated on adventure stories, including both sea and detective stories, which helped to fill the pages of the increasing number of juvenile papers, particularly the Trapps Holmes boys' papers and comics. Hamilton, however, found that his favourite form of juvenile fiction was the school story. He once said that "there isn't anything better" than writing for boys. Hamilton could, and did, write many good adventure stories, but realised the restricted appeal of blood-and-thunders and felt that a good enduring story required pace, believable characterisation and conflicts that went deeper than the superficial heroes v. villains scenario. It was this which perhaps gave him the edge of respectability which Brett, Emmett and Fox never quite achieved. It was the school story that emerged as the story at which his talents could be put to the best use, and for which there was the greatest demand for him.

Hamilton, though he loved children and wrote a number of romantic stories, remained both single and childless (as curiously did Angela Brazil, whose contribution to the girls' school story was as significant as Hamilton's was for the boys'). There is also no real evidence of his attendance at a public school. Despite these factors, Hamilton, with the aid of a large number of books about real-life schools, produced more public school stories than any other writer before or since. As more and more of his work comes to light, estimates as to his output have to be revised; although a total of 72 million words has been quoted, many believe the final tally to be over 100 million. Certainly there is evidence for his having invented over 100 different schools. Even more remarkably, he retained consistency in the character and identity of the pupils and teachers of each of the many schools about which he wrote. This was no mean achievement considering the overlap between different schools in many of his stories.

For a man whose output was so vast, it is difficult in a few words to summarise the common features of his stories. In the main, he set them in boys' public schools in fictitious locations. Normally his chosen location was England, although Hamilton wrote hundreds of stories with far more exotic settings. The atmosphere throughout was masculine, but Hamilton did not neglect the female influence. Hamilton developed a Victorian resistance to strong-minded women, and presumably on the basis that the best form of defence was attack, he found much comic material and some memorable comic characterisations in the suffragette movement and the concept of the New Woman. Hamilton provided plenty of heroics, with his young characters finding inner strength and resourcefulness that would have been the envy of every single reader; characterisations were often grossly exaggerated in order to extract maximum entertainment value. Yet the characteristics of the Reed/Avery school were not absent; stories were always told from the boys' angle (usually juniors but sometimes prefects), the author stressed a definite unwritten code of moral behaviour that underpinned each story, and he placed a considerable emphasis on outdoor and sporting activity. Hamilton had an exceptional ability to transform his readers into the heart of the narrative with much evocative writing and keen, sometimes satirical, observations on human behaviour. He could combine great humour with high drama and even pathos. At the same time, he had a strong social conscience - indeed he had socialist tendencies - and also strong values, discouraging smoking, drinking and gambling by his readers. Perhaps it was his ability to incorporate these more moral and traditional elements into his often far-fetched narratives - elements that were wholly acceptable to his intended readers - which gave him the edge over his less adventurous contemporaries.

By 1902 Hamilton was already beginning to produce school stories for magazines such as *Boy's Herald*, and in 1906 he was asked to write a series about a set of schoolboys for the magazine *Pluck*. *Pluck* was an Amalgamated Press paper; it had begun in 1894 as one of many founded by Alfred Harmsworth as part of his own crusade against the Penny Dreadful. Harmsworth's papers claimed to be "patriotic and uplifting... funny but not vulgar." The school about which Hamilton wrote for *Pluck* was a public school near the fictitious locations of Rylcombe and Wayland named St Jim's, the star of which was the Honourable Arthur Augustus D'Arcy, the epitome of the young aristocrat.

At the same time as writing for *Pluck*, Hamilton was also commissioned to write for the *Gem*. The *Gem* was also an Amalgamated Press paper, edited by Percy Griffith, who recognised Hamilton's flair and was keen to exploit it to the full. It was in the third issue of that paper that Hamilton's work first appeared, under the pseudonym Martin Clifford. Incidentally Hamilton was the only author of the six highlighted in this book to have used pseudonyms for the most significant parts of his work. Some pseudonyms were based on existing fictional characters from the work of other writers; for instance the name Martin Clifford was concocted from R M Ballantyne's *Martin Rattler* and Bulwer-Lytton's *Paul Clifford*. The fictional school chosen was Clavering, the hero one Tom Merry. Tom is an orphan, mollycoddled by a besotted nurse named Miss Priscilla, but although sent off to boarding school looking like Little Lord Fauntleroy, he strives to prove himself among his peers and does so by becoming expert at boxing and cricket. Percy Griffith saw exciting possibilities in locating Tom Merry at St Jim's, and in due course, Clavering was dropped, with Merry being transferred to St Jim's.

Griffith then asked Hamilton to provide stories for a new paper he was creating alongside the *Gem*, called the *Magnet*. This Hamilton agreed to do; Griffith wanted him to use a different pseudonym to the *Gem* stories which he had continued to write as Martin Clifford. The pseudonym he chose, Frank Richards, was based simply on the pluralisation of the name of Hamilton's brother Dick! It was with the advent of the *Magnet* that Greyfriars was born, remaining with the paper from its inception on 15th February 1908 until its closure in 1940. The first

No.1. NEW STORY BOOK!

The very first 'Magnet' cover

lines of the first Greyfriars story, *The Making of Harry Wharton*, read:

"Send Master Harry to me!"
Colonel Wharton filled his glass from the decanter, held it up to the light, and then slowly sipped the contents; a dark shade of thought upon his bronzed face the while.

As well as this story, the first edition contained the first part of a story called *Maxennis, Detective* by Lewis Hockley.

Perusing a copy of the *Magnet* over fifty years after the last issue rolled off the press is an interesting and illuminating experience. It is hard now to conceive a weekly magazine for children with almost unbroken narrative and complete absence of strip cartoons. However, the *Magnet,* for the princely sum of half a penny initially, later 2d, contained, each week, a Greyfriars story of 25,000 words or more and by no means a profusion of illustrative material (what illustrations there were tended to be somewhat indiscreetly placed, in some instances prematurely giving away what was going to happen!). The fact that the title of the paper did not relate directly to Greyfriars is somewhat misleading - Greyfriars did in fact monopolise the paper, although from time to time other stories, including adventure stories, appeared also. Taking the edition for the week ending February 3rd 1940, very close to the end of the *Magnet's* life, the cover (page 1) carried a full-page illustration of a piece of the action from that week's story. Page 2 contained that week's *Greyfriars Herald*, an ingenious "paper within a paper" supposedly edited and collated by Greyfriars pupils. The story, the *Japer of Greyfriars*, began on page 3 and, broken up only by chapter headings (although not chapter numbers) and illustrations, continued to the back page, page 24. Although the stories were complete in themselves, the reality was that batches of stories made up a "series" and hence there was something of a "serial" element about them. There would always be loose ends left untied which the Editor promised would be addressed in greater depth in subsequent issues. Series titles were colourful; they included *Mr Nugent Leaves Mrs Nugent, Featuring Cora Quelch* and *Wun Lung Takes Opium*. Individual stories within series contained titles like *His Blundering Best* and *The Caterpillar's Rest Cure*. Towards the end there might be grudging concessions to advertising (one paper included an offer for a piano accordion by monthly payments of four shillings), a pen-pal's column, and an editorial extolling the longevity, value for money, and wholesomeness of the journal. In the issue dated 24th February 1940, the editorial contained "RAPID FIRE REPLIES" to readers' queries, and it is perhaps an indication of the British stiff upper lip that despite living in the shadow of the Nazi menace, young readers still found time to ask who had the biggest feet in the Remove! (Apparently Bob Cherry did.) The *Magnet* reached its thousandth edition in 1927, and coloured covers started in late 1922.

Each story from edition 1221 onwards (in 1931) was written by Hamilton, but some stories in earlier editions were written by substitute writers, still under the name of Frank Richards. There were 25 in all, including three of the *Magnet* editors as well as journalists, teachers and staff members of the Amalgamated Press. The editors were colourful; firstly the quick, energetic, bohemian, slightly mysterious Percy Griffith; then from 1911, on Griffith's disappearance, Herbert Hinton, addicted to black cigars; on his enlistment in 1916 a cricket buff, John Nix Pentelow, took over; then after a plagiarism scandal in 1921 he made way for Charles Down, a gentlemanly figure who initiated the popular *Greyfriars Holiday Annual*. Sadly when the *Magnet* shut in 1940 he stored away all its records and papers and they were never seen again.

All in all there were 1683 numbers of the *Magnet*, compared with 1711 numbers of the *Gem*, (this latter figure did of course contain reprints - all the *Magnets* were new stories) although Bunter and his chums also featured in passing in other fictional schools of Hamilton's imagination, as well as the *Greyfriars Holiday Annual* and the *Schoolboys' Own Library*. Circulation of the *Magnet* at one stage was as high as 250,000 but by 1940, with a preference by readers to faster adventure stories and presumably with more important things to occupy the minds of its older readers, it had come down to little more than 40,000. With the wartime shortage of paper and newsprint, the *Magnet* and *Gem* were natural victims of the cut-backs made

Readers of the 'Magnet', and the hearty outdoor life it portrayed, would have been sorely tempted by its offers!

by Amalgamated Newspapers. Ironically the last story to feature - just before Dunkirk - was called "The Shadow of the Sack!" Despite the demise of the *Magnet*, a Canadian paper entitled *Story Paper Collector* which started in 1941 stimulated interest in the Greyfriars stories and inspired clubs, associations and correspondence between *Magnet* as well as *Gem* enthusiasts. Old copies were even taken by soldiers to cheer them up when they went to war! Tragically the retention by Amalgamated Press of the rights to Greyfriars characters prevented publication of further Greyfriars stories in any other competing paper. Although Billy Bunter starred in a comic strip in the wartime paper *Knockout*, it appeared that Greyfriars was finished.

It was a strange quirk of fate that led to the re-emergence of Greyfriars for a new generation of readers. To mark the launch of a series of stories on a new fictional school of Hamilton's, an article appeared shortly after the War entitled *Do You Remember Billy Bunter?* in *Picture Post*. It so happened that while on honeymoon in Scotland, this article was noticed by a publisher Charles Skilton who thought it would be a great idea for Greyfriars books to be published in bound form. The Amalgamated Press indicated in late 1946 that they had no objection to Skilton publishing them, providing they were in hardback. As a result, ten Greyfriars novels were produced, beginning with *Billy Bunter of Greyfriars School* in 1947. Incidentally, the word "novel" is wholly appropriate as each represented a complete story in itself rather than lots of incidents all making up one term which is how the concurrent Jennings books of Anthony Buckeridge were structured. All ten novels sold very well, so well in fact that Skilton was unable to cope. The rights were sold to Cassell in 1952 and with Hamilton (as Frank Richards, of course) producing two or three books a year, the series ran to thirty-eight titles, the last appearing in 1965. In 1953 *Billy Bunter's Own Annual* was launched. Various papers carried new adaptations of Greyfriars stories, and Hamilton provided them also with new stories, but these were not nearly so successful.

The *Gem*, also retailing at no more than 2d per copy, was similar to the *Magnet* in many ways with sequences of stories that individually had a sort of completeness but each sequence made up a novel-length story. The cover again contained a full-page illustration, sometimes but not always bearing a hallmark of masculinity such as a racing car or steam engine. The first year of the *Gem*, from its inception on March 16th 1907, saw an alternation between adventure stories and St Jim's stories, and there were always other stories (usually sporting rather than school) contained within, attributed to such individuals as Alfred Edgar and Sydney Horler. However, after Year One, at the same time that the *Magnet* began, each paper was almost entirely taken up with a "topping", "corking", "rousing" or of course "ripping" yarn relating to Tom Merry and his chums. In 1933 there was a merger between the *Gem* and *Nelson Lee*, which brought the work of Edwy Searles Brooks and his school St Frank's under the same cover as Martin Clifford's work. Illustrations, which again regrettably anticipated the action to come, did nothing to add to the text but broke up its otherwise tight small print which would surely be the envy of any self-respecting insurance policy draughtsman. The *Greyfriars Herald* equivalent was *St Jim's News* which might contain some sporting gossip, an editorial extolling the virtues of sporting participation, and a spot of doggerel concerning the school and its characters. As with the *Magnet* by no means the dullest part of the *Gem* consisted of the small ads. The edition for the week ending 12th December 1925 (it was published each Wednesday) contained on page 27 an ad for a "Bully Boy" pea pistol at 1/6d, and then on the very next page an ad headed "Don't Be Bullied!" which invited subscribers to send four penny stamps for two illustrated lessons in ju-jitsu. On the same page there was an ad for a foolproof Safety Revolver and the Famous Clive System for a course in height increase! The Editorial page of the Gem might contain jokes, sneak previews of the following week's bill of fare, a "tuck hamper coupon" and a gentle homily from the editor himself, exhorting readers to higher standards of behaviour and a more positive approach to life.

There were two series of the *Gem*; the first ran to 48 issues, the second to 1663. Hamilton (as Clifford) wrote all of the St Jim's stories in the first series, but only 739 in the second series, the balance being made up of reprints and stories by substitute authors. It was ironic that in early 1939 Hamilton (as Clifford) was asked to write a new series of stories for the *Gem* about St Jim's, the run of reprints having come to an end, only for wartime paper shortages to cause the *Gem* to close down in December of the same year. It appeared that St Jim's, like Greyfriars, was never to rise again. However, in the same way that the *Magnet* series of Greyfriars stories was to be succeeded by thirty-eight books, so did Martin Clifford produce a hardback series of St Jim's stories, the first six published by Mandeville Publications between 1949 and 1951, and the rest by Spring Books. There was also a *Tom Merry's Own Annual* in the 1950s, and the St Jim's stories were adapted for various newspapers and periodicals including a series of flimsy paperbacks issued by Goldhawk Press. The Howard Baker press also published some *Gem* facsimiles (see below). Sadly, none of this material achieved the charisma or the popularity of the Bunter books. Few people in the 1990s would know of the existence of St Jim's, and still fewer would actually have read stories about the school.

With the continuation of the *Gem* until 1939, Charles Hamilton as Martin Clifford (for the *Gem*) and Frank Richards (for the *Magnet*) was engaged in writing school stories for these two papers for over thirty years, although many other series of school stories were written by Hamilton during that period, with varying degrees of success. It meant that 70,000 words were being written by Hamilton each week - the equivalent of an average-length novel. His huge output led him to suffer eye strain in the 1920s, and he even had to use a heavily inked typewriter ribbon so that he could read what he had written. On occasions, and much to Hamilton's chagrin, substitute writers would be used by Amalgamated Press if, for instance, Hamilton was ill or failed to send in copy on time. Remarkably, the fact that Frank Richards and Martin Clifford were the same person seems to have escaped the majority of the readership despite obvious similarities in style and construction.

The success of the *Magnet* and *Gem* inspired the production of rival papers from D.C.Thomson & Co of Dundee, and school stories featured in the big five - *Adventure, Rover, Wizard, Skipper* and *Hotspur*. The schools featured in these

SUPER ST. JIM'S SERIES STARTS TO-DAY!

THE BEST PAPER FOR BRITISH BOYS

2ᵈ

No. 1,331. Vol. XLV.   EVERY WEDNESDAY.   Week Ending April 7th, 1934.

THE MIDNIGHT MARAUDER! See the Great Story "THE MENACE OF THE DWARF!" —WITHIN!

One of the later covers of The Gem

papers, not of course creations of Hamilton, were boarding-schools but with tougher pupils. These papers, which were to continue for decades, were all products of the "pop" school story and have largely Hamilton to thank for their success, although the quality was markedly inferior to that of Hamilton. If nothing else, their success has proved that entertaining stories, however incredible, will always be popular with youngsters. Indeed, in a poll carried out which involved nearly one thousand boys in the late 1930s, far more expressed a preference for the Thomson papers than the Amalgamated Press papers, despite - or perhaps because of - the questionable quality of the Thomson papers. E.S.Turner wrote that "Outbreaks of ventriloquism and invisibility were chronic; and no school was without its terrible twins or tricky triplets. One journal even produced a headmaster who was twins." However, even that must have been preferable to the head who "turned out to be a savage and dressed up in a leopard skin and swung about the roofs." All human life was there; readers were regaled with stories ranging in subject matter from starving and tyranny to torture and eccentricity, such as the story of a boy king who engaged a whipping boy to take punishment for him! The *Hotspur* devoted itself virtually entirely to school stories, commencing on 2nd September 1933 and containing settings for school stories which included the Wild West, the jungle, desert islands and outer space. Its best loved school was Red Circle and its most famous teacher Mr Smug. The papers continued to flourish long after the *Magnet* and *Gem* had disappeared. In a sense they marked a return to the world of Brett, Emmett and Fox. Leslie Charteris wrote: "What fine, lusty fare it was! The pirates were unregenerate cut-throats, the international spies and criminals were prodigal with murder and torture, even the denizens of other planets were bloodthirsty monsters. I would love to see some advanced evangelist, uncorrupted by airy-fairy theory, start out from the bald fact that my generation, raised on this kind of reading, produced an infinitely smaller percentage of juvenile delinquents and layabouts than the brood which is currently supposed to be raised on today's approved wishy-washy pabulum."

It is now appropriate to step inside the fictional worlds of Greyfriars and St Jim's, and then briefly to consider the other schools created by Hamilton.

THE GREYFRIARS STORIES

Greyfriars, a boarding school in the vicinity of Friardale and Courtfield, was undoubtedly Hamilton's most famous seat of learning. In over thirty years' worth of writings about it, Hamilton, as Richards, created a new world which proceeded with seeming obliviousness to things going on outside it. The very fact that Wharton, Bunter and Co. were schoolboys in 1908 and had not graduated to the outside world by the time two world wars had been fought, would have told the reader that Greyfriars proceeded in accordance with very different rules and trends to those in English society during these turbulent decades of the twentieth century. George Orwell saw Greyfriars as a "sham and unreal world"; Mary Cadogan saw it as "the projection of a perfect world at a more down-to-earth level"; James C Iraldi claimed that "it does not portray real life, nor was it ever seriously meant to."

However distasteful they may be to academics and other commentators, the themes, conventions, and norms of Greyfriars provide for the early twentieth century reader a different but also exhilarating world. For the late twentieth century reader they provide a form of nostalgic escape, where "loyalty to chums" is paramount; where things are not just good or even super but "spiffing" and "topping;" where competence at sport is symbolic of healthy-mindedness, and sporting incompetence labels one a "swot" or "duffer" however admirable one may otherwise be; where it is often the arrival of a postal order from home which saves an individual from ruin; where sneaking is the worst crime of all; where poverty, deprivation and misery are unheard of; where poking fun at the idiosyncrasies of

oreigners is not considered racist (indeed Hamilton would have been horrified to
be regarded as such, since he was remarkably tolerant towards all foreigners except
Americans); where laughter can be derived from a person's physical disadvantage
or disability; where authority is never seriously challenged; where japing, dicing
with death in exotic climes, and constant confrontations with the Law are commonplace; and where justice is dispensed in the form of harsh physical punishment.
Corporal punishment is the favoured method of retribution at Greyfriars, and
much of the entertainment value is derived from the administration of beatings
and the reaction of the victims. Despite the "escapist" quality of much of the
writing, many would still admit to pride in following the Greyfriars ethics; as
Cadogan said: "Greyfriars may fall short of Shangri-La, but it remains a vivid and
satisfying world of its own and has put its stamp on several generations of children
and young people."

By
FRANK RICHARDS.

Contrary to popular belief, it is not Billy Bunter but one of his colleagues in the
Remove, Harry Wharton, who is the central character of most of the *Magnet*
stories. The very first story, *The Making of Harry Wharton*, concerns the decision
to send this wilful, headstrong boy to Greyfriars. Like Tom Merry at St Jim's,
Harry Wharton is an orphan who has been overprotected by an elderly female and
is sent to Greyfriars by his uncle to toughen him up. Like Merry, he is not afraid
to make decisions - including a life-saving mission - and is not irresponsible,
although unlike Merry, his temperament is somewhat mercurial. For a while,

Wharton was the most popular of all Hamilton's fictional pupils, and a character with which many boys of Wharton's fifteen years could identify. He is no stereotype or cardboard hero, and although he is honest, his character is flawed by pride. His other great weakness is for Marjorie Hazeldine of Cliff House Girls' School although in this he is not alone. It was clear that Wharton, like Tom Merry, was intended to be the Greyfriars folk hero. However, what Cadogan described as the "sheer weight and loudness of manner" of Billy Bunter, a fellow-pupil of Wharton forced Hamilton to reconsider his action plan.

This was not the first appearance of a character called Bunter in Hamilton's work; a school porter in a fictional school named Cliveden had been given the same surname, and indeed Hamilton had had stories concerning a character called Bunter rejected by an editor in the late 1890s. Coincidentally, a writer known as H.Philpott Wright used the name Billy Bunter as a pupil of Blackminster School in a paper called the *Vanguard*, although Hamilton denied any connection. What is certain, however, is that by the 1930s it was Bunter who had become the most popular of all the Greyfriars characters within the *Magnet* readership. As Cadogan wrote: "From his early days as a sneaky and insignificant schoolboy he was quickly elevated to the level of farcical anti-hero to become one of the *Magnet*'s main attractions." Although many *Magnets* even during the 20s and 30s had Greyfriars stories in which he hardly featured, the prominence which the character had achieved is evident in that virtually all of the Greyfriars books have some reference to Billy Bunter in the title, and none refer to Harry Wharton, who had begun as the hero. The popularity which Bunter had achieved by the 1930s was so great that the *Magnet* offices became recipients of parcels of tuck to be handed on to Bunter!

Bunter appears in the very first Magnet story, described as "somewhat stout" and being shoved violently by Master Wharton. This first confrontation between Bunter and other boys from the Remove provides little inkling of what is to come. Originally, it would seem that Bunter was intended to be merely a peripheral character, plump rather than excessively obese, and almost apologetic in comparison to his demeanour in later stories.

With no conscience, no regard for honesty and truth, and enormous obtuseness, he is destined to be described as fatuous, lying, stupid, philistine, arrogant, cunning, condescending, nasty, conceited and infuriating - and that by a critic writing nearly eighty years later! For all his faults, many people found Bunter strangely likeable. Turner wrote in 1975 of Bunter that "He would borrow money with no intention of paying it back; he would pirate another boy's tuck without a qualm... therefore no one felt markedly sorry when dogs ran away with his sausages, when he sank his teeth into decoy pies filled with pepper... although he was supposed to be 'the guest nobody wants at Christmas,' everybody would have been disappointed if he had failed to crash the party." That summed up the Bunter enigma beautifully. Al-

"I say, you fellows," howled Bunter, as the Famous Five rushed off. "What about the cake?" The Removeites heeded him not. Turning back into the study, the fat junior gazed at the cake and smiled.

though nobody would deny that he was an almost totally amoral character, he inspired enormous affection. Some critics remained unmoved. Arthur Marshall was one writer who failed to see anything endearing in Bunter at all, describing him thus: "Obese and one suspects impotent, he is like no schoolboy that ever was, and seems in character and person to have more in common with a gin-swilling, petty-cash-fiddling, perspiring middle-aged businessman." There is no limit to the imagination employed by his contemporaries in labelling him; "blithering, bur-bling, bandersnatch", "fat, frabjous frump", "barrel" and "fat villain" are just samples of the many singularly unflattering epithets applied to him. Whatever one thinks of Bunter, there is one thing that not even his most ardent admirers can dispute: discounting his early years of comparative insignificance, he is wholly deserving of the most common nickname for him, the Fat Owl. His insatiable hunger for sticky, sweet and fattening food is perhaps his most prominent trait.

Indeed, Bunter's name has entered the English language as a synonym for anyone gluttonous and obese and even in other languages the word Bunter or "le Buntair" has connotations of fatness. Right at the start of *Billy Bunter's Banknote* - one of the Greyfriars books - Bunter has no scruples about informing his colleagues that the headmaster requires to see them, in order that he can lay his hands on a particularly appetising cake belonging to another. He is throughout let down by his own stupidity, since he is totally incapable of covering up his own guilt:

"Smithy had jam in one of his gorgeous parcels today!" remarked Bob Cherry. "You fat brigand, that's Smithy's jam."
"T'ain't!" roared Bunter. "Think I'd touch Smithy's jam? I never knew Smithy had jam - I never saw Gosling hand him the parcel, and never knew he had the parcel at all, and it certainly wasn't in his study when I looked. Besides, I haven't been to his study."

(Billy Bunter of Greyfriars School)

It must be pointed out that Bunter can be both generous and plucky, and maintains a great love for his mother. Colleagues are not entirely without sympathy for him; in *Billy Bunter's Benefit*, whilst the other boys are quite content to see Bunter being caned for his latest misdemeanours, they rally round to help him when he is faced with possible action over an unpaid seven guinea bill after the money *already provided* to him for the purpose has been blown on tuck!

Despite his redeeming features, this Falstaffian character remains the antithesis of anything and everything wholesome and acceptable to most people. However, even Bunter's fiercest critics might raise a smile at some of his failings:

Dear Father, I have not herd from you in repply to my last letter, so I rite these phew lines to hoap that you are kwite well. You will be pleezed to here that I am getting on well in class, all threw hard wurk, and that Mr Quelch has prazed me a good deal lately. He is partikularly pleezed with my spelling. Since you toald me last time to be more kareful with it I have been extreemly kareful, and whennever I am in dowt I look out the wurd in the dickshunary at wunce, to make shore.

(Billy Bunter's Benefit)

The most perennial foils (or attempted foils!) for Bunter are the Famous Five in the Remove. Wharton is one, the other four being Bob Cherry, Johnny Bull, Hurree Jamset Ram Singh, and Frank Nugent. Cherry is described as extroverted, anti-suffragette (although not knowing much about the suffragette movement) warm-hearted and genial, with an all-round talent for sport. He has much personal charm, which is used to excellent effect when in the company of Marjorie from

Cliff House School. Johnny Bull is the phlegmatic "know-all" Yorkshireman. Frank Nugent is a quieter individual, and although Bob Cherry was the author's favourite character, Nugent was the closest Hamilton came to portraying his own self in any of his work. Indeed Hamilton once wrote: "Frank Nugent is, or was, no other than Frank Richards himself, as far as one could draw one's own portrait." Nugent is however certainly not above the occasional prank; in one story he disguises himself as a pupil of Cliff House Girls' School.

The most exotic character of the Famous Five is of course the inscrutable Hurree Jamset Ram Singh, of Bhanipur, India, otherwise known as the Nabob of Bhanipur or simply Inky. His creation was inspired by Hamilton's meeting in the 1890s - for no more than five minutes - with a "dark gentleman" whose greeting - "the top of a beautiful morning" stuck in Hamilton's mind. Inky did not begin his fictional life at Greyfriars, but at Netherby School, in a series of stories Hamilton had written for the *Marvel;* his character offered so many intriguing possibilities that Hamilton was quick to transfer him to his most successful series. Amiable, good-natured, shrewd and proud, he finds a comfortable niche with his Greyfriars contemporaries and feels just as much at home with them as he does in his home territory where he is a monarch! It is his wonderful use (or misuse) of English - the incorporation of which into a work of fiction would decades later be condemned as racist- which provides a great deal of the entertainment value in the stories, and an integral part of some of the most vigorous dialogue ever to appear in schools fiction (see below). The Babu English given to him by Hamilton finds its equivalent in the pidgin English given to other foreign characters in the stories. Hamilton did this quite unashamedly; foreigners amused him, and any accusations of racism simply did not bother him.

Besides the Famous Five, a number of other pupils feature, the most outstanding of which is Herbert Vernon-Smith, otherwise known as the "Bounder" or "Smithy." Vernon-Smith, the son of a millionaire but with no aristocratic blood in him, has a particular charisma. He achieves notoriety through his rebelliousness, his encouragement to other boys to smoke and drink, and his attempts to manoeuvre the expulsion of his contemporaries. He is also something of a barrack-room lawyer, his response to a punishment he considers unjust being some revenge on the teacher who has inflicted it. He is constantly coming close to expulsion for this very thing. His great friend at Greyfriars is the scholarship boy Tom Redwing, son of a fisherman. Other pupils include Horace Coker, the bossy, blundering fifth-former, king of the "whops" and known as the Greyfriars Samson; Alonzo Todd, who together with cousin Peter are study mates of Bunter; the aristocratic Lord Mauleverer (Mauly) who once saves Bunter's life with the aid of a cunningly secreted chunk of canned beef; the caddish, cowardly, snobbish, sneaking Skinner; the dauntless school captain Wingate; the unpopular sadistic prefect Loder; the

Lancashire scholarship boy Mark Linley, referred to by Bunter as "you beastly factory rotter" but who was one of Hamilton's favourite characters; the brash money-grubbing American, Fisher T Fish, whose seemingly endless capacity for financial scheming incurs considerable unpopularity amongst his colleagues Bunter's younger brother Sammy; the deaf boy Dutton whose disability generates some hilarious although somewhat tasteless misunderstandings; and the Chinaman with the equally tasteless name Wun Lung.

The teacher who appears most frequently is Henry Samuel Quelch, master of the Remove, and not infrequently infuriated by Bunter's excesses. Although rather more benign than Mr Ratcliff of St Jim's, and indeed a compassionate and understanding man, he is not sparing in his use of the rod, and anybody who crosses him or pulls his leg is well aware of the fate that awaits him - hence the tag "a just beast." His liking for the classics mirrors Hamilton's, as does his singleness and dedication. Also prominent is Dr Locke, the Headmaster, to whom the outside world hardly exists. He is extremely intelligent, is head-magisterial to his finger-tips, and has as great a liking for the classics as Quelch and Hamilton. Less prominent, but nonetheless featured in a number of stories, is the overweight fifth-form master Paul Pontifex Prout, the pompous enemy of Quelch. Prout has little time for Horace Coker and his sidekicks; his attempts at friendliness with the boys are frustrated because, quite simply, he is such a bore, using any excuse to regale his charges with reminiscences of his days in the Rockies. Other masters include the incompetent Monsieur Charpentier (the Greyfriars equivalent of St Jim's' Monsieur "Mossoo" Morny) and the excessively fierce Shell master Mr Hacker. Ratcliff of St Jim's is great friends with him, this friendship providing another reminder of the not inconsiderable overlap between many of Hamilton's fictional schools. Among those not on the teaching staff but who figure in the Greyfriars stories, there is Gosling the porter, the tuckshop owner Mrs Mimble, and Horace Coker's Aunt Judy whose obsession with her nephew and intimidating personality make her, in Cadogan's words, the "female buffoon of the *Magnet*." One would like to think that if Bunter predeceased her he would remember her in his will; her tuck parcels for her beloved nephew were prone to end up in Bunter's clutches instead!

THE ST JIM'S STORIES

The two principal characters have already been mentioned; Arthur Augustus d'Arcy, alias Gussy, the aristocrat, and Tom Merry, the robust yet equable, good-tempered yet magnetic Lower School leader. Once ensconced at St Jim's, Merry (Harry Wharton's equivalent at St Jim's) was never in serious danger of being upstaged by the arrival of a Billy Bunter equivalent at his school, and remains the central character throughout. His magnetism is not confined to the cosy Sussex countryside where, near a ruined castle, St Jim's is situated. One of the stories, for example, is set in the casinos of Monte Carlo; another takes us to the borders of Italy and Austria after a Zeppelin lands on the cricket field at St Jim's, and Merry and his chums find themselves on board when it unexpectedly takes off. Hamilton, as Clifford, even took Merry and his companions to Arizona, where Merry's wealthy uncle has a ranch, and Merry distinguishes himself by lassoing a savage mustang.

Whereas Merry is the hero, d'Arcy is the figure of fun. His aristocratic tendencies are reflected by his patriotism and his voice, and his speech is written throughout in the manner he would say it:

"Yaas, wathah - wight in! Wight in, neahly up to his neck! I wegard that a vewy wippin' of Watty! He was wathah cwoss about it, but, of course, he is wathah a cwusty old codgah...."

"I wefuse to ansah that widiculous question, Lowthah. I wepeat that pewwaps I had better take the mattah in hand."

(Tom Merry & Co. of St Jim's)

"But nevah say die, deah boy! Make a firm wesolve and stick to it, and - Bai Jove! this chair seems to feel wathah damp, Cardew."

(The Scapegrace of St Jim's)

His apparently superior manner hides a caring (though not entirely unpatronising) concern for the disadvantaged, and a realisation that his peers are not blameless in some situations. Indeed, much of the hilarity of the St Jim's stories arises from his attempting, in his own misguided and foolhardy way, to put right some injustice. For instance, when the Great War breaks out and he sees that "selfish wottahs" are making money out of the war, he suggests that surplus wealth of his St Jim's colleagues be used to go towards the war effort. He also suffers a beating for questioning the attendance of the School housemaster, Mr Railton, at a football stadium during the war, unaware that Railton is leading a recruitment drive!

Another charismatic character in the St Jim's stories is George Figgins of New House. Those coming to St Jim's after Greyfriars will spot the resemblance between Figgins and Herbert Vernon-Smith; both come perilously close to being expelled for misdemeanours, and neither are afraid of attempting revenge on a teacher who has meted out some injustice. Things tend to be in threes at St Jim's; Figgins' friends in New House are Kerr and Wynn; Merry's buddies in the Shell are Manners and Lowther; the Fourth Formers who as School House men are deadly rivals to Figgins et al are Blake, Herries and Digby (these three being the first "heroes" of the St Jim's of *Pluck* fame), and there is another group, containing the prankster Ernest Levison, with his mates Clive and Cardew. From time to time we hear of a boy who rejoices in the unfortunate name of Kangaroo. One character which Greyfriars aficionados will instantly recognise is Baggy Trimble, whose craving for solid refreshment and lack of any endearing characteristics whatsoever, is very reminiscent of Bunter. There is Ralph Reckness Cardew, a fastidious aristocratic individualist. In a St Jim's novel, *The Scapegrace of St Jim's*, his preoccupation with betting leads directly to his very nearly losing a vital cricket match against Carcroft School. There is Dick Julian, a sterling Jew who has to endure torment at St Jim's from the unpleasant Mellish and Crooke; Monty Lowther, the practical joker who engineers an unpleasant trick for Julian and who ends up fighting with him but, in the best traditions of school confrontations, makes up later; and St Jim's prize duffer, Herbert Skimpole, many of whose characteristics are reflected in Alonzo Todd at Greyfriars. Skimpole, who sets much store by the work of Professor Balmycrumpet and quotes freely from him, has strong Socialist tendencies, and also the somewhat peculiar pastime of inviting into St Jim's the various tramps he meets on his travels. One of the Martin Clifford stories in the *Gem* is entitled *Skimpole's Little Scheme* and has a picture of the bespectacled Skimpole standing benignly beside a vagrant whose hand is outstretched for generous cash contributions.

Despite the inevitable male dominance, ladies are not neglected; Tom Merry's nurse Priscilla Fawcett plays a not inconsiderable part in the narrative, and d'Arcy's Cousin Ethel Cleveland is another popular character throughout the series. As well as playing the part of the pampering nurse, Priscilla Fawcett features in one delightful story where, taking refuge at St Jim's following a threatening letter, she turns the school's domestic arrangements upside down. Ethel, though portrayed as extremely pretty and much admired by the pupils at St Jim's, is no dumb blonde; we hear that not only does she cycle and ride, but she also understands cricket and football! The front cover of one issue of the *Gem* is devoted to Ethel on horseback, negotiating a fence with consummate ease, leaving a number of other riders, including the monocled D'Arcy, behind her. She appears to have a wondrous effect on the behaviour of other boys, filling Cardew with guilt after she has seen him smoking, and making Figgins promise not to fight. The relationship between Ethel and Figgins occupies a significant amount of space in the *Gem*. His inordinate fondness for her is demonstrated by his being the first to invite her to join St Jim's boys on organised events, and his saving her life in a train crash on the Continent. She joins the Girl Scouts and as well as being a good Samaritan to d'Arcy in her capacity as member of the Girl Scout Patrol, she is part of the Girl Scout team that takes on and defeats scouts from St Jim's. Another device for bringing ladies on to the scene is a story of how d'Arcy, forced into hiding, takes refuge in the woodshed of a neighbouring girls' school and having been found out, has to endure the wrath of the formidable gym mistress Miss Bullivant who swings a nifty and extremely menacing golf club. Chivalry, though, is triumphant; having been suitably thrashed d'Arcy is left to reflect on the "fearful thwashin'" he would have given her had she been a man! In fact another fertile subject for the pen of Hamilton was d'Arcy's flirtatiousness, beginning as early as 1907 with a liking for the Headmaster's niece - also called Ethel!

As for teachers, the one outstanding - or perhaps, one should say, outstandingly terrible - teacher is Mr Ratcliff, whose sadistic nature is emphasised by his smiling while he administers beatings. He is at his worst in *Tom Merry & Co. of St Jim's* wherein the first quarter of the book alone he administers whoppings to two boys:

Figgins bent over the chair. Six times in succession there was the rhythmic sound of cane meeting trousers. Figgy set his teeth and was silent, till the last swipe came - but Mr Ratcliff seemed to put all his beef into that last swipe, and it was too much for Figgy. He roared.

Mr Railton is another tough character; whilst lacking Ratcliff's obvious repellent features, he will not hesitate to refer any misbehaviour amongst his School House charges to the headmaster, Doctor Holmes. Foreign colour is provided by Monsieur Morny the French teacher, otherwise known as Mossoo, which speaks volumes for the standard of French pronunciation at St Jim's. His Franglais would make Miles Kington envious:

"Entrez, mon cher Ratcliff! Is anyzing ze mattair?"

(*Tom Merry & Co. of St Jim's*)

Animals are not overlooked either. D'Arcy's brother Wally owns a dog named Pongo who causes much distress to both brothers by continually disappearing, and Herries in the fourth form has a pet bulldog Towzer, useful when evildoers are at hand, not so useful when it is the fourth formers, rather than the criminals, who are savaged by the canine in question.

HAMILTON'S OTHER SCHOOLS

Although Greyfriars and St Jim's dominated Hamilton's writing career, he still found time to write numerous stories about many other schools; so many, in fact, that nobody has been able to trace and identify all his work. It will be recalled that Hamilton had already written stories for other boys' papers; one of these was the *Boy's Friend*, and in 1915 Rookwood School, set in Hampshire, was created for that paper. This was at the request of Herbert Hinton who had taken over from Griffith as editor of the *Gem* and who had also acquired control of *Boy's Friend*.

Rookwood stories, written under the pseudonym Owen Conquest, ran from 1915 until 1926, and were the most popular stories of Hamilton after those of life at Greyfriars and St Jim's. The stories are shorter than the *Magnet* ones, but contain the same wealth of personalities; Bunter's equivalent Reginald "Tubby" Muffin with a particular inkling towards jam tarts and who "goes gay" not by a sudden burst of effeminacy but by smoking and gambling in order to impress a rich uncle; Herbert Manders M.A., the unpopular housemaster, resplendent with gown, mortar board and fearsome-looking cane; yet another less-than-adequate French teacher, Monsieur Monceau (alias Mossoo again); the monocled top hatted Adolphus Smythe (d'Arcy's equivalent), leader of the "Nuts;" Mark Lattrey, the Cad of the Fourth Form; the aristocratic Valentine Mornington, Cardew's equivalent; Richard "Dicky" Dalton who ranges his fourth form delinquents in a row before his desk and then whops them; the Headmaster Dr Chisholm who receives his comeuppance at the unlikely hands of the bootboy and dogsbody Timothy Tupper; a number of top-class sportsmen; the "Famous Fistical Four" (not five as in Greyfriars!) namely Jimmy Silver, George Raby, Arthur Newcome and Arthur Lovell; and lastly the "Modern ticks," Tommy Dodd, Tommy Cook and Tommy Doyle. Rivalry between Houses is stressed far more at Rookwood than at Greyfriars, with Silver and Co. staunchly defending the honour of the Classical House. As with the boys of St Jim's, the Rookwood pupils are taken across the Atlantic and spend 35 weeks in Canada. Despite the cessation of the series in 1926, Rookwood reappeared in the *Greyfriars Holiday Annual* in 1938. There was also a single novel published by Mandeville in 1951 entitled *The Rivals of Rookwood*. It is perhaps slightly disappointing that the plot of this novel duplicated a plot used in many other Hamilton stories, namely an attempt by boys to achieve revenge for an act of injustice perpetrated by a teacher. The ending, where all is resolved thanks to a fierce dog who has hitherto played no significant part in the story, is particularly feeble. Rookwood never produced characters of the charisma of Bunter or d'Arcy.

A number of other boys' schools were created by Hamilton but again failed to achieve either the popularity of Greyfriars or the output of St Jim's or even Rookwood stories. Many, with their fleeting appearances in print, are lost to the modern reader and critic. Before settling down to work on the Greyfriars and S Jim's stories, Hamilton wrote for a number of papers; his writings in the boys' paper *Best Budget* in 1902 represent possibly his earliest discovered schools writing. Although new fictional schools were created by Hamilton throughout his life, it was noticeable that when he started writing regularly for the *Magnet* and the *Gem* he took on far fewer other commitments. A list of the fictional schools he is known to have invented is given at the end of this chapter, together with a list of the periodicals to which he contributed. One or two schools deserve special mention.

uch as the Cedar Creek series of stories in *Boy's Friend* in 1917, using the Martin Clifford pseudonym. Cedar Creek is a day-school set in British Columbia in Canada. The hero is called Frank Richards, and indeed it is said that much of Hamilton's boyhood experience is mirrored by that of Frank in the Cedar Creek series. Other characters include Vere Beauclerc, and the extremely eligible headmistress who is another Ethel - Miss Ethel Meadows. The setting of Cedar Creek - deep in backwoods and vulnerable to attacks by rustlers and grizzlies - invites endless possibilities for exciting yarns. The series ran until 1921. Hamilton's aptitude for telling a good adventure story is illustrated by his creation of Len Lex, a schoolboy detective. Similar to Cedar Creek is Packsaddle, which featured in the *Gem* from January 1935. Set deep in a small community in the Wild West, the school, in log-cabin-style buildings, offers minimal standards of comfort. As Cadogan put it: "All this is a far cry from Greyfriars and St Jim's, with their cricket and football pitches, cloisters, ancient elms, ivy clad buildings, and masters rustling to and fro in gowns and mortarboards." Discipline is harsh, and justice rough; the headteacher, Sampson, is an ex-cowpuncher with no education to speak of. By contrast, Mr Brown is a diffident academic recruited by Sampson to attempt to instil some learning into a bunch of boys regularly subjected to kidnappers, rustlers, and other death-defying adventure. Heroes among the boys include a British boy, Dick Carr, and his Yankee sidekicks Slick Poindexter and Mike Kavanagh. Returning to England, in 1935 Hamilton also invented High Coombe School for *Modern Boy*. High Coombe is also known as School for Slackers and the series consists of the struggles between the young, enthusiastic headmaster James McCann who tries to dump the unenviable image High Coombe has for itself, and the slacking boys themselves, led by Aubrey Compton. McCann is by no means always victorious at the end, the only crumb of comfort for him being the enthusiasm one of the principal slackers shows for sport! It was not one of Hamilton's more inspired creations. Even their appearance after the war in *Billy Bunter's Own Annual* and *Tom Merry's Own Annual* when classroom anarchy was more topical, failed to give the stories the immortality won by the Greyfriars chronicles. The most ignominious creation of Hamilton's was Harry Nameless of St Kit's, written under the pseudonym Clifford Clive, for a boys' paper *School and Sport* established by Herbert Hinton in a fit of pique following his departure from Amalgamated Newspapers. Not only did the paper fail miserably, but Hamilton received no fee!

The outbreak of the Second World War brought with it the abandonment by Amalgamated Press of all Hamilton's school storypapers of which the *Gem* and the *Magnet* were examples but not of course the only ones. Since Amalgamated Press held the copyright of the Greyfriars stories, Hamilton was forced to think elsewhere for ideas for school stories. Despite his considerable income, Hamilton spent money quickly and needed ideas fast in order to survive. He found salvation

ANOTHER ROUSING SCHOOL YARN, FEATURING OTTO VAN TROMP—

THE GREYFRIARS REBELLION!

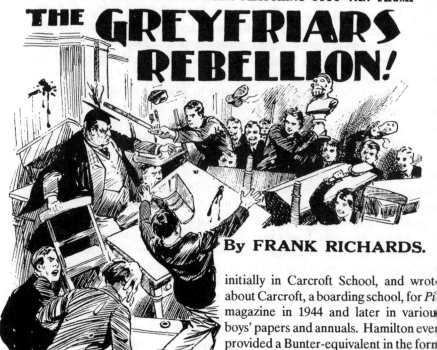

By FRANK RICHARDS.

initially in Carcroft School, and wrot
about Carcroft, a boarding school, for *Pi*
magazine in 1944 and later in variou
boys' papers and annuals. Hamilton ever
provided a Bunter-equivalent in the forn
of "Turkey" Tuck, and Herbert Vernon
Smith was given an "opposite number" in
the form of Dudley Vane-Carter. Th
school actually found its way into th
post-war novel *The Scapegrace of St Jim's*. However, Carcroft was a poor substitut
for Greyfriars. Other schools followed; these included Lynwood, Felgate, Head
land House, Topham and Sparshott, all produced by small publishers in mini
paperback form. Although none of these were successful for Hamilton, it was th
promotion of the Sparshott series - in which Bunter reappeared - by reference t
Greyfriars' success which prompted the commissioning of the series of Bunte
novels in hardback form. This marked the start of the exciting revival of Bill
Bunter and the Famous Five of Greyfriars, and from then on it was Greyfriars tha
was to occupy Hamilton's energies again, to the exclusion of almost all the othe
schools of his imagination.

Though primarily a writer for boys, Hamilton did not confine himself purely t
the boys' school story. In 1903 he had written about a boys' school called Clif
House for the *Marvel*, and it was to be Cliff House that would be the venue fo

Hamilton's principal series of girls' school fiction. Reginald Eves, the deputy wartime editor of the *Gem* and the *Magnet* realised, from correspondence he had received, that both these papers had a considerable female following. He saw that there was no equivalent paper for girls and thought that the establishment of such a paper would assure him of a job when the existing editor of the *Gem* and the *Magnet* returned from war service. The result was *School Friend* which began in 1919, and which would, over the next decade, provide numerous tales from fictional girls' schools. Hamilton, under the pseudonym Hilda Richards, was asked to provide a girls' school storyline. This led to the creation of Cliff House, which had already featured in the *Magnet*. It was thus that readers of *School Friend* were introduced to a number of characters that were already well known to *Magnet* readers. These included Amy Locke, sister to the Greyfriars principal, an ardent suffragette who would later become second in command to the headmistress, Penelope Primrose. Miss Primrose had been a central figure in a *Magnet* story entitled Alonzo's Plot where she was a victim of a hoax by boys trying to bring her and Mr Quelch together. Other characters at Cliff House, whom *Magnet* readers had already met, included Marjorie Hazeldene and Clara Trevlyn. It was also felt that Cliff House needed an equivalent to Rookwood's Tubby Muffin and Greyfriars' Billy Bunter, whose popularity had become so evident by the time of the advent of *School Friend*. The need was met by the introduction into the school of Billy Bunter's sister, Elizabeth Gertrude Bunter, known to everyone as Bessie. She is introduced to readers by way of a picture of her sitting smugly in a bun shop. Like her brother, she does not walk but she rolls; she has fat paws rather than hands; and she always has her eyes open for food. In the first chapter of the novel *Bessie Bunter of Cliff House School* she is detained by Mademoiselle Lupin, the incompetent French teacher, having been caught eating a pear in class. Indeed in the same novel it is her practical joke on Mr Quelch within the precincts of Greyfriars which forces Marjorie's brother, known as Hazel throughout, to go into hiding and risk death through starvation. Other characters include Miss Bullivant, who gave d'Arcy such a hard time in the *Gem*, Marjorie's form mistress Miss Bellew, and chums and rivals of Marjorie, namely Dolly Jobling, Babs and Mabs. Babs, or Barbara Redfern, is the Captain of the Fourth Form and the Lower School, and who Cadogan and Patricia Craig described as the "epitome of every conceivable virtue... unswerving sweetness, courage and loyalty... nauseating nobility of spirit." Rather more human is Clara Trevlyn, another member of the 4th form, and a tomboy although not without traces of femininity; Cadogan and Craig observed that "Hamilton cannot resist lumbering her with all the undesirable attributes which he considers exclusive to women; calculated duplicity, illogicality, craven fear of mice and insects and an obsessional interest in pretty hats." Clara is in effect a more acceptable mixture of courageous, athletic, temperamental and cowardly. She also appears to have considerable difficulty expressing herself in plain English:

> *"I think this fountain pen leaks," said Dolly Jobling. "Look at my fingers."*
> *"Behold, they are black but comely," said Clara.*
> *"I say......!" howled Bessie.*
> *"You still there?" asked Clara, looking round. "Fatima, you're de trop."*
> (Bessie Bunter of Cliff House School)

Unfortunately Hamilton's stay with *School Friend* was destined to be a short one; he was taken off the paper after composing a mere handful of stories for it. This was ostensibly because the editor of the *Magnet* and the *Gem* (which were of course, like *School Friend*, owned by Amalgamated Newspapers) felt Hamilton could not possibly keep going with so many different papers at once. However, it had become clear that despite Hamilton's tremendous aptitude for writing boys' school stories - his works retained their popularity despite the general decline in the boys' school story in the 1920s - he had not the same sureness of touch when writing about girls. Cadogan and Craig suggested that "Hamilton's... Cliff House characters were ciphers rather than believable schoolgirls, either overdrawn embodiments of squealing femininity or at the other extreme, tomboyishness."

Humphrey Carpenter and Mari Prichard were also critical: "His characterisation of Bessie was too crude for girls' tastes, and the other girls at her school, Cliff House, were too sketchily drawn."

The irony was that other writers kept the Cliff House stories going in *School Friend* using the Hilda Richards pseudonym, and perhaps just as galling to Hamilton was the fact that the writers who followed, though not allowed to use Greyfriars, developed the characters quite effectively and impressively and became successful in their own right. The success of *School Friend* with its new writers resulted in the establishment of a number of new schoolgirls' papers by the Amalgamated Press. These included *Schoolgirls' Own* in 1921, as well as the *Schoolgirls' Weekly*, the *Schoolgirl* (which replaced *School Friend* in 1929 and ended in 1940 when the German invasion of Norway cut off pulp paper supplies and *Crystal*, later renamed *Girls' Crystal*. All of them were well illustrated, full of robust adventure, and immensely popular, their exuberance contrasting sharply with the more strait-laced inter-war schoolgirl fiction. Not to be outdone, Hamilton's response was to include Cliff House in Greyfriars stories and also to use the pseudonym Hilda Richards for some of his later works. Only one Cliff House title appeared in hardback form; that was *Bessie Bunter of Cliff House School* in 1949. However, Armada Books and Merlin Press reissued some of the *School Friend* stories in paperback book form for a new audience in the late 1960s. *Bessie Bunter f Cliff House School,* like many of the Greyfriars novels, was reissued by Hawk 3ooks in 1991 and thus became available to a new audience. None of Hamilton's uccessors on *School Friend* achieved lasting popularity despite their favourable eception at the time they first appeared.

It was not only in the strength of Hamilton's characterisation that he made such n impact on his readership; his style was, quite simply, unique.

"Throughout (Greyfriars') 32 year run," wrote Mary Cadogan, "boys and mas- ers roared and raved, howled and hooted, snorted, sneered and sniffed, gurgled nd gasped, bawled and burbled, exclaimed and ejaculated, and, in the case of 3unter, squeaked and cachinnated." One of the most appealing aspects of the tories is the richness and pace of dialogue, and the superabundance of catch- ›hrases and expressions which the reader would instantly recognise as the work ›f Martin Clifford or Frank Richards. Although the extracts below are all taken rom Greyfriars stories, the principles remained the same throughout Hamilton's vork.

The catchphrases are legion. The most famous is Billy Bunter's "I say, you ellows!" which perhaps says less about Bunter himself than about the way in which Greyfriars pupils talked. If Bunter is flustered, it is quite likely that the "I" will ake the form of a protracted stammer. Bunter has a number of other favoured

"That's enough, you rotter!" roared Coker at the headmaster.
"Hands off, or I'll knock you spinning!"

remarks. "Blessed if I see anything to cackle at!" is uttered when Bunter find
himself on the receiving end of the Remove's hilarity. "Oh, really...." and then a
name, is Bunter's way of expressing disapproval of the last speaker's comment or
action. "Oh, lor'!" a discreet form of schoolboy blasphemy, usually follows an
announcement that the cane is about to be employed on his posterior. "Oh
crikey!" is a frequent alternative. "Beasts!" follows conduct by his colleagues to
which Bunter takes exception. When something hard and/or sharp is applied to
Bunter either by a teacher or by a colleague, the expletives "Yarooooooh!" and
"Yoo-hoooooop!" are likely to follow. Of the other members of the Famous Five
the outstanding catchphrase contribution is provided by Hurree Jamset Ram Singh
who having referred to his chums as "esteemed" will seize upon a statement made
by the previous speaker and turn it into a wonderful new word followed by an
opinion that the state of affairs expressed in that word is, or would be, terrific.

For example:

"There'd be a row," said Frank Nugent.
"The rowfulness would be terrific!"

(Bunter the Bad Lad

Inky will go further, however, and produce some magnificent mixed proverbs:
"My esteemed chums... let not the exacerbation of arguefulness cloud the idiotic
smile of ludicrous friendship. Speech, my esteemed Johnny, is silvery, but silence is
the bird in the hand that spoils the broth, as the English proverb remarks."

(Bessie Bunter of Cliff House School

"A stitch in time saves a cracked pitcher from going longest to the well, as the English
proverb remarks, my esteemed Bunter," remarked Hurree Jamset Ram Singh, "and it
is no use locking the stable door after too many cooks have spoiled the broth."

(Billy Bunter's Benefit

Or he will be guilty of simple misuses of lengthy words:

"The helpfulness of our absurd selves will be terrific, if you can tell us anything we
can do... we are all preposterously keen to restore the idiotic equanimity of the
beauteous Marjorie."

(Bessie Bunter of Cliff House School

A large number of other catchphrases are shared out amongst the Famous Five
- and others - with no particular owner; all these come from Billy Bunter's Benefit
but they can be found in almost every other Greyfriars title:

"Oh, scissors!"
"Oh, my hat!"
"You fat villain!"
"You howling ass!"
"Oh, crumbs!"
"Go and eat coke!"
Horace Coker of the Fifth frequently threatens to "spiflicate" Bunter following the Fat Owl's latest nefarious deed, but Fisher T Fish, coming as he does from across the Atlantic, has his own brand of phraseology which gives the appearance of a completely different language:

"Absquatulate!"
                                    (Billy Bunter of Greyfriars School)
"I guess I'm on in this," he said. "It sure is the bee's knee!"
                                    (Billy Bunter of Greyfriars School)
"School books is rather a drug in the market," he said, "and these are purty tattered."
                                    (Billy Bunter of Greyfriars School)
"Aw, pack it up!" snapped Fisher T Fish. "I guess Amurrican clocks can lay over anything that ever ticked on this side of the pond."

"I'll say," murmured Fisher T Fish, "that they sure are boneheads in this pesky old island - they sure are boobs from Boobsville! I guess its cruelty to animals to fool them sich all-fired jays!"
                                    (The Japer of Greyfriars)

Mr Quelch, because his sentences tend to be lengthy and pompous, might be thought to be above catchphrases, but his "Bless my soul!" and "Upon my word!" are frequently heard; the phrase which sends shivers down any spine is his "Bend over that chair!" which inevitably means that a caning is on its way, and, after the chastisement has been administered, yells of anguish are silenced by the unsympathetic command to "Cease that ridiculous noise!" Hamilton, being a keen exponent of the Latin language, found it easier to write about misbehaviour in Latin lessons than in any other, and frequently Quelch's command to "Construe!" (i.e. translate from Latin to English) rings round the classroom. Quelch is often referred to as having "gimlet-eyes."
One of the highlights of Hamilton's books is the graphic detail conveyed by him through the use of single words. Bunter does not walk; he rolls. It is not a hand that stretches out for a twelfth jam tart or third slice of cake, but a paw. The characters do not just say, reply, answer, respond, utter or even retort. They jaw, roar, gasp, stutter, hiss, yell, splutter, bawl, grin, squeak, chortle, cacchinate, and, of course, ejaculate. When a character laughs, we do not just hear about it; we

hear it:

> *"Sure it wasn't a pirate landed from a lugger?" asked Bob.*
> *"Ha, ha, ha!" yelled the Removites.*
>
> (Bunter the Racketeer)

When a character is in pain, we certainly know about it:

> *"Ooooogh!" Coker spluttered soot. "I-I-I'll-woooogh!"*
> *"That will be a lesson to you, Coker," chuckled Bob Cherry.*
> *"The lessonfulness will be terrific, my esteemed idiotic Coker."*
> *"Ooooooooooogh!"*
>
> (Billy Bunter's Benefit)
>
> *Coker glanced round.*
> *"This cheeky fag came here to whop me with a fives bat!" he said. "He looks like*
> *doing it, doesn't he?"*
> *"Yow-ow! I never......Yarooooooh!"*
> *Whack, whack!*
> *"I never.....Yurrrrooop!"*
> *"Looks like it - what?" grinned Coker. "What do you men think - eh?"*
> *"Ha, ha, ha!"*
> *Whack!*
>
> (Bunter the Racketeer)
>
> *Bob gave the fat Owl a gentle push with his right, on the widest part of his*
> *circumference.*
> *"Urrrrrggghh!" gurgled Bunter.*
> *He sat down again suddenly on the settee.*
> *"Wurrrrrgh!"*
>
> (Billy Bunter's Benefit)

When a caning takes place, the sound effects of the cane are also provided to
supplement the sounds of the victim:

> *Swipe! Swipe! Swipe!*
> *"Yow-ow-ow-ow-ow!" roared Bunter.*
> *Swipe!*
> *"Yaroooh!"*
> *Swipe!*
> *"Yooo-hooooooooop!"*
> *SWIPE!*

Quelch put his beef into it. Immemorial custom prescribed "six" as the limit. Quelch kept to the six; but every one was a swipe, and the last swipe was really terrific. Billy Bunter's frantic roar woke every echo in the Rag.

(Billy Bunter's Benefit)

OUR GRAND FORM-ROOM NUMBER!

The GREYFRIARS HERALD

Harry Wharton, Editor

Supplement No. 54.   Week Ending January 7th, 1922.

A Fateful Blunder!

By
FRANK NUGENT.

MR. QUELCH UNDER FIRE! The door of the Form-room opened, and a figure in gown and mortar-board crossed the threshold. The air was thick with the small peas, which rained upon the intruder in a shower!

It was indeed extraordinary that a man as compassionate as Hamilton should have adopted such a zany approach to the subject. Perhaps the only crumb of comfort which can be derived from this as far as opponents of corporal punishment are concerned, indeed giving strength to their case, is that caning seems to have precious little effect on the behaviour of Master W.G.Bunter!

The narrative itself always has a hectic edge. Even when little happens to push the action forward, there is always the appearance of activity and business by simple virtue of the very short, snappy speeches of the characters, which pepper the stories relentlessly. Often, the speeches are not accredited to a particular speaker; indeed, sometimes it is impossible to tell who has spoken many of the lines.

"Oh!" gasped Bunter, "I-I say, you fellows...."
"Here he is!"
"Where's that cake?"
"The wherefulness is terrific."
"You fat brigand...."
"You podgy pirate..."
(Billy Bunter's Banknote)
"These verses, Bunter, copied from the seventh eclogue of Virgil, you have endeav-oured to palm off as your own!"
"Oh, crumbs!" breathed Bob Cherry.
"Oh, scissors!"
"Ha, ha, ha!"
(Billy Bunter's Benefit)

Charles Hamilton's faithful Remington typewriter, on which he produced his vast number of Greyfriars stories, would have seen prodigious use of the inverted comma keys as well as the exclamation mark! Sentences are short and pithy, paragraphs never more than a few lines long. It should not be forgotten that Hamilton was for over thirty years writing for children with limited attention spans in magazines which would often be read in circumstances that were not in the least conducive to uninterrupted concentration and undivided attention. Yet when a paragraph of prose, unsullied by the unholy exclamations of the Removites, does appear in print, there is as much humour to be found there as in the crisp passages of dialogue that precede and follow.

Billy Bunter liked jam. In fact, he loved it, with a faithful and abiding love. But the course of true love never did run smooth. Bunter did not meet the object of his affection nearly so often as he wished.
(Billy Bunter of Greyfriars School)

Frequently, Hamilton either as Richards or Clifford demonstrated his knowl-edge of the classics, the Bible, Gilbert & Sullivan and many other famous writers by comparing his characters' predicament with that of celebrities of former times.

He thus created a wonderfully ironic contrast between the innocent juvenile world of his own making, and the deliberations of great men and women of the past.

The wrath that gathered in Horace Coker's rugged brow, as he realised it, was tremendous. Achilles' wrath, famed in ancient song, had simply nothing on it.

(Billy Bunter Afloat)

But contact with Mother Earth did not have the effect on Billy Bunter that it had on Antaeus of old. Every time he went down, the Fat Owl was slower in getting up again.

(Bunter Does His Best)

Had he remembered it, he might have supposed that Mary would return to finish hoovering the study while he was in the form-room, when the hoover might have hummed like a hive of bees, or roared like the Bull of Bashan, without bothering him.

(Billy Bunter's Postal Order)

Through the millions of words written by Hamilton, and the vast number of schools he created, Billy Bunter emerged as the people's favourite, and he continued to thrive whilst Hamilton's other inventions faded into obscurity. In 1952 Billy Bunter broke into a new medium by becoming a BBC television star, with scripts written by Hamilton and with Joy Harington as producer. The show's anticipated popularity with both nostalgic adults and a new generation of children meant that it went out live, twice every Friday, at 5.25pm for children and two hours later for adults. The series, which made easy transition from book to screen, lasted on and off for ten years. There was some difficulty in finding a suitable person to play Bunter. Joy Harington said: "Every fat boy in England came for the part, but none was right. Then a friend suggested Gerald Campion. Of course, he isn't fat enough in the tummy - we'll have to arrange that. But he's got the face for it."

Gerald Campion was no schoolboy - when given the part he was twenty-nine years old, and married with two children. Anna Home, head of Children's Programmes at the BBC for several years in the late 1980s and 1990s, claimed later that casting an adult in a juvenile role would not be acceptable today. At the time, however, Campion was a resounding success. He had read the *Magnet* when at school and had even been nicknamed Fatty but had dieted to keep his weight down. When given the part of Bunter he said: "I shan't bother (to diet) any more. And I love jam tarts - I even make them myself." Unbelievably, the use of the word "Crikey!" got the series into trouble when an Enfield vicar criticised it as being bad language. He pointed out that the dictionary defined the word as "vulgar." However Campion himself had no shortage of fan mail; people sent him cakes through the post and even kicked him around if they saw him because that was what always happened to Bunter. It is perhaps most apt that Campion went on to become a successful restaurateur with entries in the Good Food Guide! Towards the end of the 1950s Campion starred in a number of Bunter Christmas shows at the theatre before handing over to ‑Peter Bridgmont. The plays were written not by Hamilton but by a former *Magnet* reader Maurice McLoughlin. However, to demonstrate that his zest for writing about Greyfriars was still unquenched, Hamilton managed, despite his advancing years, to write some Greyfriars material in Latin, including a complete story *Ultio Bunteri* which was published in 1961 in the *Times*.

Before any of the juniors could realise what was happening, Dr. Armstrong produced a cane from under the folds of his gown, and rushed on to the field and commenced to lash at the bare knees of the players. "Stoppit ! Ow !" roared Bob Cherry. (*See Chapter 2.*)

Indeed in 1958 his enthusiasm for his fictional companions of half a century's standing was as strong as ever: "A couple of world wars... poles north and south have been explored. Flying men have girdled the earth; and Russian sputniks the heavens. And all the while Billy Bunter has been rolling on his plump way unperturbed..."

Even after Hamilton's death, Bunter lived on, despite attempts at censorship by librarians and schoolmasters alike by banning them from the shelves; this of course made children want to read them all the more. In 1969, the publisher Howard Baker began republishing the *Magnet* in facsimile and by 1988 250 volumes of not only *Magnet* but also *Gem* editions were available in this form. Even though many copies have succumbed to the indignity of the remainder bookshops, the fact is that Bunter is still available to the modern reader in just the same form as it was available to earlier generations. Between 1965 and 1972 Armada, a children's imprint of William Collins, issued paperback editions of some of the hardback novels but also some of the old *Magnet* stories. The Merlin Press also issued paperback editions of Bunter stories. *Valiant* magazine had a Bunter comic strip - not of course the work of Hamilton - in the mid-1960s.

For a while during the late 1970s and early 1980s no Greyfriars titles were available in "ordinary" book form, although Howard Baker continued to turn out facsimile reprints of *Magnet* titles. There then followed a curious episode in 1982 when the Quiller Press published a series of six Greyfriars reprints but in an expurgated form. The books, edited by Kay King and issued in paperback form a year or so later by Granada, excited considerable controversy. Some of the memorable catchphrases, including "I say, you fellows!", "Beast!" and "Oh, crikey!" were preserved, but Hurree Jamset Ram Singh's "the wherefulness is terrific" was blue-pencilled out, as were the blesseds, the ejaculations (which sadly would have conjured up quite different images to the 1980s youngster), the "Oh, really"s and of course the canings. These bowdlerised adaptations, designed to introduce 1980s children to the joys of Greyfriars but without sinister overtones of racism and child abuse, had none of the vigour and the character of the originals and were classic examples of throwing out the baby with the bath water. With the deserved disappearance of these titles as the 1980s progressed, it appeared that the continued existence of Bunter on the High Street bookshelves would once again depend solely on Howard Baker.

Fortunately, 1991 saw a magnificent initiative by Hawk Books, who began publishing faithful facsimiles of the Skilton and Cassell titles at very reasonable prices. The hardbound volumes, with good quality paper and copious illustrations, are now widely available and accessible to yet another generation of Greyfriars enthusiasts. For real Greyfriars aficionados, there is the *Greyfriars Gazette*, a periodical with news and comment about the Frank Richards stories. Bunter also enjoyed a brief radio revival in the summer of 1993, with Greyfriars stories read on Radio 2 by Tim Brooke-Taylor, Graeme Garden and Bill Oddie.

Charles Hamilton, described as a sensitive, gentle and scholarly man, died in 1961 in Kingsgate near Broadstairs in Kent aged 85, achieving a half-column obituary in the *Times*. In those eighty-five years, however, his output was enormous, producing at one stage an average of one and a half million words a year;

no other children's writer achieved this output. It is estimated that using 20 different pen names he wrote 5,000 stories - the equivalent of 1000 full-length novels - in his lifetime. Many of his stories were never actually published, for example editions 1684 to 1687 of the *Magnet*. At one time he was writing six stories and serials *every week*. Indeed even the great George Orwell could not believe a man could write so prolifically. It was the need to produce so much in so short a time, in response to the demands placed upon him by Amalgamated Press, which contributed to his unique style, especially his short paragraphs and use of repetition. It was however that style that made the books so popular and, to quote Carpenter and Prichard, "had an almost hypnotic effect on devotees." Another admirer, Denzil Batchelor, remarked that Hamilton had a gift for characterisation comparable with Homer. Richard Hoggart, writing in 1988, recalled throwing a stink bomb in class, and claimed that "his impulse to throw the stink bomb would have come as much as anything from reading Frank Richards in the Magnet and Gem... pseudo-public-school culture had overhauled street culture." Craig commented on the "extraordinary hold especially among young working- and lower-middle class readers," which Hamilton's work enjoyed. The comedian and entertainer Bob Monkhouse remarked upon the unique harvest of glorious, obsessional fiction which Hamilton had provided. Finally, the great playwright Noel Coward admitted that he had an obsessional liking for the work of Hamilton, and avidly read the *Magnet* and *Gem* every week when he was a schoolboy!

Not everyone liked Hamilton's work. Isabel Quigly, who regarded Hamilton as the father of the "pop" school story, deplored the repetitiveness and predictability of so much of the narrative. Arthur Marshall, number one fan of Angela Brazil, had an avowed dislike of Hamilton's work, and went so far as to state that it created an implausible and tasteless picture of public school life; like Quigly, he found the repetitiveness wearisome. Such sentiments may be justified, bearing in mind the fact that Hamilton himself claimed that he would sit at his faithful old Remington typewriter, think on the subject he wanted to write about, and the story would then come to him; in fact he never knew what each character was going to say until he said it.

Hamilton's most famous critic was George Orwell. In 1940 Orwell claimed that Hamilton's work appealed mostly to state school children who liked to fantasise about public schools, arguing that the Greyfriars and St Jim's stories were implicitly right-wing in a snobbish Edwardian way. He certainly implied that the value of the stories was reduced by the absence therefrom of religion, sex, war and poverty, and the treatment of foreigners as cardboard figures. He suggested there should be a left-wing paper to redress the balance.

Although Hamilton loved positive feedback and welcomed enthusiasts with open arms (always wearing a skullcap in his later years), he reacted aggressively to his critics. His reply to them was that he felt his business was to "entertain his readers, make them happy as possible, give them a feeling of cheerful security, turn their thoughts to healthy pursuits, and above all to keep them away from unhealthy introspection." He also hoped that a boys' left-wing paper would remain impossible to produce, stating that "boys' minds ought not to be disturbed and worried by politics."

Hamilton's stories, but particularly the Greyfriars stories, call to mind an era which has long disappeared from even public schools. Although Hamilton was far from given to puritanism - he was a great gambler - his stories deplored gambling, and he managed to exert a profound influence for the good on the youth of Britain by adopting a clear moral code without preaching. Although the stories even then were considered far-fetched, the snobbery, the intense comradeship, the beatings (so colourfully and graphically described!), even the public school terminology, and above all the cloistered cut-off-from-the-real-world feel about the stories, are all evidence of an age which has long since passed but which provide magnificent escapism and entertainment today. The simple language and what P.W.Musgrave called "the stereotypical nature of the stories" made them easily accessible to young folk of a wide range of educational backgrounds and aptitudes. No real successor to Hamilton has ever come along; while the Thomson papers carried on, in a sense, from where he left off, and comic papers have continued to feed the public demand for purely entertaining school stories, nobody has successfully adopted his style or ethos. It is the combination of this straightforwardness, the escapism, the strong characterisations and above all the charismatic figure of Bunter which makes Hamilton the most outstanding contributor to the English school story of this century.

"Yarooooooh!"
Bunter's wild yell echoed into Berkshire on one side of the Thames, and into Oxfordshire on the other.
"Ha, ha, ha!" came from Pon and Co.
"Yoo-ow-ow! Who's that? What's that? Is that you, Bob Cherry, you beast? Ow! wow! yo-ow! Yaroooh!"

(Billy Bunter Afloat)

It is impossible to list all Hamilton's work; not only is there too much of it (a whole book has been devoted just to listings of his *Magnet* work!) but the list would never be complete. Below is a list of his schools together with the year in which each became a regular feature in his writing; also a list of the magazines and periodicals for which he wrote. The list may need updating at some future time.

SCHOOLS
(NB - Hamilton often used the same name for different schools)

1902: Redcliffe. 1903: Cliff House. 1905: St Winifred's, St Cynthia's, Castle-moor, Clavering, Fernley. 1906: Westmoor, Chilcote, Clivedale, Northmoor, Rookwood, St Edith's, St Hilda's, Melthorpe, Carbrooke, Lyndale, St Jim's, St Oliver's, Headland, Chumley. 1907: St Kits, Carnforth, St Egbert, Grayle College, St Hilda's, Clivedale, St Freda's, Dormer College, St Winifred's, Greyfriars, St Kits, Clavering, Swarthmoor, Northcote, Northorpe, Norchester Board School, Friardale, Larkshall, Netherby, Cliveden, St Seriols, St Ronan's, St Kate's. 1908: Blackdale, Beachwood, St Friar's, Greyfriars, St Ronan's, Birchemwell, Winwood, St John's, Cranmere, St Cecilia's, St Winifred's. 1909: Mornington, St Dorothy's, Professor Crammer's School for Young Gentlemen, Chigville, Pelham, Ravens-bourne, Clarence Dugdale. 1910: Rylcombe Grammar, St Cuthbert's, St Mi-chael's, St Tim's, St Dennys, St Steve's, St Mick's, St Andrew's, St Freda's, Clyffe. 1911: St Wode's, St Mary's, Headland College, St Luke's, St Dennis, Clifton College, Banleigh. 1914: Courtfield Council School, St Mildred's. 1915: High-cliffe, Rookwood. 1917: Cedar Creek. 1919: Cliff House, Benbow. 1921: St Kits. 1932: Grimslade. 1935: Packsaddle, High Combe. 1936: Cockshot. 1937: Ben-dover. 1944: Carcroft. 1946: Sparshott, Headland House. 1947: Topham. Be-tween 1944 and 1949: Lynwood, Tipdale, High Lynn. 1949: Barcroft, Felgate. c1950: St Kate's. Dates unknown: St Ethelbert's, Ferndale.

PERIODICALS
Best Budget, Marvel, Union Jack, Funny Cuts, Pluck, Boy's Friend, Boy's Realm, Smiles, Gem, Vanguard, Boy's Herald, BFL, Magnet, Diamond Library, Boy's Realm, Football Library, Picture Fun, Empire Library, Chuckles, Boys Friend Weekly, School Friend, School & Sport, Ranger, Pilot, Pie, Sparshott, Headland House, Mascot, Nugget Library, Coloured Comic, Larks, World Comic, Popular.

JUBILATE!

"Carry this kitten back at once to St Chad's," she commanded. "Honor Fitzgerald, you will learn two pages of Greek chronology, and repeat them to me before school to-morrow morning. Lettice Talbot, take a forfeit! Girls, I am astonished at you! Open your books instantly, every one of you! Gwen Roby, read out your answer to Example 37."

(The New Girl at St Chad's)

Thus spake Miss Farrar, and verily the girls in their boots did tremble. Mention of Angela Brazil, for modern-day critics, immediately throws up a picture of disgustingly wholesome and insufferably virtuous public school pupils rejoicing in names such as Maisie, Flossie and Lettice, conversing in absurd and often incomprehensible school slang, and spending their time in genteel games of hockey and cricket in seeming ignorance of the cruelties and privations of the outside world. Is this a fair picture?

Angela Brazil was not the first to write schools fiction for girls. The work produced by her predecessors, however, reflected an attitude towards young ladies which contrasted quite considerably with that of the subject of this chapter. Until the turn of the century, girls' story authors had given no real support to the concept of female emancipation, and not even the magazines, the *Girls' Own Paper* or *Girls' Realm*, both established before 1900, foresaw for their readers a life away from married domesticity. As Mary Cadogan and Patricia Craig wrote: "Girls were expected to become women early in their lives; not for them the fantasies and freedom of childhood, but rather conditioning as embryonic little mothers and home-makers." The only girls' school story writer of note during the 1890's was L.T.Meade. Not only did she make no concessions to emancipation, but her work was of the didactic mould from which Talbot Baines Reed had sought to break free in the 1880's. An example was *The Girls of Mrs Pritchard's School*, running to 441 packed pages. The story concerns Rhoda Mangerton, desperate to win an essay prize, so much so that she offers ten pounds to Peggy West to write a good essay for her. Peggy herself needs money to cure her little sister, and accepts. "Bella is alive, and I did it for her," she reminds herself. "It is always worth while to do something for one you love, as I love Belle." As Belle's condition deteriorates - "When I go up to the sky to the Lord Jesus you will come too, won't you, Meg?" - Rhoda and Peggy negotiate further deceptions of similar nature. Inevitably Rhoda's deceit is discovered - "But, Rhoda, you must pray very earnestly to God to help you conquer that deceit which is, I fear, a part of your nature." Throughout,

L.T.Meade's writing was turgid, formal and stiff, and although the moral message was clear enough, it was hardly an enjoyable or relaxing read.

Angela Brazil was responsible for two crucial developments in the girls' school story. Firstly, she transformed such stories from sermons-in-disguise to vibrant readable fiction with seemingly endless possibilities for storylines and good entertainment; she has even been called the feminine equivalent of Talbot Baines Reed. She expressed the girls' attitude from the inside, adopting as far as possible their views and jargon, to achieve, in the words of Cadogan and Craig, "a zest and immediacy which the Edwardian schoolgirl must have relished." Secondly, she saw girls not as trainee domestics or housewives, but as human beings, with personalities, aspirations, abilities and talents of their own, and therefore reflected the drive towards emancipation which was to become such a potent political issue in the first two decades of the twentieth century.

Angela Brazil (whose surname should be pronounced to rhyme with "razzle") was born on 30th November 1869 in Preston, into a comfortable middle-class Victorian household. Her father was a cotton manufacturer. Her mother, Angelica, whose childish freedoms had been curtailed by an English boarding-school, was determined to bring her children up in a creative atmosphere, and at an early age Angela was introduced to art, music, literature and botany. This early introduction to the appreciation of life's riches was to prove significant in her later childhood. Her schooldays began at Preston, in Miss Knowles' Select Ladies School, and almost from the start she demonstrated a keen understanding of the schoolgirl spirit and youthful exuberance. She moved on via Manchester High School to Ellerslie School in Victoria Park, Manchester, a day-school, and there became head girl. Despite the benefits she received from the teaching there, she found its formal atmosphere and lack of opportunity for leisure activities somewhat stifling. From Ellerslie she moved to London to complete her education at Heatherley's art school, where she was a fellow student of Baroness Orczy, who wrote *The Scarlet Pimpernel*. She then returned north to keep house for her brother Walter, a doctor. After her father's early death she travelled extensively in Europe with her mother. Like her great contemporary, Charles Hamilton, she never married. She said: "I don't say I wouldn't like to (marry), but I don't think it's at all likely. I'm not an attractive kind of girl. I know that well enough. I'm so shy." When Walter moved to Coventry, Angela moved with him; she was to be based at 1 The Quadrant in Coventry as housekeeper at her brother's practice from 1911 right through to her death in 1947 and she died peacefully in her sleep at that house. She was to be no lady of leisure; she hated idle moments, and as an ardent conservationist she belonged to the city's Natural History and Science Society as well as the City Guild, of which she was secretary. Additionally she undertook poor visiting and did tireless work for the city's cathedral and YWCA. There was also the little matter of her writing.

It is not difficult to see how Angela became a writer. Helped by her mother, creativity, romance, exuberance and a natural curiosity for things going on around her had been cultivated in her from an early age, and it is arguable that in implanting such characteristics in her fictional schoolgirls she was biting back at the lack of opportunities for self-expression at Ellerslie. Her memories were very important to her, with minor incidents transfigured into significant experiences and providing enormous inspiration for the subject matter of her books. However, while her schooling may have stifled her in one sense, it helped her to cultivate a strong interest in literature, history and mythology, as well as a fascination for fairies and fairy lore. It was also significant that her sister Amy persuaded her parents to take a country cottage in Wales; Angela's stays in Llanbedr, in the heart of the Welsh countryside, inspired her even more. The combination of the wonders of nature with the background of Celtic legends and superstitions was to provide a wealth of material with which to entertain her readers. Although at a very young age she had collaborated with a friend, Leila, on a magazine which contained a serial as well as riddles, acrostics and short stories, it was indeed surprising that it was not until 1899 that her work was first published. The work in question was the first of a series of four children's plays entitled *The Mischievous Brownie*. These were published by T W Patterson of Edinburgh. In the five years that followed she contributed to *Our School* magazine and *Burgons* magazine. Equally surprising was the fact that it was only at the suggestion of her family and friends that she sat down to write a novel. It was in 1904 at the age of 35 that she wrote her first full-length book, *A Terrible Tomboy*, published in 1905; her first school story, *The Fortunes of Philippa*, appeared in 1906. It was published by Blackie & Son, who went on to publish all her full-length school stories, of which the final tally was well over forty. (Cassell & Co published a collection of short stories by her which included tales of school life, and Armada, the paperback imprint of Collins, published some abridged editions of her work in the 1960s and early 1970s.) Advancing years did not deter her; *The School on the Loch*, her last book, appeared in 1946, the year before her death. It was even suggested after she died that she was already working on a book called *The School at the Pearly Gates*! In contrast to the work of Charles Hamilton, the novel was by far her most favoured means of communicating with her readership; she wrote that she preferred books to magazine articles. However, between 1909 and 1919 she was a regular contributor to *Little Folks* magazine; during and after the war she wrote for *The Jolly Book*, and her name also appeared in *Girls' Realm*, the *Violet Book For Girls, The Green Book for Girls* and, towards the end of her life, the *Girls' Own Paper*. The majority of her "non-novel-writing" activities throughout her writing career were channelled into the girls' annuals produced by Blackie & Son and Cassell & Co, although this work stopped completely in 1931. Despite the demand for her talents, her work was never seen on screen, radio or the stage. Marie Stopes once approached her and asked to be allowed to adapt one of her school stories for stage. The request was gently refused, on the basis that the books were not written with the idea of any adaptation for the stage; she claimed she always tried to cram in outdoor adventures to suit the taste of her young readers. She did, however, regard her work as admirably suitable for film adaptation.

In her account of her early life, *My Own Schooldays*, she gave some of the reasoning behind her late start. She admitted that she had already at school established a reputation as a raconteuse, and she recalled in her autobiography how, at school, someone had said: "Let Angela Brazil tell us a story." However she explained that the impetus to start writing came principally from her times in Wales; it was only amongst the Welsh mountains that she found the peace and quiet which enabled her to devote herself to serious writing for the first time. She had an outside studio in which she would sit with notebook and pencil on her knee, and would often produce as many as three drafts before pronouncing herself satisfied with what she had written. First she would plan her plot; then evolve her heroine; then and only then would the incidental material be considered. Often she would take her work to the mountain streams and prepare her plots with the sound of rushing waters as her only distraction. She preferred working definite hours to writing only when the spirit moved her. As well as Wales, she also enjoyed writing in her cottage in the Cornish village of Polperro. She could not, however, be described as parochial; her publishers paid for her to travel in Europe to research stories set on the Continent, and her business canniness ensured that she stayed in the best hotels in France and Italy! Despite her business awareness, she was a compassionate woman, giving half her royalties to charity and even donating a cottage to the Coventry YWCA in 1938.

The secret of Angela's success in writing for children was largely attributable to her attitude towards her readers. Angela liked to think of herself as "a chronic child... liv(ing) in a world of exciting fantasy in which everything... experienced or remembered was recycled at a girlish level of fun." It is hardly surprising that she wrote about children and for children in such a sympathetic as well as prodigious fashion. In *My Own Schooldays* she confessed that "all my heart was with young folks." During her time in Wales she befriended many children and spent much time with them, joining in their play and their activities. She claimed to find their doings more interesting than those of adults. This contact with children provided her with much valuable material, and she claimed that all her stories had foundations in fact. She also claimed to hate books written ostensibly for children but really with an eye to the general older public, and was determined to aim her writing at children. An indication of how well she succeeded is given by a letter she received from one of her many fans: "Please don't ever write for grown up people because we like to feel you belong entirely to us." Angela's skills were in telling her stories from the children's viewpoint and in writing about things children enjoyed reading about. It was therefore hardly surprising that she should choose the English girls' school as the setting for most of her work. In *The Fortunes of Philippa*, incidentally her only novel to be written in the first person, there is a most telling observation, by Mrs Montgomery:

"*I consider a boarding school is the world in miniature.*"

"Those aren't my papers," Winona faltered.

This statement was fully borne out in Angela's books. The intense rivalries and even more intense friendships, stern spinster teachers, cliff-hanging sporting contests, and sheer exuberant outdoor activity and adventure, were all part of school life, and thus made for exhilarating reading, to be eagerly understood and enjoyed by the young reader.

Whereas Charles Hamilton was to concentrate most of his energies on a select number of fictional schools, with Billy Bunter of Greyfriars and Tom Merry of St Jim's exercising his mind most frequently, Angela wrote of many different schools without dwelling on a particular one. In some ways this gave her considerable advantages over Hamilton; not only did she not have to invite the reader to suspend her disbelief at the fact that the same boys and girls were in class long after they had reached middle age, but she had no problems over consistency of characters and she was never in danger of being strait-jacketed by any characters or schools she had created. Although she became most noteworthy for writing about well-to-do children in independent schools, she did not confine herself merely to English schoolgirls in English public schools. Many of her schools are not public schools or indeed boarding-schools, by no means all of the schools are in England or even Great Britain, and the heroine will not necessarily be an English rose. Indeed some of the heroines, even though they are English, lack the upper-class background common to most of Hamilton's characters. Whilst the name Frank Richards immediately calls to mind Billy Bunter, it is almost impossible to recall one of Angela's heroines. The word "heroine" is used advisedly; menfolk do appear in the tales, but usually only as brothers, cousins, fathers and uncles of the principal characters. Although they are occasionally important to the plots, they never occupy a central position in the stories.

Despite the diversity of characters Angela created, there were a number of aspects of her writing which can be described as distinctive hallmarks. Firstly, there is her use of slang, coupled with the extraordinary names with which her characters are blessed. Secondly, there is her plot construction which with its digressions and unlikely twists aimed not only to portray girls as human beings rather than second class citizens, but also aimed to broaden the general knowledge of the readers. Thirdly, considerable coverage is given to relationships between girls. Fourthly, like Harold Avery with the boys' story, is the adherence of her characters to an unwritten code of conduct.

Unlike Charles Hamilton and Anthony Buckeridge, the successful boys' school writers, Angela was not noted for her catchphrases. She was however famed for her extraordinary brand of slang. One should be cautious in this area; the frequent uses of words like "queer," which have perhaps sadly only since acquired a secondary meaning, and "nigger," which was quite acceptable to a nation yet to be confronted with the concept of racism, were not the least bit unusual for a writer of that era. However, even leaving those words aside, and making allowances for the fact that almost a century has passed since her first school story appeared in print, it seems incredible to think that schoolgirls could ever have talked in the way her girls did. It should not be forgotten that Angela was telling the stories from the girls' viewpoint. She was also trying to be up-to-date, and portray the girls, in the words of Cadogan and Craig, as "vying with one another to express their personalities through the use of current expressions." Angela insisted that the dialogue was based on conversations she overheard in the Coventry-Leamington trains. It is perhaps a pity, but nonetheless a fact, that it is the way her schoolgirls talked, rather than their exploits, that most school story enthusiasts remember now:

"Of all silly-judkins you're the silliest!"
(Nesta's New School)

"Irma! Janet! Ethelberga! We've got exeats! Oh, jubilate! Scurry quick and get ready."
(For the School Colours)

"What a blossomy idea!"
(For the School Colours)

"A very jinky notion. We might get an idea on the spot."
(For the School Colours)

"Oh, you lucker!"
(The School at the Turrets)

"Hope I shan't make such a muddle of mine," whispered Peggie. "Who's No.9?"
"A girl from Tancaster. Doesn't look as if she could play for nuts," replied Edna.
"Rather not. I never saw anyone so heavy and stolid," quoth Eileen.
"Impudence of her to have entered," snorted Katie.
"She'll be no go," volunteered Enid.
(Schoolgirl Kitty)

"Glad they've put us in diggings together. I'm ready to chum no end."
(For the Sake of the School)

"I'm afraid my brains don't work very fast. Oh, what a jubilee!"
(The New Girl at St Chad's)

"It's a good thing you tore it up, all the same," said Ruth. "Vivian would have been simply horrified. We have a crusade against slang at Chessington, and 'ripper' is one of the words absolutely vetoed. We only say 'jolly' by stealth."
(The New Girl at St Chad's)

"Now you're sark! Almost as sarky as the snark herself!"
(A Popular Schoolgirl)

"I'm afraid I'm rather rocky today, somehow."
"Got nerves? Girl alive! Do brace up!"
"I suppose I must have caught cold. It'll be a grizzly nuisance if I can't play on Saturday."
(The Luckiest Girl in the School)

"We could get up a hockey concert in aid of it."
"What a frolicsome notion! I'm your man."

(The Luckiest Girl in the School)

"Well, this is a pretty go!" agreed Winona.

(The Luckiest Girl in the School)

"Why, that would be simply glorious! What a splendiferous idea! Oh, do let us try! Then we could have a Past versus Present match. Oh! Wouldn't it be precious?"

(The Luckiest Girl in the School)

"Go ahead! Lay it on thick!" twittered Betty Carlisle. "We knew when you hove into sight that we might expect some jaw-wag!"

(The Luckiest Girl in the School)

"Good old Dollikins!" murmured Linda as the girls put on their coats. "She's A1 at a foray. Got something ripping for next season in her head. I can tell by the twinkle in her eye. She'll ruminate over it all winter, and drop it on us a surprise one day! Oh, thunder! Yes, we ought to be starting!"   *(The Luckiest Girl in the School)*

"Old Vergil's utterly stumped me today!" she mourned to Garnet, as they met in the dressing room before nine o'clock. "If Bunty puts me to construe anywhere on page 21, I'm a gone coon. I'm feeling in a blue funk, I can tell you."

"Poor old bluebottle!"

(The Luckiest Girl in the School)

"Oh, the grizzly bad luck of it!" she wailed to Garnet.

(The Luckiest Girl in the School)

"I say, we're having a regular spree this evening at home," she whispered.

(The School on the Loch)

"Go on, Materkins!" encouraged Clem. "You're A1 at a yarn - and you do enjoy telling it - bet you do!"

(The School on the Loch)

"Good biz! Here's a chocolate for you as prize winner!" declared Sadie.

(The School on the Loch)

"Isn't it withering?" she remarked. "And just on the very afternoon when we'd made up our minds to decide the tennis championship, and secured all the courts for the Lower School. I do call it the most wretched luck! I'm a blighted blossom!"

(The Leader of the Lower School)

Linked with the choice of language, the choice of names is colourful to say the least: we have already met a Winona and a Garnet, but the keen reader will also meet Cissie, Cicely, Effie, Ethelburga, Loveday, Tattie, Irma, Avis, Avelyn, Nesta, Aldred, Ernestine, Mercy (whose surname is Ingledew), Lettice, Maisie, Flossie, Gertrude and Leonora, to name but a tiny percentage. In *A Popular Schoolgirl* there is a Saxon family with children named Egbert, Ingred and Quenrede. The greatest fan (and also the greatest mimic) of Angela was the humorist, writer and broadcaster Arthur Marshall; in *Life's Rich Pageant*, his 1984 autobiography, he wrote that "One could hardly improve on some of Miss Brazil's own nominal inventions - Gipsy Latimer, Mabel Farrington, Loveday Seton, Tattie Clegg, Winnie Waters, Agnes Dalton - and if, after every name, you added, in bossy and schoolmistressy tones, the word 'dear' and pronounced it 'dee-ah,' the effect was heightened. A sentence such as *'Blanche Doubleday, dee-ah, WHAT are you doing?'* implied that she was up to something forbidden, such as preparing an apple-pie bed for Mademoiselle, or at tea-time, secreting an extra doughnut in the elastic of her knickers."

Next, one should consider the plots themselves, and the construction of her stories. Whereas Hamilton would carry his readers breathlessly through the action in what seems like an amphetamine-charged roller coaster, Angela was happy to plod gracefully and none too expeditiously through her stories, using any conceivable excuse to digress into areas of particular interest and fascination for her. A good example is in *Nesta's New School* in which the death of Nesta's mother-by-adoption results in her having to forsake the luxury of the Villa Alpina and return to her real mother. In chapter sixteen Nesta goes with her "real" family on a hiking holiday. For the next twenty-four pages we are given an account of the holiday. What is going to happen, we ask ourselves impatiently. Will Nesta's mother peer too intently over the two-hundred-foot precipice and crash to her death? Will Nesta be swept off her feet by the farmer's boy and repair hastily to the hayloft? No such dramas. The most exciting moment is awaiting the result of a competition to see who can write the most convincing doggerel about the holiday. On page two-hundred-and-forty-three, at the end of chapter seventeen, the plot has gone no further forward. At least we are told who won the poetry competition. Who is the winner? Read the book and find out for yourself.

One of Angela's favourite digressions was sporting activity. Angela's own schooldays had been spoilt by lack of such facilities, and, just in the same way that her childless state seemed to impel her to write about children from their angle, so did her own lack of sporting activity, and her strong belief that girls should have non-academic outlets, lead to a large amount of writing about organised games (although proportionally perhaps not as much as Harold Avery). To quote Cadogan she "seemed almost carried away by the sporting motif." Returning to Nesta, two chapters in her saga are devoted solely to sport (winter sports in chapter four, sports day in chapter nine), neither having the slightest relevance to the plot. What does it matter, for instance, that the visitors' race at the sports day is won by a long-legged child of nine, whose seven-year-old brother came in as a good second? In a number of Angela's stories, girls who would otherwise be something of a disappointment manage to "come good" by virtue of their prowess on the sports field. A classic example of such a girl is Winona Woodward. In *The Luckiest Girl in the School* she is granted a scholarship by accident, but her expertise on the sports field at Seaton High qualifies her to go on to Physical Training College. As well as sporting activity in school there are plenty of impromptu games, and there is much outdoor activity outside its four walls, providing the girls with ample appetites for hearty teas with heaps of bread and butter.

Another favoured source of digression is journeys into the past. In *The Manor House School* Angela recognised the extent of the digression by according a special heading to the *Story of Sir Mervyn's Ward*. The habit of digression seems particularly evident in *The School on the Loch* which was Angela's last book. This is devoid of any plot whatsoever, but merely the story of two girls leaving the heat, the dust and the locusts of Kenya for the rain and lushness of bonnie Scotland, and being informed at the end through a previously missing will that their family's financial future is secured. Angela might be forgiven for allowing some Celtic legend to pop up with little more than a third of the book gone and with no possibility, as yet, of anxious readers beginning to chew their fingernails in anticipation of

SCHOOLGIRL KITTY Angela Brazil

build-up of the drama. With time running out, however, a vigorous depression sweeps in from the Firth of Clyde. The resultant rain means that the nature ramble has to be cancelled in favour of some Highland legends, although it is fair to suggest that most readers by this time will have given up hope of seeing the ghost of Rob Roy, a tartan-clad mermaid dancing a Highland fling on the waters of Loch Lomond, or Nessie putting in a special guest appearance.

The fact is, of course, that for Angela the plots were not especially important. Indeed at times they appear to be no more than an inconvenience, solved when time finally runs out by the appearance of a missing will or a long-lost relative. Angela was certainly not looking to further her plot with each line she wrote; she would start with a school and use her plot as a vehicle for describing life in and around the school. As a result, a new world was created for her readers, built on experiences she had, or perhaps would like to have had, herself, and full of the inconsequential incidents and digressions which typify everyday life. It was also a useful means of broadening the general knowledge of the readers. Gillian Freeman contended that the structure of her books was influenced by the four elements; earth(botany), air (folklore, mythology, idealism and romance), water (shipwrecking, seascapes) and fire (acts of bravery). There are acts of horseplay, poems, nature studies, history lessons, mini-homilies and descriptions of timetabling arrangements, all painstakingly and meticulously chronicled. Each is designed not only to edify, enlighten and entertain the reader, but also to portray girls as having just as much to offer as boys. Here are some examples of Angela's varied digressions:

"There's a girl at St Chad's who's named Flossie;
She tries to be terribly "bossy;"
She sets us all straight
Which is just what we hate
And makes us exceedingly cross(y)."

(*The New Girl at St Chads*)

A white streak ran like a corkscrew over the clouds, and a louder peal resounded...
the... sound of heaven's artillery.

(*The Luckiest Girl in the School*)

"Though driven westward, the Celtic church did not perish, and every now and then
some devoted monk would try to establish himself among the worshippers of Thor
and Odin."

(*The New Girl at St Chads*)

What they loved best was the garden. Its high walls sheltered it from cold winds,
and lovely flowers were growing there, roses, godetias, morning glories, violas, gera-
niums, marguerites, and half-exotic shrubs the names of which they did not know.

There were walks bordered with box-edging, and there were sheltered corners wit
shrines, and seats where some of the gentle grey-clad sisters were generally sittin;
reading their little books of devotion and looking like peaceful apparitions from th
Middle Ages.

(Schoolgirl Kitty

At the end stood the beautiful ancient church built in days when each artisan wa
a master of his craft, and made his work a labour of love. Strangers often came fror.
a distance to admire the delicate tracery of the windows, the exquisite carving of th
pillars, and the splendid old oak choir stalls that had formed part of a twelfth centur
abbey.

(The Manor House School

We, still in the preparatory class of God's great school, cannot yet grasp the highe
forms, but those who have been moved up surely smile at our want of comprehension
and look back on this earth as the College undergraduate remembers his kindergarten
for the spiritual evolution goes ever on, working always Godwards, and when th
human dross falls away, the imperfect and the partial will be merged into the perfec
and the eternal.

(The Luckiest Girl in the School

They saw the Virgin's Fountain, still the public source of water supply, where th
Virgin Mary, pitcher on head, must often have gone to the spring, with little Jesu
toddling at her side.

(The School on the Cliff

"When people are dead I think if they were good they are either resting unti
resurrection or have something so much better and nobler to do in another world tha
they could not revisit this world any more."

(The Manor House School

Breakfast was at half past seven, and at half past eight everybody was due in chape
for a short service; lectures and classes occupied the morning from nine till one, an
the afternoon was devoted to games; tea was at four, and supper at half-past sever
with preparation in between.

(The New Girl at St Chads

Angela's strong religious beliefs, combined with the fact that she was writing fo:
children, rendered it unsurprising that virtually all of her plots would result in :
happy and often sickly-sentimental ending. Indeed Elinor Brent-Dyer, who wa:
to outpace Angela in terms of popularity after both women had died, found thi:
sentimentality somewhat off-putting. Readers with a squeamish disposition wil
find some of Angela's work hard to take except in small doses. A classic exampl(
is in *The Nicest Girl in the School* where Patty Hirst, despite being far from gifte(
intellectually, wins a prize and huge acclaim at her Morton Priory school becaus(

he is so nice to everyone. Good triumphs superbly and unerringly over evil and doubt, even if it is necessary to contrive the plot to a ludicrous extent, as well as expect its principals to assume the physical ability of the territorial SAS. Angela's girls, full of the joys of emancipation, are remarkably resilient; writers such as L.T.Meade would have been amazed to see young girls coping apparently effortlessly with perilous coastal walking (*The New Girl at St Chad's*), mountain mists (*The Manor House School*) and sea rescues (*The Nicest Girl in the School*), and no amount of daring is too far-fetched if it helps achieve the neat conclusion. As has been mentioned, a missing will may ensure the financial security of the chief protagonist: girls who have been making life unpleasant will be either converted to a life of righteousness or taught the error of their ways; false accusations will be cleared up; a relative thought by everyone to be dead suddenly turns up in the school grounds; and conveniently mislaid papers will materialise to confirm the alleged miscreant's innocence. Angela's heroines are incidentally remarkably forgiving; having been "set up" mercilessly by jealous colleagues, they will often have forgiven and befriended them by the time the last page is turned. In *The Fortunes of Philippa* Ernestine Salt makes Philippa's life a misery throughout but it is left to Philippa to save Ernestine from the ravages of a great black bull, with the result that the two become firm friends. A more detailed discussion of Angela's adherence to a notional code of conduct will follow later in this chapter.

The next feature of Angela's writing that is worthy of note is her exploration of deep friendships between pairs of girls. Schoolgirl jealousy and rivalry was of course a fertile area for any writer, and the relating of the story from the girls' viewpoint was bound to touch on relationships generally. However, nobody described deep friendship between schoolgirls quite so graphically as Angela. This would appear to be the result of the intense friendships which she herself had experienced at school. In her autobiography which she wrote in 1926, at the age of 56, she recalled her childhood passion for a girl named Effie: "How immensely, frantically, intensely I had loved her - loved her even then! My friendships were so white-hot, I see now it must have been difficult for a girl of different temperament to keep face with me." It could well be argued that in her portrayal of similarly intense relationships she was conjuring up memories of Effie. Indeed there was a character called Effie in *The Manor House School*.

Angela's very first school story, *The Fortunes of Philippa*, pairs Philippa Seaton with Cathy Winstanley; Philippa admits to have fallen in love with her, and claims that...

"...to have Cathy all to myself for seven long glorious weeks seemed the absolute summit of earthly bliss."

Subsequent titles contain scenes in similar vein; Winona Woodward and Garnet Emerson in *The Luckiest Girl in the School* is another such "coupling." In a fashion which would have evoked admiration from Barbara Cartland, we are told how the two of them come together:

The result of the stand-off attitude on the part of the rest of the form was the cementing of a close friendship between Winona and Garnet. It seemed natural for the holders of the two County Scholarships to become chums, also they found each other's society congenial. It marked a new epoch for Winona. The two girls spent every available moment together, and soon waxed confidential on the subject of their home affairs.

Then comes the sad realisation that they are drifting apart:

Winona, wrapped up in the supreme fascinations of hockey matches and gymnasium practice, had chummed with Marjorie Kemp, Bessie Kirk, and Joyce Newton who shared her enthusiasm for games. She remembered with a pang of self reproach that she had not walked round the playground with Garnet once this term. Winona admired fidelity, but she certainly could not pride herself upon having practised that virtue of late.

When Winona offers to make amends by allowing Garnet to come and sleep at her house to assist them both in their matriculation exam revision, Garnet is ecstatic:

"Win! You don't really mean it? Oh, you're big! I didn't think anyone in the world would have done that for me. Do you realise what you're undertaking? It's the one thing that can save me! And only a girl who's in my own Form, and going in for the matric. herself could do it. Nobody else understands exactly what one wants. Win, I'm ready to worship you!"

In *Leader of the Lower School* an American pupil, Gipsy Latimer, is befriended by Meg Gordon, and the latter is so besotted with "Yankee Doodle" as she xenophobically comes to be known, that she even dresses up in Gipsy's clothes and gets arrested by the police on Gipsy's behalf. Angela does not skimp on printers ink when it comes to describing Meg's feelings for Gipsy:

Meg Gordon in particular was inclined to accord her that species of hero worship often indulged in by schoolgirls. She brought offerings of late roses or autumn violets from home, and followed her idol about the school like a love-sick swain. She would sit gazing at Gipsy during classes in deepest admiration, and was ready to accept her every idea as gospel. Her sudden and violent devotion to the newcomer caused no little amusement to the form.

"You agree with every single thing Gipsy says," laughed Norah Bell. "I believe if she declared the trees were pink and the houses green, you'd uphold her!"

In *Nesta's New School,* Rita is the object of Nesta's love:

She was naturally affectionate, so this new friendship with Rita came somewhat in the nature of a revelation. Miss Derrick... watched it carefully. She did not encourage too sentimental devotion among schoolgirls, but, knowing Nesta to be an only child she considered it wise to allow her to attach herself to a special chum. Nesta was evidently a girl who could be led by her affections, and if she could catch the tone of the school more readily by an intimacy with Rita, that was all to the good.

In *A Fourth Form Friendship* the girls in question are the new girl Aldred Laurence and the aloof Mabel Farringdon. Mabel's friendship for Aldred is based on an incorrect belief that Aldred has rescued a child from a burning house. The climax of the book sees Aldred actually saving Mabel's life, and Aldred dramatically proclaims:

"I'd have given my life for you gladly."

To which Mabel replies:

"I know, and I feel almost unworthy of such love."

In *For the Sake of the School*, the partners are Ulyth Stanton and Rona, a rough diamond from New Zealand. At first Rona's nationality and background receive a somewhat hostile reaction from her colleagues - the "patriotic" aspect of Brazil's writings will be examined towards the end of this chapter - but when Rona receives an invitation to Ulyth's home, she is suddenly the focus of considerable admiration:

In her new plumage the Cuckoo appeared turned into a tropical humming-bird. Una had thought her good-looking before, but she had not realised that her room-mate was a beauty. She stared almost fascinated at the vision of blue eyes, coral cheeks, white neck and ruddy brown hair. For her hostess Rona evinced a species of worship. She would follow her about the house, content simply to be near her, and her face would light up at the slightest word addressed to her.

In *The Harum-Scarum Schoolgirl*, Wendy becomes smitten with Diana, another American lass:

"I'm falling in love with her. I was taken with her, of course, the moment I saw her, but I believe now I'm going to have it badly. I think she's beautiful. If there were a peach competition she'd win it at a canter."

Later we detect the taste of forbidden fruit:

"If Diana - a modern Eve - hankered after the apples of new experiences, Wendy succumbed to her persuasions as readily as Adam."

Angela clearly saw the hand of Destiny in such relationships. In *A Pair of Schoolgirls* she begins a sentence:

The fickle goddess of fortune having drawn together the lives of Dorothy Greenfield and Alison Clarke...

Alison does not defy the gods, and is unstinting in her praise of Dorothy:

"Miss Tempest is rather tempestuous... but the acting is going to be fun. As for Dorothy, she's ripping!"

Angela seemed unconcerned that something more than laughter and fellowship might one day be imputed into these relationships. An example occurs in *The Manor House School:*

Cicely admired Lindsay immensely and copied her absolutely, being generally ready to follow her through thick and thin. The pair shared a bedroom and were so inseparable that Cicely was often called Lindsay's shadow.

Not content with this relationship, Angela in the same story told of Monica Courtenay who...

...took her sudden popularity serenely and scarcely seemed to notice that her schoolfellows were quarrelling over who should sit next to her in class, or take part with her in a game of tennis.

The mind boggles when Mildred Roper asserts:

"I admire her very much myself but I don't go and kiss her coat when it's hanging in the vestibule, or beg her old torn exercises for keepsakes."

We turn now to the traditional ethos inherent in the stories; a link with Angela's own assertion that "virtues to be copied and admired" are "religious zeal, calm courage, patriotism, affection and great capacity for love." Let us see how the link is demonstrated in the stories.

Angela's heroines are not paragons of virtue by any means. All have some failing or another. They may, like Winona Woodward, hit on-drives with a ferocity which might cause Ian Botham to take up a fielding position in the car park, but academically they may lack any kind of accomplishment. They may indulge in horseplay and prankishness which belies their seeming effortlessness in obtaining high marks in mathematics and geography. They may, like Patty Hirst, not win any prizes for academic brilliance but in terms of saintliness are more than a match for the early Christian martyrs. They may, like Nesta Meredith, get along superbly with their classmates but become resentful at any attempt by their single parents to develop a relationship of their own. Yet the imperfections of her heroines do not detract from the fact that as with Harold Avery's work, there is an unwritten code governing the behaviour of the characters in her schools. There is a strong hierarchical structure, with headmistresses ruling their schools with rods of iron, assisted by sixth formers and prefects who themselves are bossy, officious and domineering. Foreigners are treated with suspicion or the greatest circumspection, and the girls themselves tend to be conservative and cliquey.

Turning firstly to the headmistresses, one can do little better at the outset than quote Cadogan: "Angela's headmistresses were... formidable, humourless ladies who struck more terror into the hearts of their charges with their tongues than Greyfriars masters could bring about with their birches."

It should be stressed that many of Angela's fictional teachers are tolerant, benign and sympathetic, and even the occasional bad apple among the staff is not beyond redemption. The number of historical and geographical outings organised for the girls, and the consequent need for the relating of historical anecdotes and legends, requires teachers to be competent and versatile as much outside the school walls s within. One suspects that in Miss Harper in *The Nicest Girl in the School* Angela as painted the picture of the perfect mistress:

Her bright, vivacious, interesting style, her fund of appropriate stories for every occasion, and her many amusing remarks and comments, made her extremely popular with her form in spite of her strictness, and he moment she took her place on the platform all eyes were fixed on her clever, intellectual face.

However, headmistresses, who like the teachers seem rarely to get married (or perhaps reverting to their maiden name after an unsuccessful marriage?) are far more formidable and aloof. Although some might be kind, understanding and sporting, others are menacing and all are demanding of awe, obedience and admiration.

An example of one particularly terrifying lady is Miss Poppleton of Briarcroft School, in *The Leader of the Lower School*. Although nicknamed Poppie, she has nothing of the meekness, approachability and innocence which this title suggests. Indeed she displays some of the most unsavoury aspects of the manager of a fee-paying school, by making a fuss of Leonora Parker, a daughter of wealthy par-

"Oh, Garnet, I'm so sorry! Will the doctor let you take the matric. at all?"

ents, and according particularly unpleasant treatment to an American, Gipsy Latimer, whose father has ostensibly disappeared without any indication that her fees will be paid. When she has a pretext - or so she thinks - for punishing Gipsy, the punishment is particularly harsh. There is no corporal punishment, of course, but her sentence of solitary confinement without any communication with her fellow-pupils until she confesses to a wrong she did not do, might raise eyebrows amongst even the hanging judges in the Court of Appeal. Her attitude towards Gipsy even when she arrives suggests that she is not entirely well-disposed towards our transatlantic brethren:

"You're not in America now; you'll have to learn English ways here, and English speech too. You must make an effort to drop Americanisms, and talk as we do on this side of the Atlantic... While you are here, you will be expected to keep the rules of the school, or, if you break them, you will be punished. Leave my study at once, and don't report yourself here again until you are sent for."

Another difficult confrontation occurs in *The Luckiest Girl in the School*. Before it transpires that Winona has obtained the scholarship incorrectly, Miss Bishop wastes no time in castigating her pupil for her poor performance:

Miss Bishop looked up from some papers, motioned her to a chair, and went on writing for several minutes. To Winona it seemed worse than waiting at the dentist's. The suspense was ghastly... Miss Bishop's eyes were... large and clear, but the pupils were unusually small, appearing mere black specks in the midst of a wide circle of blue. This peculiarity gave her a particularly intense and penetrating expression.

"We can't win honours without paying the price! You must know that already by experience. Here is Miss Huntley's report; French, weak; Latin, beneath criticism; mathematics, extremely bad."

For *The School Colours* introduces us to Miss Thompson, who...

...might not be very tall but she was thoroughly capable of managing the school. Every inch of her bristled with dignity. Avelyn entered the room a trifle jauntily, but one steady glance from those convex glasses caused her feathers to fall.

One of Angela's great headmistresses is Miss Cavendish in *The New Girl at St Chads*. We are told, even before we hear any details about her, that she...

...can reduce one to quaking jelly when she feels inclined.

When Angela does get down to details, Miss Cavendish is described as...

...an imposing and commanding figure (with) clear cold blue eyes.

Having been told of her phenomenal academic pedigree, we learn that she is...

...not a remarkably tender woman... perhaps more respected than loved by her pupils.

When a pupil unfortunate enough to be summoned for an audience with her approaches her desk, she is favoured...

...with a scrutinising gaze so comprehensive and so full of authority that despite he.

ntention of showing a bold front, the girl involuntarily quailed.

There follows an intensive ten-minute inquisition; even the lack of cane-shaped objects within immediate vision or reach is no real consolation. The Head declaims:

"Every girl, as a member of this community, is bound to preserve its rules, which have been wisely framed, and deserve to be faithfully kept. You have been guilty of a very grave breach of our regulations, and by your own showing you merit punishment. Do you consider this to be just?"

Compassion is clearly not the middle name of the Principal in *The Harum Scarum Schoolgirl*; Diana receives the dreadful punishment of not being allowed to wear evening dresses for one week, and to add insult to injury we learn that the Principal...

...would not remit the least atom of the sentence until it was paid to the uttermost farthing.

Headmistresses are not the only ones who strike fear and trepidation into the pupils. We are told in *The Fortunes of Philippa* that Philippa's form-teacher, Miss Percy, had...

...manifold rules and regulations... narrow sympathies and strict discipline.

Sixth formers and monitresses also are minded to assert their authority to a far greater extent than some of the teachers. One particularly obnoxious example is Vivian Holmes, the monitress at St Chads in *The New Girl at St Chads*. After Honor Fitzgerald has been told by Miss Cavendish to remove green trimming from her hat, Vivian not only rips the trimming off herself, but also tells her:

"You needn't think that what you have done is at all clever. I am responsible for St Chads, and I don't mean to have this kind of nonsense going on there; so please understand, Honor Fitzgerald, that if you give any more trouble, you may expect to find yourself thoroughly well sat upon!"

When Honor plays a fairly innocuous trick on a house-mate, Vivian storms:

"If you try any more of those senseless practical jokes, I shall report you to Miss Maitland. I'm monitress here, and I don't intend to have this kind of thing going on at St Chads."

After her harangue, we are told that she leaves the scene wondering whether she has adequately fulfilled her monitorial duty! Another persuasive argument against giving power to pupils seems to be Linda Fletcher, the Head Girl of Seaton High, who reacts most angrily to Winona Woodward's attempt to set up an Old Girls' Hockey Club. This creditable piece of private enterprise is rewarded with these harsh words:

"It was a most unwarrantable liberty! Why, you're not even a prefect! And no prefect would have dreamed of calling such a meeting on her own account without consulting her colleagues. I hardly need impress upon you the necessity in future of referring

everything to headquarters."

In *For the Sake of the School* Una does not mince words on the subject of monitresses:

"Catherine's so high-handed and Helen's nearly as bad. They snap the girls up for the least trifle. The result is that juniors have got it into their tiresome young heads that monitresses are a species of teacher."

No wonder, when Helen as librarian castigates Una for spilling ink over a library book:

"I thought better of you, Una Stanton. One doesn't expect such things from VB."

In *Leader of the Lower School* Angela brought together two important traits of hers; the telling of the story from the pupil's point of view, and the bossy, superior attitude of the Upper School. The Upper School, led by another unpleasant young lady named Helen Roper, think that the Annual Meeting of the Guilds will be a formality, and it comes as a shock to them to find that not only do the Lower School want fairer treatment in the Guilds but, horror of horrors, they want representation on the Committee! Helen Roper, who believes that it would be the greatest mistake to give way, bows to pressure and agrees to hold a vote, but pleads with the girls:

"Remember our old traditions and to resist these innovations. Be loyal to your monitresses!"

Whilst there is a strong hierarchical feel in the stories, the girls unite in their distrust of foreigners. The words "nigger" and "negro" do crop up every so often, and when a girl arrives at one of Angela's establishments from across the waters - even if those waters are only the Irish Sea - it is almost bound to end in tears. Gipsy Latimer, whom we have already met, is warned in no uncertain terms that she must expunge "guess" and "reckon" from her vocabulary, and is told that it is simply out of the question to be provided with the wherewithal to make fudge. We have already met Honor Fitzgerald, who is hauled abruptly over the coals for committing the cardinal sin of wearing green trimming on her hat. However, while Gipsy integrates quickly amongst her peers, the Irishness of Honor is a source of considerable derision for the girls. When Chatty Burns asks her if she is Irish, she gasps. Things go from bad to worse:

"Is that Ireland? Then I suppose your name is Biddy?"

"Certainly not!"

"I thought all Irish girls were called Biddy; are you sure you're not?"

"My name is Honor Fitzgerald."

"Really! I'm surprised it isn't Mulligan, or O'Grady."

In *For the Sake of the School*, Ulyth Stanton makes the mistake of regarding a foreigner as an object rather than as a person. She invites Rona Mitchell, a New Zealander to England, thinking that she will conveniently accord with the image of her that Una has cultivated; a beautiful, dashing, daring heroine, who might have stepped straight out of an adventure film, representing an exciting culture in total antithesis to Una's own strait-laced background. However, when it becomes clear that her new toy is not really like that at all, Ulyth does all but take court action on the grounds that the product is not of merchantable quality:

"I've had the shock of my life. She's - oh, she's too terrible for words! Her voice makes me cringe... I never dreamt she'd be like this. It sounded so romantic, you see, living on a huge farm, and having two horses to ride. I shall go to Miss Bowes, first thing tomorrow morning, and ask to have her moved out of my room."

Antipathy towards people of more exotic climes is well-documented in The *School on the Loch* in which Jessie and Ailsa Lindsay have come to school in Scotland after a stay in Africa.

"So you're WHITE!"

"What? What d'you mean?" asked Jessie sharply.

"Why, Gwen said you came from Africa, and we thought you'd be BLACK!"

"Of course we're white!" cried the indignant voice of Ailsa.

"Well, how were we to know? Gwen told us you were Africans!"

"I never said they were black!" denied another girl.

"You said they came from Africa, and that means niggers, doesn't it?"

"We've lived in East Africa, but our father is Scottish, if you want to know!" declared Jessie.

"Well, yes! You look Scottish! Not much woolly hair and rolling black eyes about you!" shouted another.

Fortunately Miss Renton arrives shortly, admonishes these racist excesses, and tells the girls to finish their milk.

Preconceptions about Africans are neatly summed up in *The Girls of St Cyprians*, where one pupil, bemoaning the tortuous graft she has to undergo by way of piano practice, says:

"I sometimes wish I'd been born a savage in East Africa."

To which the not inappropriate reply is:

"Then they'd have made you learn the tom-tom."

The novelty value of visitors from other climes is demonstrated in *The Third Class at Miss Kaye's* when Myfanwy exclaims excitedly:

"I believe the niggers are still here!"

As will be seen, it would be left to the writing of Elinor Brent-Dyer to demonstrate a more enlightened attitude towards internationalism and the spirit of co-operation between nations.

The approach to, and outbreak of, the First World War, caused the author to make considerable reference in the texts to joining the battle against the evil Hun. Whereas Angela never gave her approval, explicit or implicit, to the treatment of overseas visitors as mentioned above - indeed she was a great supporter of the underdog, and oppressed characters in her stories always come good in the end - her own personal patriotism and commitment to defeat the common enemy permeated all her wartime writing. The enthusiasm of the girls to "do their bit" was given full rein by Angela, even when that enthusiasm carried no notion of the horrendous realities of war, ceased to be naive and became merely distasteful. There is no better example of this than in *A Patriotic Schoolgirl* when Marjorie - who founds the Secret Society of Patriots - goes into a hospital for wounded soldiers and announces:

A CHANCE FOR RETALIATION

"This is Peters; he keeps us all alive in this ward. He's lost his right leg but he's going on very well and takes it sporting, don't you, Peters?"

Worse is to follow; when Marjorie asks her headmistress if it is right to forgive the enemies of their country, she is told that it is right but only when they are dead!

In *The Luckiest Girl in the School* which seems to encapsulate almost all of the

Angela Brazil traits at their best (or worst?) Winona's brother Percy joins up by pretending to be of the correct age, having got himself into what he describes as a "grizzly hole" at school. He is wounded and conveyed to hospital. Our first meeting with him at the hospital does seem to convey something of the horrors of war:

A few months in the trenches, and a baptism of fire, had transformed the careless, happy-go-lucky lad into a man. Tears glistened in Winona's eyes as she bent down to kiss him. It was hard to see her active brother lying helpless and suffering.

Yet Winona later reports, with wonderful sensitivity:

"Percy is just wild to go back. I believe he'll do something splendid, and get a commission, or win the Victoria Cross."

Winona's enthusiasm for the war extends from waving her handkerchief to Lieutenant Mainwaring of the Flying Corps as he swoops in his biplane over the park adjoining the hostel at which she is staying, to knitting a pair of socks for her brother. We are told she starts on this latter task as soon as she hears that Percy has joined up:

I regret to say that Winona's patriotic knitting had languished very much during the last two terms, but this personal stimulus revived her ardour. She even took her sock to the tennis court, and emulating the example of Patricia Marshall and several other enthusiasts, got quite good pieces done between the sets.

We then hear that knitting is forbidden on the cricket pitch because on one occasion a fielder missed an easy catch through being preoccupied with her needles and balls of wool. First things first!

Germans themselves are held up to ridicule. Examples of this include the treatment of Gerda in *The School by the Sea* - the girls imagine her to be German and give her an extremely hard time until she turns out to be pure English. Even in the immediate pre-war years, this anti-German trend seems prevalent. No better example is contained in *Leader of the Lower School*, where the unfortunate victim is Fräulein Hochmeyer, described thus:

So intensely German in both accent and methods that she offended the British susceptibilities of her pupils and inspired more ridicule than respect. She treated her classes exactly as she would have dealt with similar ones in Germany; but what might have pleased apple-cheeked, pig-tailed Gretchens did not at all suit the tastes of the Briarcroft-ites.

Fräulein - who receives the non-too complimentary nickname "German Sausage" - comes to grief when teaching the girls some music. The reaction of the girls seems to go beyond mere indifference:

"That sort of rubbish may go down in the Fatherland but it doesn't here."

However, a whirl of resentment breaks out amongst the class members when Fräulein declaims:

"Hosh, my baby, sveetest, best, leetle moozie's gone to rest."
Gipsy Latimer strives to improve the situation in a way which will not hurt Fräulein's feelings, but the reaction of the other girls still betrays some suspicion:
"Can't see much romance about our homely German sausage!" giggled Daisy Scatcherd. *"You'll be standing perennially on the platform now, holding your teeth like a dentist's advertisement, to show us how to 'open ze mouz!'"*
"I've brought this picture of a sausage," piped one of the smaller girls. *"I'm going to pin it on to the piano. She knows we call her 'Sausage!' She'll be in such a rage!"*
The last aspect of the "unwritten code" of values to be considered is the conservatism and cliqueyness of the majority of the girls. Angela's girls tend to be pro-establishment, happy in their environment, and enthusiastic partakers of all that their school has to offer. It should not be forgotten that although Angela did write of schools other than fee-paying independent schools, her emphasis was strongly on children of families who were either well off or who at any rate found the necessary cash to finance their tuition. It is hard to find a Brazilian establishment where there is any real privation or ill-treatment; the girls tend to be perfectly happy with their lot in life and with the school they attend. Of course, circumstances do diminish the happiness of girls from time to time, but that is all part of the "ripping" excitement of the stories, and at the end of each book we are left in no doubt that God is in his heaven and all is right with the world. It was this presumption which put Angela's work, and that of her would-be imitators, into the "Reward" category. Reward was originally the name given for books or tracts given to Sunday School children, but in the early part of the twentieth century they came to mean any mass-produced cheap book for children, designed for Christmas and birthday presents as well as Sunday Schools. The basic premise of order in Angela's books would have been perfectly suited to the Reward category; if there is any anarchy, it tends to be more in the way of whinging and harmless practical joking than threatening the established order. The honour of the school is paramount, and a girl ignores that fact at her peril. The introduction of a girl "from outside" tends to exaggerate this conservatism rather than dilute it; the hostile reaction to foreigners has already been fully documented. Competence at sport is as acceptable to the school as competence in the classroom. Sneaking is the cardinal sin. Change, like any threat to the equilibrium, is looked upon with fear and suspicion; in *For the School Colours* the amalgamation of a posh school with one that is not so posh provokes reference to girls...
"...whom we never spoke to, wouldn't have touched with a pair of tongs!"
There tend to be pockets of friendship, or cliques, into which a girl on the outside will try and enter at her peril. *The Nicest Girl in the School* sees Patty Hirst full of despondency because she cannot break into a circle:
She rose next day and went to breakfast, feeling still an alien and an outsider. The

three girls who shared her bedroom appeared determined to show by their manner how much they resented her presence.

However, she need not worry, it seems, or be panicked into joining the school's lonely Hearts club, because thirteen pages later, she has found her way "in:"

Muriel and her three friends, for no good reason at all, considered themselves slightly superior to the rest of the form, and put on many airs in consequence, a state of affairs which was much resented by Enid Walker and Winnie Robinson, who, with Avis Wentworth, had a clique of their own, in which they now included Jean Bannerman and Patty. Doris Kennedy, May Firth, and Ella Johnson, the three girls who shared Patty's bedroom, made a separate little circle with Beatrice Wynne, while Cissie Gardiner and Maggie Woodhall were such bosom friends that they did not want anybody else's society.

The idea of pupils as objects, who can neatly be placed into groups or compartments, is given additional force in *Joan's Best Chum* where one girl announces to another:

"Let's take each other on appro. for the term."

With her telling the story from the schoolgirls' angle, refraining from imposing adult comment or ethics, and writing to entertain without an underlying purpose of edification, it is not difficult to see why Angela's work became so instantly popular. Her books sold all over the world, including India and the USA as well as in Europe. It is reckoned that over three million copies have been sold, with the most popular story, *The Nicest Girl in the School*, selling 153,000. Cadogan and Craig wrote that the name of Angela Brazil has, inter alia, become "synonymous with the school story genre as it was in its heyday." One of her fans wrote to her: 'it has always been the dearest wish of my heart since I was a little girl to go to boarding school' and it was clear that the books helped to fill that gap in her life. There is evidence that many girls, their attention engrossed by these narratives of school life, were inspired to become boarders as a direct result of reading Angela's work.

However, Angela's books were not popular with everyone. Schoolteachers did not like them; they felt that the slang was Angela's own invention which girls tended to copy, and not a sincere reflection of the kind of language used in schools. At some schools they were forbidden, and Ethel Strudwick, the headmistress of St Paul's in 1936 stated that she would like to burn all Angela's books. Isabel Quigly, cited in the previous chapter as an outspoken critic of Hamilton, had barely more time for Angela's work, which she regarded as insubstantial, childish, narrow-minded and silly, or indeed Angela herself whom she regarded as self-centred and snobbish. While less overtly critical, Cadogan and Craig felt that her efforts to free the girls' story from what they describe as "archaic conventions which had governed it" gave the stories "a laughable quality which certainly was not intended...

her girls can be ruthless (and) stupid without incurring overt narrative disapproval."

The great champion of Angela after her death was the humorous writer and journalist Arthur Marshall, who wrote and spoke of her work with enormous affection, although not enough to spark a revival of interest in it. He clearly had Angela's work in mind when describing the ideal fictional girls' school.

"The ideal school of fiction... must at all costs be near the sea, preferably standing at the top of precipitous cliffs. The cliffs can either be fallen down, climbed up, or stuck on halfway. Stuck on halfway is best, for the agonising wait enables Thirza to find the old smugglers' cave and the underground passage and to come bursting back through a secret door right into Miss Pritchard's bathroom at the moment when Miss Pritchard is least expecting her."

The strait-laced girls' public school story was satirised in Ronald Searle's magnificent collection of cartoons depicting incidents from the anarchic world of St Trinians, later turned into a memorable series of films featuring Alistair Sim playing the ineffectual headmistress and Joyce Grenfell (who can forget her wonderfully lumbering gait?) pretending to be the "jolly hockey-sticks" games mistress. However the film-makers did not only have Angela's schools in mind, rather the whole concept of the girls' school in fiction. More interesting for Angela Brazil buffs was the 1983 comedy *Daisy Pulls It Off* in which a take-off of Angela's work came to the West End stage. It opened in Southampton in January 1983 and then moved to the Globe Theatre, London, on 18th April 1983. It starred Alexandra Mathie as Daisy Meredith, an East End girl who wins a scholarship to Grangewood, a suitably exclusive school for young ladies. Act One introduces us to, among others, the snobbish Sybil ("not only do we have to suffer this girl in the same form room, but we have to share the hitherto unpolluted air of our dormy with her as well"), the cruel Miss Glanville ("I would usually give an order mark for such an offence, but as you are new I shall let you off"), and Daisy's friend Trixie ("Oh, heavenly! We must have a motto too, a password. Um... *audacia et virtute adepta*... too long! *Absque virtute nihil*... no! Ah, how about this, *hinc spes effulget!*" Other characters include the mysterious male Russian music teacher, and the officious prefect Clare ("Well, my dear child, it's high time you gave up kiddish stunts"). There is the element of mystery ("In his portrait he's holding a jolly queer looking instrument of some kind") which is developed in Act II at the same time as a hockey match is played out ("Matron will never let her play with a broken ankle") and we meet the scatterbrained Mademoiselle ("For I come in to see za all is well after ze splendid 'ockey match and pouf! I see a big gap on ze shelf.") Daisy is soon in hot water over a missing library book. To help solve the mystery, and to cheer her up, an inter-dormy bottle fight is organised. ("Matron's a sport, she'll gather the joyful gist.") Resentment against her is such that other girls plot gainst her to give the impression of her having cheated, and she comes close to being expelled by the icy headmistress, Miss Gibson ("Until that time you will be iven a room in the Sanatorium where you will sleep, your meals will be brought you and you will be given specially prepared classwork to do"). However Daisy ersuades Miss G to allow her to take part in the vital hockey match against 'earncombe, and she scores the winning goal ("I did it for Grangewood"). She escues her tormentors in dramatic style, becoming dangerously ill as a result ("If he dies then it's my fault"); solves the mystery, and is reunited with her father who everyone believes is dead. Having heard his preposterous story - ("I survived by linging to a spar of wood in the sea for two days") she successfully campaigns gainst the expulsion of the girl who nearly caused her to suffer that fate. Well ight Trixie say "Oh Daisy, how perfectly scrummy everything has turned out to e!" The play has been dwelt on at some length because, although deeply satirical, nyone reading it would instantly recognise many of Angela's favourite themes; ang, chumminess, honour, sport, eccentric and clueless foreigners, schoolgirl valry and jealousy, horseplay, life-saving drama, severe prefects and headmisesses, and absurdly contrived plots always ending happily. Such themes were agerly seized upon by Angela's successors.

With the disappearance of the Armada titles, access to Angela's work is now erely by means of the second-hand shelves. Humphrey Carpenter and Mari richard felt that "Her stories now seem to have come to the end of their opularity." Perusal of the extracts given above may confirm to the general reader at they are best consigned to posterity, notwithstanding Joseph Connolly's escription of them as "something of a cult, not to say an object of wonder". It is adly impossible to feel great affection for any of Angela's creations in the same ray in which the connoisseur will feel affection for Billy Bunter or J.C.T.Jennings. o character stands out; there is no particular jewel in the Angela Brazil crown. ut it is also impossible for schoolchildren of today to relate to her characters, teeped as they are in an age that has long gone by. The writing style is absurdly ated; by trying to be progressive and to see things as schoolgirls saw them, ngela's writing sowed the seeds of its own doom. The growth of the comprehens- e school with the differing needs and priorities of its pupils, the change in ost-war attitudes, and continuing competition from other sources such as the irls' papers, also served to diminish her following among young folk. Yet, aradoxically, it is exchanges such as the one which ends this chapter, from *The uckiest Girl in the School,* which come closer to ensuring immortality for Angela razil than any other aspect of her work. Perhaps it is as well that she is no longer live to see just why it is that enthusiasts do find her books so entertaining!

However, to remember her principally for her schoolgirl slang and the enthusistic, sporty type of pupil is in a way unfortunate. Angela, like Talbot Baines Reed,

was a pioneer of the "entertaining but respectable" school yarn, telling the stor
from the point of view of the pupil rather than the adult, and yet still maintainin
a keen sense of moral values as well as acceptable standards of writing. Th
difference between the girls' school story and the boys' school story is that it wa
only during the years immediately following the Great War, as the woman's rol
became more liberated and less predictable, that the girls' school story became

major driving force in children's literature. Indeed, a phenomenal number of girls' schools fiction writers, anxious to capitalise on the evident demand for such work, followed hopefully in Angela's footsteps. In all of it, the private school was to dominate, and the books usually came within the "Reward" category. As Cadogan and Craig remarked: "Girls were just beginning to explore and sa-vour the concepts of tradition, 'team spirit,' even academic pres-tige, and responded enthusiasti-cally to the type of fiction which stressed these."

One of the very few writers who came close to emulating both the style and popularity of Angela Brazil was Dorita Fairlie Bruce. A Scot, she was born in 1885 and coincidentally, like Charles Ha-milton, reached the age of 85. The similarities to Angela's work were legion - the telling of the stories

"Excuse me, but are you afraid of scarlet fever?"

from the girls' angle, the slang (albeit somewhat toned down), the bosom friend
ships, the intense nationalism, the emphasis on organised games, and the whole
someness. Unlike Angela, however, she concentrated on only a few schools, he
most celebrated creation being the Jane Willard Foundation, at which Dimsie i
the star pupil. The first title, *The Senior Prefect* but later renamed *Dimsie Goes T*
School, appeared in 1920; overall seven Dimsie books appeared in sequential forn
taking the heroine neatly into adulthood. The books were popular at the tim
although Carpenter and Prichard wrote rather unkindly that they were publishe

Oxford University Press "before it had a more discriminating policy towards children's fiction." Also popular in the Twenties and Thirties (and beyond) was Elsie Oxenham and her Abbey series, although her work can only loosely be described as schools fiction. A handful of other writers at that time - Christine Chaundler, May Wynne and Ethel Talbot being examples - produced acceptable readable schools fiction in fair quantities, although their popularity waned even more rapidly than Angela's. It was clear that any writer who wanted to succeed would have to do more than just conform to pattern; one writer who attained significant popularity by daring to be different was Elinor Brent-Dyer, whose work will be considered in the next chapter.

A much larger number of writers produced totally forgettable - and now forgotten - stories of girls' public school life. Many did not even pretend to develop plot or characterisation, relying simply on the success of the more proficient writers in this area. Even first editions of their works - and authors were lucky if they ever were reprinted - today fetch only a few pounds, and collectors are uninterested. Those authors who did make anything can thank Angela Brazil, who undoubtedly pioneered a style to which real-life schoolchildren could easily relate and respond, even if a study of the passage below renders this seemingly now impossible to believe.

"Are you in for the mermaidens' fete?" Winona asked Marjorie Kemp.

"Mermaidens fete, indeed! How romantic we are all of a sudden! The frogfight, I would call it."

"There speaks the voice of envy! You're evidently out of it."

"Don't want to be in it, thanks! It'll be wretched work shivering round the edge of the bath for a solid hour!"

"Sour grapes, my child!" teased Winona.

"Go on my good girl - if you want to make me raggy, you just shan't succeed, that's all!"

"Now I SHOULD like to have been chosen!" mourned Evelyn Richards. "I don't mind confessing that I've had a disappointment. I thought I could swim quite as well as Freda, and it's grizzly hard luck that she was picked out and I wasn't. Rank favouritism, I call it!"

"Poor old Eve! Look here, I'll tell you a secret. You head the reserve list. I know because I saw it. If anybody has a cold on the day of the event, you'll take her place."

"You mascot! Shall I? Oh! I do hope somebody'll catch cold - not badly, but just enough to make it unsafe to go into the water. You can't think how I want to try my luck. I don't suppose I've a chance of a prize, but if I did get one, why I'd cock-a-doodle-do the school down!"

SCHOOL STORIES BY ANGELA BRAZIL IN BOOK FORM
(All published by Blackie & Son, except where stated)

1 The Fortunes Of Philippa (1906)
2 The Third Class at Miss Kaye's (1908)
3 The Nicest Girl in the School (1909)
4 The Manor House School (1910)
5 A Fourth Form Friendship (1911)
6 The New Girl at St Chads (1911)
7 A Pair of Schoolgirls (1912)
8 The Leader of the Lower School (1913)
9 The Youngest Girl in the Fifth (1913)
10 The Girls of St Cyprians (1914)
11 The School by the Sea (1914)
12 The Jolliest Term on Record (1915)
13 For the Sake of the School (1915)
14 The Luckiest Girl in the School (1916)
15 The Madcap of the School (1917)
16 A Patriotic Schoolgirl (1918)
17 For the School Colours (1918)
18 A Harum Scarum Schoolgirl (1919)
19 The Head Girl at the Gables (1919)
20 A Popular Schoolgirl (1920)
21 The Princess of the School (1920)
22 Loyal to the School (1921)
23 A Fortunate Term (1921)
24 Monitress Merle (1922)
25 The School in the South (1922)
26 Schoolgirl Kitty (1923)
27 Captain Peggie (1924)
28 Joan's Best Chum (1926)
29 Queen of the Dormitory & Other Stories (1926) (Cassell)
30 Ruth of St Ronans (1927)
31 At School with Rachel (1928)
32 St Catherine's College (1929)
33 The Little Green School (1931)
34 Nesta's New School (1932)
35 Jean's Golden Term (1934)
36 The School at the Turrets (1935)

37 An Exciting Term (1936)
38 Jill's Jolliest School (1937)
39 The School on the Cliff (1938)
40 The School on the Moor (1939)
41 The New School at Scawdale (1940)
42 Five Jolly Schoolgirls (1941)
43 The Mystery of the Moated Grange (1942)
44 The Secret of the Border Castle (1943)
45 The School in the Forest (1944)
46 Three Terms at Uplands (1945)
47 The School on the Loch (1946)

In addition to the Blackie series, Angela Brazil had four plays published by T W Patterson between 1899 and 1904; *A Terrible Tomboy*, published by Gay & Bird in 1904; two stories published in 1909 - *Bosom Friends* (Nelson & Co) and *Our School Record* (Dow & Lester); *The Treasure of the Woods* and *The Language of Flowers* (both Oxford, 1919); *Two Little Scamps and a Puppy* (Nelson, 1919).

Angela Brazil also contributed a mixture of school and non-school stories to :

Our School Magazine (T W Patterson) - 1900, 1901, 1902, 1903,1904.
Burgon's Magazine (Atlantic Press) - 1902, 1903, 1904, 1905.
Little Folks (Cassell) - 1909, 1910, 1911, 1912, 1915, 1916, 1918,1919.
Girls' Realm (Cassell) - 1910, 1911.
The Chummy Book (Nelson) 1918.
The Jolly Book (Nelson) - 1916, 1918, 1919.
British Girls' Annual (Cassell) - each year from 1911 to 1919.
Children's Annual (Cassell) - 1918. Mrs Strang Annual - 1919.
Christmas Bookman - 1922.
Girls Budget - 1924, 1925.
Graphic - 1923.
Red/Green/Rose/Violet/Blue Book for Girls (Oxford) - 1910, 1911,1913, 1914, 1915.
Blackie's Annual - 1916, 1917, 1920, 1926.
Blackie's Girls' Annual - 1923, 1924, 1925, 1927, 1930, 1931.
The Girls' Own Paper (Blackie) - 1938, 1939, 1940.

KAFFEE UND KUCHEN

"If only I knew what to do with you girls!" said Dick in worried tones.
"Oh, you needn't worry about us!" replied Madge.

These are the opening words of the first book in a series of school stories whic
were conceived during the reign of Angela Brazil and Charles Hamilton, b
which now, seventy years later, are still to be seen on the shelves of children
sections in the bookshops and not just confined to the mustier corners of secon
hand dealers. With just under sixty novels, all on the subject of one school, writte
over half a century, and most of them still in print (albeit in abridged form), Elin
Brent-Dyer has become the most celebrated and continuously successful girl
school story writer of the century.

In the 1930s, the girls' school story was enjoying unprecedented popularit
Angela Brazil had lit the flame, and Dorita Fairlie Bruce was one of many othe
who were fuelling it. Her Dimsie books were proving successful, and it was cle
that part of the appeal was the serial aspect; the fact that one story followed o
from another, retaining the most endearing characters and encouraging the read
to find out what happened next in their lives. Doubtless many of Dorita Fairl
Bruce's contemporaries recognised this, and it would have been a blinkered writ
indeed who did not have a vision of their own fictional creation, be it St Saviour
or St Symphorian's, capturing the reader's imagination in twenty or more glorio
volumes. A writer with a special vision was needed; a vision of a school whic
would not only retain many of the popular features of the inter-war fictional girl
school but would incorporate a more exotic location as well as characters wi
which the reader would strike an instant rapport. Not only did Elinor succeed
achieving all three objectives, but her sensitivity to the age in which she was writi
and her broader, wiser outlook ensured that new books of hers would continue
enjoy the attentions of young folk long after the lesser writers had faded in
obscurity.

Elinor was born in 1894 in South Shields and died in 1969. She wrote arour
100 girls' stories, chiefly with school settings, but it was with the Chalet School th
she achieved immortality. It is with this series that this chapter is principal
concerned. Her first Chalet School book, *The School at the Chalet*, appeared
1925; the last, *Prefects of the Chalet School*, was published posthumously in 197(

Elinor's early life and upbringing was undistinguished. Her childhood wa
comfortable, and somewhat shielded from the considerable poverty and diseas
that were prevalent in her neighbourhood. She left school at seventeen and we

nto teaching, which was to become her career. As a schoolgirl she was boisterous nd forthright, and also cleverer than her peers. Described by Helen McClelland s having a "larger than life manner," she cultivated an interest in storytelling lmost from the age at which she learned to speak; she would ask her mother to write down a story I've 'magined" and would tell stories to the family cat! This est for storytelling would continue throughout her life. At the age of five it is said he won a magazine competition with a story entitled *Lotty's Fright*. The only urviving manuscript, however, that she wrote before 1921 is a collection of poems. McClelland suggested that her writing energies during her early adulthood were argely directed towards poetry, thus delaying her start in fiction. In 1919, however, n important event took place in Elinor's life; a theatrical family, Edith, Julian and Hazel Bainbridge came to live in South Shields. Elinor befriended them, and ctually wrote plays for them, the first of which was a historical piece called *My Lady Caprice*. The experience taught her that she was capable of completing omething on a large scale. It was for Hazel Bainbridge (mother of well-known ctress Kate O'Mara) that Elinor wrote her first full-length novel. It was a school tory. The choice of subject matter was obvious in the light of trends at that time; n the early twenties vast amounts of girls' school fiction was being written with a teadily increasing demand. Unlike most school story writers, however, Elinor hose to begin with a day-school story, reflecting the fact that she had not been to oarding-school. It was entitled *Gerry Goes To School*. Although not a classic, it howed the emergence of many of the themes that would recur in her writing; ealousy, rivalry, close families, and the consequence of impetuosity. The heroine, Gerry Challenor, was not drawn from Hazel Bainbridge, but Hazel found it easy o identify with her in her various predicaments in the story. The story was ubmitted to W & R Chambers in 1922, and in the autumn of that year it was ublished. The Bainbridges left the area in July 1922 and just over a year later Elinor had moved to Fareham in Hampshire to take up a post at Western House Girls' School. In the autumn of 1923 her second book, a sequel to *Gerry Goes To School* named *A Head Girl's Difficulties*, was completed and soon afterwards a hird, *The Maids of La Rochelle*, not a school story, was in preparation.

It was in 1924 that her choice of summer holiday destination was to prove articularly felicitous. Not being particularly well off at the time, she chose the Tirol in Austria, then a very cheap country for British people to visit. Following her return to England she decided that the place in which she had stayed, Pertisau on the Achen See and roughly 35 kilometres from Innsbruck, would make a fine etting for a school story. Although other school stories written by English authors t that time had overseas settings, the Tirol had never been selected and there was, herefore, as McClelland pointed out, "an element of novelty (in addition to) the roven advantages enjoyed by all fictional schools in foreign lands."

The fictional school was, of course, the Chalet School, and *The School at th* *Chalet* appeared in print just a year after the authoress' Tirolean holiday. Indeed the fictional journey taken by the founder head and pupils to reach the school wa drawn deeply from her own experience of the same journey. Early books in th Chalet School series are brimming with descriptive writing based on Pertisau o the Achen See or Briesau on the Tiern See in fictional terms as the authoress sa it. One can almost experience for oneself the aroma of freshly brewed coffee, o the flowers in the windowboxes, of the scented mountain air after a heavy rair storm, and of the newly varnished woodwork. *The Times Literary Supplemen* called the opener a "delightful story," the chief characters "well described" an the story "interesting" for parents and teachers as well as girls. Elinor, encourage by not only these comments but favourable comment from other sources, decide to write a sequel, and *Jo of the Chalet School* appeared in 1926. Soon after it publication, Elinor returned to South Shields, giving up her job in Fareham. Fo six years she apparently did no regular teaching, but devoted her main energies t writing, producing a further seven Chalet School books, three La Rochelle book and a number of "one-off" titles. Having been an Anglican all her life, she wa received into the Roman Catholic Church in December 1930. Around 1933, he mother and stepfather, for reasons that were far from clear, decided to move t Hereford, and she followed suit. In Hereford she met a Mrs Griffiths who wante a daily governess to teach her two daughters in their house at Peterchurch, som fourteen miles from the city. Elinor was offered, and accepted, the post. Sh remained there until 1938, when, following the death of her stepfather, she decide to open a school of her own in Hereford, known as the Margaret Roper Schoo Having started with just two pupils - the Griffiths girls - numbers increase dramatically as the dangers of war and evacuation came closer. However, althoug she enjoyed teaching, she was never happy in her role as headmistress. After th war, numbers declined and it may well have come as a relief to her to close th school in 1948 and concentrate on her writing which had continued to be her chie interest throughout the thirties and forties. During her time as headmistress sh managed fourteen books; in the decade following she completed thirty-eight sixteen of them within two years! These included not only Chalet School books bu adventure stories, educational readers, and school stories with a religious slan This output, despite her not being in full-time work, is still remarkable when on considers that she was at the same time nursing her elderly mother, who died i 1957. After her mother died, she remained in Lichfield House, the Victorian vill which had housed her school. In 1964 two of her friends persuaded her to sell up and together they bought a house in Redhill, Surrey. Between 1957 and 196 another twenty books were written, and interestingly, all but two were Chale School stories. By 1967, however, her health had begun to fail, with two hear attacks followed by bouts of pain and depression. As a result, *Althea Joins the Chalet School,* which was to prove to be her penultimate title, took two years (from 1967 until 1969) to prepare. In January 1969 she began work on her very last book, appropriately enough another Chalet School title, *Prefects of the Chalet School.* She never saw the printed article; she died peacefully in September 1969 seven months before it was published.

In total, fifty-eight Chalet School books plus three annuals and a Chalet School cookbook were written (as well as an "additional" title *The Chalet School and Rosalie* which is not strictly part of the sequence). Elinor also wrote seven La Rochelle books, three books in a Chudleigh Hold series, four geographical readers, two books about a school named Skelton Hall, and around twenty-five miscellaneous titles, some with a school setting, some without. Interestingly, just like Angela Brazil and Charles Hamilton, the writer remained single and childless throughout her life.

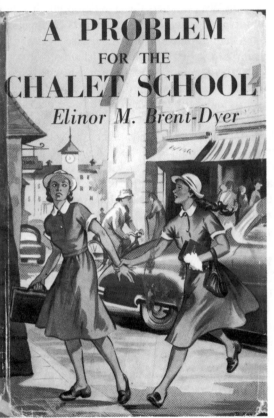

The Chalet School, although it accepts day pupils, is a boarding-school, taking children of all ages. Mary Cadogan described it as being "an intriguing amalgam of British grit and foreign glamour". The pupils come from well-off families; no working-class girls are admitted, notwithstanding the many with whom the authoress would have co-existed during her early years. It is a girls' school, but there is a boys' section in the kindergarten and there are, interestingly, male teachers. It is founded by a twenty-four-year-old, Madge Bettany, with no experience and hardly any money;

it is the health of her twelve-year-old sister Jo that she has chiefly in mind. Though it begins in the Tirol, it does not remain there, and even in the Tirol there are several changes in its structure and size. Elinor used a number of different settings for the Chalet School. The Nazi menace prompts a move to Guernsey, and thence, following the outbreak of the Second World War and in the face of the Nazi Occupation, to the vicinity of Armiford. This was clearly based on the Golden Valley in Herefordshire, Armiford as Hereford and Howell (where the school is situated) as Peterchurch. Enthusiasts seeking original editions of Elinor's work in the second-hand book mecca, Hay-on-Wye, will pass through Peterchurch if they take the direct route from the motorway at Ross. In 1994 a whole book appeared devoted solely to tracing the real locations on which the Armishire stories were based. From Howell the school moves to St Briavel, a fictional island off the coast of South Wales, and thence to Switzerland. Senior pupils form an advanced guard, setting up a finishing-school known as Welsen or Unter die Kniefen, with more of the school following soon afterwards and setting up shop at Gornetz Platz. The school soon contains 200 girls, with another 100 juniors at the Carnbach "branch" in Wales. For the migrants, things therefore come almost full circle, with many of the customs, traditions and trappings of school life on the Continent returning to the series and remaining with it from story number 26 onwards. It is however the adventures in Austria which have captured the imagination of readers most vividly, and one suspects that the readers would sympathise with Miss Annersley's sentiment, expressed in *Changes for the Chalet School*, that...

"...we have never given up hoping that the day would come when we could go back to our first home in Tirol."

A series of this nature was bound to throw up some difficulties. The first was obviously the time lapse. With the stories spanning some forty-five years, there was a choice between varying the characters throughout or keeping the same ones and asking the reader, like Charles Hamilton or (as we shall see) Anthony Buckeridge, to treat the characters as Peter Pans, remaining hapless school pupils while the readers moved on inexorably into middle and old age. Elinor decided that her characters could not remain static, but she kept a close link between its best-loved characters and the Chalet School throughout. The second was the problem of language, and what Cadogan and Patricia Craig called "racial disaffinities". It would have been stretching credibility rather too far to fill a foreign school with girls who were all English! However, any concerns are soon shown to have been needless; both English and foreign girls mix very well, and appear to have remarkably little difficulty in understanding each other. Notwithstanding that, the communication process is undoubtedly aided by the constant supply of English recruits to the Chalet School, many of them orphans and several of them extremely talented and interesting; Nina Rutherford, in *A Genius at the Chalet*

School, is a good example.

Jo Bettany, sister of the first headmistress and "Joey" to her friends, is the central character from start to finish. At the start, Jo is a schoolgirl and of course founder pupil of the Chalet School. In due course, she grows up and leaves, but remains in the Chalet School limelight, taking on various roles including those of teacher, author, mother (eleven times!), guardian and mentor. Like the little lamb following Mary, she assiduously follows her beloved school wherever it goes, helped by the fact that Jack, her husband, is able to move with his work so that he is usually within reasonable distance of the Chalet School. As a child she is impetuous and rebellious - as early as the second book she risks life and limb by going unsupervised to an ice carnival - but her impetuosity helps to save the life of her first schoolmate, Grizel Cochrane, in the very first story. In the first five books she actually saves the lives of six girls and a dog. She does, however, draw the line at exposing undergarments to an unsuspecting public even where her safety is at stake! Elinor's accounts of Joey's constant flirtations with death are thought to stem from a bereavement she suffered early in her life. Joey is straightforward, unsentimental, tomboyish and physically strong. She is also moody, impatient, sarcastic and snappy. Many of her characteristics reflected those of her creator. For all her undesirable qualities, she is a sensitive soul with a strong faith; we are told in *The Chalet School and Jo* that her faith in God's ultimate goodness is unshakeable. She is not especially good-looking - indeed in *Jo of the Chalet School* she says:

"No one on earth could call me beautiful, could they?"

In adulthood, she becomes a clever, friendly, loyal and compassionate woman, but still a schoolgirl at heart. As McClelland said: "(she is) a mature adult, though still at heart a schoolgirl with a would-be delicious dottiness and sense of fun. It is all quite simply too good to be true." In *Jo Returns to the Chalet School* we are told that Joey, though still only 18 and just out of school herself...

"...would not have turned a hair if she had been asked to take on an entire form."

Was Elinor trying to recruit more youngsters to the teaching profession? Interestingly, although Jo, like Elinor, becomes a bookworm and an authoress at a very early age, her development as a person is quite different from that of her creator. Her school is a boarding-school, whereas Elinor attended a day-school; Jo marries and has children, whereas the author did neither. The children incidentally arrive rapidly with three of them being born before Joey's twenty-third birthday.

Other characters come and go, although the turnover of head teachers is hardly speedy. Madge, having at an early stage in the series surrendered herself to motherhood, is consequently relieved of her headship by her partner Mlle Lepattre. Described as middle-aged, plain and a stern disciplinarian she is nevertheless always utterly just and fair. Illnesses forces her to make way for Miss Annersley, otherwise known as the Abbess. Regarded as the very model of a successful and popular headmistress, there was an element of wish-fulfilment on the part of her creator. In *Changes for the Chalet School* we hear she is tall, stately and very good-looking with a voice that is deeply pitched and resonant and flexible. Not all the staff are saints; for instance, Matron Webb in *Princess of the Chalet School*, possibly drawn from her creator's hated Hampshire landlady, and another Matron, Matron Besly in *The New House at the Chalet School*. As with Angela Brazil and Dorita Fairlie Bruce, masculine impact on school life is minimal; one notable exception is Mr Denny, the eccentric music master. Among the girls, Grizel, with wicked stepmother, is the first apart from Jo to make an impact, as she quickly rises to the rank of head girl. Nevertheless, it is only in the fiftieth book of the series that she is allowed by her creator to get married, as though, in keeping with the parallels between Elinor's experience and Chalet School happenings, the authoress was seeking to place on show her own frustration with spinsterhood.

The second book sees the arrival of Cecilia Humphries, or "little Robin," as she becomes known; six years Joey's junior, and referred to as Joey's little adopted sister, she appears throughout the series, and having come very close to death as a child, becomes, in McClelland's words, "one of Elinor's most successful and best-loved characters." The authoress described the Robin to her readers as a dear little girl, very happy and sunshiny, and not at all shy. It is suggested that the relationship between her and Joey was modelled on that between her creator and Hazel Bainbridge. Much later in the series, a new girl named Mary-Lou Trelawny temporarily takes the limelight off Joey. With natural leadership qualities, an assertive and often sharp attitude towards those who cross her, popularity with her peers, and her straightforward, grown-up outlook on life, she proves to be as potentially strong a personality as Joey, although she never acquires Joey's charisma. It is hard to keep count of the girls of various nationalities who pass through the Chalet School. Some seem to appear more frequently than others and then return to the Chalet School as teachers - Juliet Carrick, Grizel Cochrane, Biddy O'Ryan and Gillian Linton, for instance - but many others receive just a few fleeting glimpses before merging into insignificance. A favoured device of the authoress is to introduce a new pupil who does not quite fit in to Chalet School life - Thekla von Stift, Joyce Linton, Jessica Wayne, Eustacia Benson and Evelyn Ross, for instance - and then to describe whether they cope with the pressures or are gently eased out. Doctors are the preferred choice of husband, with Madge, Joey and Grizel marrying doctors. Animals come into the stories as well; Elinor loved dogs, and Joey's two St Bernards are sympathetically and affectionately described. One should also not forget Minette, the school cat, in later titles.

Some similarities with the work of Angela Brazil are only to be expected. Until the departure to Switzerland, there is a strong emphasis on Girl Guiding with all the activity that entails. There is an equally large emphasis on sport, with plenty of hockey, cricket, lacrosse, tennis, rowing and swimming. The bracing outdoor air of the Tirol lends itself to wholesome, healthy activity, inevitably rewarded by soup, hard-boiled eggs, boiled ham, rolls or cakes at the day's end. Indeed, the reader of any one book would feel cheated - and the girls would be a great deal slimmer - without at least one helping of that time-honoured snack Elinor liked so much, "Kaffee und Kuchen" (coffee and cake). With the differing locations, and plenty of holiday activity too, some parts of the books contain digressions worthy of Angela Brazil herself. Reference has already been made to the mass of descriptive writing early in the series, with Austrian food and drink whetting the appetite of even the staunchest

couch potatoes among the intended readership. In *Mary Lou at the Chalet School* we are told of...

Dampfnudeln mit Pflaumen - yeast dumplings cooked in plum syrup with butter and then popped into a hot oven to bake twenty minutes.

Did any of the readers give it a try?

There are many other digressions within the stories. Elinor became an unofficial holiday brochure, with expeditions to other towns and beauty spots prompting a large chunk of historical and geographical information of only marginal relevance to the plot. In *Changes For the Chalet School* a tour of the Bournville Chocolate Factory is described, although not perhaps as charismatically as Roald Dahl's fictional factory is portrayed. School concerts, the activities of the Hobbies Club and Peace League, pantos and sales of work are described with meticulous attention. However, this is counterbalanced with careful study of the Tirolean people, a hardy, hard-pressed community having little in common with their Mittagessen-scoffing neighbours at the school, and having to endure extraordinary extremes of weather, from spectacular electrical storms to snow, ice and hard frosts. Elinor is particularly fond of her thunder and lightning, and just as winter is likely to bring a nativity play, so will summer bring blisteringly hot days building up to terrifying mountain storms which have little respect for the smooth running of the school. In the course of such a lengthy series, Elinor was certainly successful in bringing wonderful new vistas to British children who were living through difficult times, and who of necessity were confined in their experiences and outlook. When the Chalet School moves to Herefordshire (or Armishire, as it is known in the books) description continues, with what McClelland called "almost obsessive accuracy." It is arguable that without the authoress' flair for descriptive writing and her guiding the reader to new locations the Chalet School books would never have achieved the success they did. As McClelland wrote: "Although Elinor's descriptions can sometimes be flat or, at the other extreme, over-written, it cannot be denied that she was often most successful in recreating the scenery and special atmosphere of the Tirol."

To continue with similarities with Angela Brazil, much of the narrative is taken up with schoolgirl foibles. An example is the language used, with the words "ripping", "topping" and even "golloptious" and in-vogue expressions such as "gum-swizzled" bespattering the earlier works, plus a bewildering array of transatlantic slang from the American contingent. As if in response to Angela Brazil the girls are constantly reminding themselves that slang is forbidden, but that does not prevent some memorable phrases that Angela Brazil herself would have been proud of; "Great Caesar's bathmat!" and "Holy smoke!" (shades of Batman) can be found in *Exploits of the Chalet Girls* and *The Chalet School and The Lintons* respectively. Even in 1950 Bride is heard to exclaim: "Oh, my stars and garters!" (*Peggy of The Chalet School*). There is plenty of daredevil adventure or plain stupidity; such activity usually ends in tears and punishments which range from scoldings to docked half-holidays and even fines. The mountainous settings for the earlier and later stories provide not only plenty of opportunities for misdemeanour but also the constant threat of tragedy which often materialises. There are other disasters of a more minor nature but attributable to schoolgirlishness at its most insufferable; spilled ink, coverings of pepper, caked enamel, burning muslin, drenching with fast green dye and paste-swamping bring a Mack Sennett element to our Chaletian community. Other incidents, such as the smoking tower in a representation of the 1812 siege of Moscow (*Adrienne and the Chalet School*) and the burning of a fancy dress costume (*Carola Storms the Chalet School*) are more cruel twists of fate than the results of schoolgirl bravado. The first dozen books of the series contain many conflagrations! If it is not fires, it is train crashes (*The School at the Chalet*), plane crashes (*The Chalet School in Exile*), avalanches (*Trials of the Chalet School*) and thunderbolts from the aforementioned electrical storms (*The Princess of the Chalet School*). Elinor was fond of using disaster as a device to draw previously warring factions together, the near demise of Eustacia in *Eustacia Goes to the Chalet School* being a prime example.

As in the work of Angela Brazil, there is a strong moral undertone to the stories, reflecting Elinor's strong Christian beliefs. As has been said, the authoress enjoyed introducing a "difficult" girl into the Chalet School, usually with little or no faith, and then showing them integrating smoothly into school life in time for a suitably syrupy ending. Such conclusions often bring about unequivocal acceptance or affirmation of faith in God; for example, near the end of *Mary-Lou at the Chalet School* we are informed that...

"Heaven is the happiest happiness and laughter is a part of happiness."

Almost every story contains reference to spiritual matters, and the Oberammergau Passion Play is described in loving detail. Even hardened readers may find it difficult to quell the odd tear in their eye when reading Elinor's painstaking descriptions of the elaborate Nativity plays put on at the school. If Christmas term exploits are being described, it is a fairly even bet that a Nativity play will find its way in somewhere. What some critics find remarkable is the degree of toleration between Protestant and Catholic in the Chalet School. Cadogan and Craig called the religious sentimentality a "serious weakness" in the stories, particularly in *The Head Girl in the Chalet School* where death is described as...

"...just falling asleep to wake with God."

To be fair, any girl or indeed any individual might invoke the name of the Almighty upon being faced with possible death through falling off mountains, drowning or exposure, as Elinor's characters seem to do on a regular basis. McClelland applauded Elinor for facing up to the issue in the first place even if one fan regarded the early books in the series as "too religious" for her.

The final similarity to the work of Angela Brazil is in the hard-nosed prefects, exciting more fear and terror than the fiercest headmistress. In *Trials for the Chalet School*, for instance, prefects take the law into their own hands to "punish" more junior pupils for causing chaos in the lost property department. Mary-Lou Trelawny, whilst a popular girl, expresses her displeasure with junior girls in no uncertain terms in *Theodora and the Chalet School*. Elinor, like Angela Brazil, believed fervently in the reality of her creations. She described them as "alive, and panting to tell their stories."

It should not, however, be forgotten that Elinor found herself writing not just for a Twenties and Thirties readership, but for a more modern and perhaps less easily pleased post-war readership too. She wrote with much more understanding of the changing times, and there are a number of examples of this in her work.

Firstly, she appeared to have a less blinkered view of the outside world and the international and religious scene than many of her contemporaries. She seemed to have greater awareness of the Nazi menace than might have been expected of an English children's author. Hitler's great might is recognised in *The New Chalet School*, published in 1938, and then developed in *The Chalet School in Exile* which is a genuinely exciting, fast-moving adventure with little time for Kaffee und Kuchen. There is not the nationalistic fervour of Angela Brazil or Dorita Fairlie Bruce; foreign teachers are not held up to ridicule, although Bridget O'Ryan's appearance produces a flood of faintly insulting Irish blarney. The fact that girls of different nationalities are living together under the same roof makes for a spirit of international fellowship rather than rivalry or mockery, and indeed a fine is payable in *The Chalet School and the Lintons* for forgetting that a certain day is a German Day, with German being spoken in preference to other languages. The Chalet School Peace League, founded in *The Chalet School in Exile* in response to the Nazi menace, shows how far the girls are prepared to go in terms of international co-operation, and everyone is at great lengths to stress how there is no quarrel with Germans per se - only with Nazis. Ian Ousby applauded Elinor for her "emphasis on internationalism, (which) as an ideal acted as a useful corrective to the strong belief in national superiority found in other popular writing for British children of the time." Elinor's characters demonstrate a more enlightened attitude towards religious differences, Joey explaining in 1930 that the Catholic Church is "only one of the roads to God."

Secondly, relationships between girls are kept firmly in perspective, and there is not the same emphasis on bosom friendship that there is in the work of Angela Brazil; indeed when Simone, a French girl, appears on the scene in the first book, her amorous advances are rebuffed by her peers. Juliet Carrick is allowed to fall for Kay O'Hara in *The Chalet School and Jo* although by then Juliet, an ex-pupil, has grown up, and she has a boyfriend, Donal, who competes for her attentions. In *A Problem for the Chalet School* we are told that at the Chalet School...

"...sentimental grand passions were severely sat on."

Interestingly, this area of sentimentality was held up to ridicule in a pre-Chalet School title of the writer's called *A Head Girl's Difficulties*. Elinor claimed to be against "all that sort of thing" but it has been suggested that underneath she was merely innocent rather than having deep feelings on the subject of sex. Friendship, though, is another matter; much of the feuding in *Theodora and the Chalet School* concerns jealousy between girls, and *The Rivals of the Chalet School* explores the jealousy between girls of different schools.

Thirdly, as has already been stated, the books are often amazingly topical. In fact, a great many incidents in the Chalet School series were based on real-life happenings, and McClelland highlighted the problems experienced by Elinor in reversing the process and trying to make the Margaret Roper School live up to the Chalet School in terms of achievement! There is a more masculine influence in some of the stories; not only the frequent presence of husbands and boyfriends, but also the impression made on the girls by the work of a real-life composer Ernest Farrar (particularly his song, *Brittany*). The writer admired him greatly, and although the affection was purely platonic, it is doubtful that many would have heard of Farrar but for the references to him in the Chalet School books! The advent of 'O' level examinations was not lost on the author who by introducing them to the narrative demonstrated that she was able to keep up with educational as well as social changes.

Fourthly, the dialogue and indeed behaviour of the characters moves with the times; "ripping" and "topping" make way diplomatically for "good", "excellent" and "marvellous." Elinor's early playwriting clearly stood her in good stead when constructing acceptable dialogue; in 1966 she showed considerable awareness of current schoolgirl phraseology by the use of the expression "a complete moron" (*Challenge for the Chalet School*). She is also credited with the introduction of the word "fabulous" to schoolgirl fiction! Elinor was anxious that the bad habits of her creations should not have a detrimental effect on her fans; girls are often being castigated for grammatical misuse, even where the misuse is so minor it would hardly be noticed today. Her characters are more credible than those of Angela Brazil and Dorita Fairlie Bruce; McClelland described them as "neither the paragons of virtue nor the monsters of depravity so often found in schoolstories." Credibility can be found in many unexpected forms. An example is smoking. Elinor's liking for smoking, and the fact that it was in vogue in post-war Britain, meant that her characters, including pupils, smoked too, something which might well be frowned upon in the more health-conscious 90s. It is quite a shock to find Joey-ba-ba lighting up in *The Chalet School in Exile*! The sixth formers who were brought to the Oberland in *The Chalet School in the Oberland* are seen to indulge both in smoking and card-playing. A curious feature of the books is reference to juvenile fiction read by her characters. Elsie Oxenham is the inspiration behind one of the incidents in the series, recounted in *The Chalet School Wins the Trick*. Angela Brazil books, however, are never owned by Chalet School pupils. Was Elinor afraid of the free advertising for a competitor, or had the headteachers discreetly banned the books?

The fifth and final essential difference from the work of Angela Brazil lies, of course, in the series element. Virtually every work of Angela Brazil brings us a new school and new characters, whereas the Chalet School books, although complete stories in themselves, have a definite serial element with the fortunes of Joey providing the golden thread that runs through each story.

The popularity of the Chalet School books - *Three Go to the Chalet School* in 1949, for instance, achieved sales of almost 10,000 within two months of publication - led to the formation of the Chalet Club in 1959. Despite the decline in the market for school stories, and the immense changes in ideas and fashions in children's literature, the books continued to be read and enjoyed, not just in English-speaking countries but on the Continent too. In five years the number of Club members rose from 33 to just under 4,000. Not all of these were children. Club members received a newsletter with con-

tributions from Elinor herself; in return prodigious quantities of fan mail were received and from this the publishers were able to gauge which titles were most popular and merited reprinting. In 1967 the books began to appear in abridged form in paperback and in the first six months almost 200,000 copies were sold. In 1969 a Lyons promotion promised purchasers of their Harvest Pies a free Chalet School book for eight coupons! As might be expected, there was some controversy about the abridgements, which incidentally Elinor undertook herself for a time. Not only was much flavour lost from the virginal texts, but in an effort to keep the books to a reasonable length, some indiscreet editing resulted, and in some cases two paperbacks were issued to cover the ground contained in one hardback. As a result, despite the continued availability of most of the titles some 70 years after the first one appeared, there is still a considerable market for second-hand "originals." In the 1990s the books were enjoying a vast following by both children and adults, some of whom were grown-up before the very first title appeared in print! In 1993 a copy of *Tom Tackles The Chalet School* which would have set a reader back less than a pound if purchased when new, was on sale in London for over fifty pounds. Because their print runs were much shorter, it is the later rather than the earlier titles which are much harder to obtain and which seem to fetch the most exorbitant prices. Although Elinor's work never appeared on radio or television, the publication of the fiftieth title earned her an appearance on television in 1964, and she was given an obituary in *The Times* when she died. The Chalet Club has now been superseded by an international organisation known as Friends of the Chalet School, with a wide - and not exclusively female! - membership. Incidentally the title Friends of the Chalet School is significant; while Elinor did write other school stories, the great majority have disappeared and never acquired any charisma. They are listed at the end of this chapter. The Friends are an active group, providing newsletters and even a lending library service; a typical newsletter might contain personal reflections on Elinor's work, speculation on the fate of the characters after they left school, and critiques of both new editions and reprints of the originals. The Friends marked the centenary of Elinor's birth by organising a celebratory weekend based at Hereford. Angela Brazil never enjoyed such enduring or loving support, perhaps partly because she created so many schools and characters. By contrast, the author of the Chalet School series, in McClelland's words, "created at the beginning of the series a set of characters who... gradually assumed an almost independent existence in her eyes and those of the readers." One fan wrote: "I found it as easy to write about Elinor's Chalet School people as about my own family and friends I know really well. That must mean something."

Despite her popularity and her attempts to cater for a more critical readership, her books were not above criticism. One criticism was that there were too many of them; that Elinor had not called time early enough. Cadogan and Craig claimed that "By the late 1940's the possibilities of the series clearly had been exhausted, yet the books continued to appear with dispiriting regularity. Although the direct sociological content of the books always had been negligible, by the end of the series they had become absurdly anachronistic." They felt that the weaknesses in the stories become apparent when Jo was removed from the actual school environment, and became a less and less convincing adult. *Joey Goes to the Oberland* does not pretend to have any plot at all, and is certainly nothing to do with current Chalet School activity, but deals, in very long-winded fashion, with her journey to Switzerland from Armishire, surrounded by squawking children. What a contrast to the hectic, exciting and almost disturbing narrative of *The Chalet School in Exile*. Certainly there is a school of thought which suggests that the quality of the writing deteriorated after the war, with fewer memorable characters being introduced, and apart conceivably from Mary-Lou, nobody to rival Joey Bettany. It is perhaps significant that the Swiss setting of the Chalet School, one of five different settings used, occupies well over half of the series. The series could well be likened to a motor car which, having spent only a few years on the road, rolls into a garage to remain for many more years until it rusts away. The first eighteen books or so are busy, fast-moving, full of incident and drama, and forming a fascinating perspective on a very turbulent period in history. A large majority of the remainder, however, in the Swiss setting, seem to be rather tired duplications of already overworked material, with an excess of nativity plays, thunderstorms and nasty accidents. In the absence of anybody with Joey's charisma, there is nothing or nobody in the second half of the series that is especially memorable. As a result, there is no real incentive for the reader to go out and buy the next book, except perhaps force of habit or to boast of having the complete set. McClelland saw an almost paradoxical link between the increase in time that Elinor had available to write, and the deterioration in quality: "Later on, although Elinor writes a multitude of new people into the series, few have any real interest. It does appear that Elinor's imagination had thrived the more when time to express herself was in short supply."

Besides anachronism, another focus of criticism might be lack of authenticity. For instance, reference is made in *Exploits of the Chalet Girls* to a Brahms quartet with flute, whereas in fact no such quartet existed. There are also references in *The School at the Chalet* to Kronen as the Austrian currency, whereas Kronen had actually been superseded by the Schilling before any of the books were published. Credibility, although commendably evident in some aspects, is stretched to the limit in others. One might argue that the whole concept of a twenty-four-year-old girl with virtually no money setting up a school in the Austrian Alps, and the subsequent relocations of that school in at least four different places many hundreds of miles apart, is absurd enough. Other examples are the extraordinary frequency of near fatal accidents with which central characters are confronted; the chance meetings of distant relations in the most unlikely circumstances; and the seemingly effortless way in which the girls, of wholly different nationalities, understand one another. Irish, Italian, American, Austrian and English are just some of the nationalities that appear in the narrative.

More worrying, although not necessarily detrimental to the enjoyment of the stories, are the almost legendary errors of consistency, with characters mysteriously changing name from one book to the next. The most glaring example is that of Mademoiselle Lepattre who begins the series as La Pattre and then Lapattre, and whose Christian name changes from Elise to Therese. Biddy O'Ryan becomes Biddy O'Hara in *The Highland Twins at the Chalet School*. In *Exploits of the Chalet Girls* Frieda is conclusively proved to be in two places at once. In *The School at the Chalet* we are told that Madge's middle name begins with 'H' but subsequent books state her middle name to be Daphne. In *Summer Term at the Chalet School* a child named Claire makes her debut but mysteriously disappears from the scene after this one story. A town called Taverton changes location from Cornwall to Devon; the fictional island of St Briavel (not to be confused with the real Gwent village of the same name) is on one occasion described as an island in the Irish Sea off Wales and on another occasion is referred to as an island off the coast of South Wales. The difficulty is that the Irish Sea is off the *west* coast of Wales! In *Two Sams at the Chalet School*, one form begins with Jean Abbot as its form prefect; on the very next page, the form prefect is Barbara Hewlett; and not fifty pages later, the incumbent is a girl rejoicing in the name of Jack. The Friends of the Chalet School Newsletter regularly includes newly-discovered "bloopers" as they are called, with more coming to light all the time. In defence of the writer it should be pointed out that not only did she have a poor memory and was somewhat unmethodical, but she had access to none of the sophisticated indexing systems used by many "soap opera" writers and producers today.

The series has attracted other criticisms too, not only from the point of view of authenticity. The writing style can be sloppy. One fan wrote that "Stylistically many of (the later Chalet books) are awful, at best pedestrian and at worst incredibly clumsy." Chapter endings seem particularly prone to attacks of poor English. The following examples are taken from *Princess at the Chalet School*:

Still, if he had realised what she was he might have reconsidered his plans again.

They were thinking hard enough, though; Madge hoped that it would never be resurrected again, but she was to be disappointed there, though that came later on.

In *Peggy of the Chalet School*, Joey, referring to a violent storm which has buffeted their island and her therefore using outdoor leisure time for extra teaching, says:

"If this weather is a fair sample of the sort of thing we can expect here in the winter, I'm making hay while the sun shines."

Some comments are briefer and to the point. "Why, oh why are they always eating?" wrote an Australian woman in 1975. "If another of them marries a doctor I shall scream!" The length of the series prompted one lay critic to say: "Later on I think the long series got absolutely nutty." McClelland wrote: "At some point a kind of Soap Opera Syndrome begins to operate, and people once hooked will find no rubbish too great to swallow. Had there been no more to the books than a glamorous background and a lot of instruction more or less attractively packaged, the Chalet series would long ago have been forgotten." Ousby asserted: "Little read now, her fiction is a testament to the type of undemanding reading once thought suitable for adolescent girls." His comment is somewhat hard to reconcile with the success of the Armada reprints.

It is conceivable that the comparatively exotic setting was all that was needed to persuade suburban youngsters to hurry out to buy Elinor's latest title. It could equally well be argued that following the high quality and deserved success of the early books, the only significant incentive to purchase later titles was to discover the eventual fate of the characters introduced in those early stories, although it cannot be denied that the satisfaction of having a full set of Chalet School books would also have been a motivating factor. Even these positive points need some qualification. By no means all the books have a foreign setting, and whereas some of the characters continue to appear long after their schooldays are gone, many others fade away without trace. There is certainly never any real guarantee of being able to discover the "fate" of one's favourite character in subsequent books. If one then considers the negative aspects such as the inconsistencies, the lack of authenticity, the stylistic lapses and the anachronisms, one might be forgiven for wondering how it is that Elinor succeeded at all.

It is important, however, not to understate Elinor's undoubted talents. She did more than take the readers to an interesting setting; her descriptive writing could be graphic and vigorous, whether she was portraying the arrival of a fierce mountain storm or describing the bill of fare for the girls' Sunday tea. Although there was tremendous variation in the extent to which she developed her characters, she ensured that her principal creations remained in touch with the action right through to the end of the series. The narrative, though not always strictly believable, moves forward in a robust fashion and can never be described as boring, especially when a thunderstorm is in the air or a mountain walk is scheduled. The progressive ethos of the Chalet School itself sets it apart from many fictional schools that were being portrayed by other authors at the same time.

Elinor had begun her writing career by following unashamedly in the footsteps of Angela Brazil and many others; ultimately she was to enjoy more lasting popularity than any of them, still going strong while the traditional girls' boarding school story lost its appeal and became the subject of ridicule. The fact that there was a thriving international appreciation society for her work over twenty five years after her last book appeared is proof enough that she was no ordinary writer. No other writer achieved similar success with a school "soap". Elinor's success demonstrated that an author who could create a series about a school, write about it imaginatively, and invent an assembly of well-loved characters, stood as good a chance as anyone of preventing a wholesale drift from the written word to the television and comic strip. McClelland identified the concept of the Chalet School as an abiding institution where well-established traditions and the continuity of the characters were the most powerful factors in ensuring the success of the series. As we shall see in the next chapter, Anthony Buckeridge was to be similarly successful.

THE CHALET SCHOOL BOOKS

Given below is a brief synopsis of each title, together with its publication date, and some quotations. All the Chalet books were published by W & R Chambers Ltd.

1. THE SCHOOL AT THE CHALET (1925). The Chalet School is founded by Madge Bettany principally to cater for her younger sister Joey. Grizel Cochrane is another recruit. Her abscondment from the CS prompts a rescue mission from Joey who is lucky to escape with her life.

2. JO OF THE CHALET SCHOOL (1926). Joey's experience of a Tirolean winter includes an idyllic Christmas and sneaking out to an ice-carnival. Her resulting injuries prompt attention from Doctor Russell who asks Madge to be his wife.

3. THE PRINCESS OF THE CHALET SCHOOL (1927). A new matron, Miss Webb, arrives, makes herself very unpopular, and is dismissed. A freak storm nearly destroys the Chalet School. Princess Elisaveta of Belsornia joins the school and Jo rescues her after she has been abducted. Madge marries Doctor James (Jem) Russell.

Just as she reached them there was a frightful red glare, a dull shrieking noise sounded, and then a ball of crimson light flashed past the window, and there was a most awful crash, which quite outdid anything that had previously happened.

4. THE HEAD GIRL OF THE CHALET SCHOOL (1928). Grizel Cochrane becomes Head Girl and despite early challenges to her authority is a success. A trip to Salzburg nearly ends in fiery disaster but thanks to Joey does not; bold new recruit Cornelia explores some caves and nearly meets her doom; there is a scare when the Robin goes missing; Madge and Jem bear a son, David.

5. THE RIVALS OF THE CHALET SCHOOL (1929). A rival school, St Scholastika's, opens in a neighbouring village. A feud rapidly develops between them and the Chalet School, its climax being a jape played by the new school intending to damage the Chalet School and involving Elisaveta. Joey saves one of their pupils, Maureen, from drowning, almost losing her life in the process.

"On the whole, I think I'm jolly glad we're going to be friends," she said seriously. "It's such a bore to remember all the time that you aren't pals with someone!"

6. EUSTACIA GOES TO THE CHALET SCHOOL (1930). Eustacia Benson, a thoroughly disagreeable girl, is sent to the school in order that she might learn some manners. She succeeds in alienating almost everyone, and decides to run away. Unsurprisingly she encounters difficulties in the nearby terrain and when conveyed back to school she becomes a changed woman, adopting the name Stacie.

7. THE CHALET SCHOOL AND JO (1931). At last Joey Bettany becomes head girl of the Chalet School, and under her headship the school enjoys sporting success. The Robin's health continues to give cause for concern. The Chalet School expands with an annexe being opened. An Irish orphan girl, Bridget O'Ryan, appears with her own distinctive Irish lilt.

8. THE CHALET GIRLS IN CAMP (1932). Joey and her friends go off to guide camp. Joey is cross when she falls into a pit; even more cross when on a fishing trip she believes that a corpse has been hooked and it turns out to be a dummy. Grizel, returning to the school as a teacher, helps to play a trick on her which indirectly leads to an interesting discovery. Ilonka gets high on syrup of figs.

The sun came out again, shining on a fairy world, where every grass-blade and flower-petal was hung with gleaming drops, and the grass, so parched and brown early that morning, was transmuted into a sheet of living green.

9. EXPLOITS OF THE CHALET GIRLS (1933). Christmas term has once again arrived at the Chalet School and various festivities are organised. Thekla remains aloof until an accident with her undergarments makes her think that the Girl Guides are not so bad after all.

10. THE CHALET SCHOOL & THE LINTONS (1934). Joyce and Gillian Linton go to the Chalet School while their mother is treated at Dr Jem's sanatorium. Gillian settles in well but Joyce's behaviour is such that only a woman-to-woman talk with Joey saves her from the boot. Thekla, however, after more cavortings, is not so lucky.

(N.B. The paperback edition was split into 2 volumes, the second being entitled 'Rebel at the Chalet School')

11. THE NEW HOUSE AT THE CHALET SCHOOL (1935). A new house, to be called St Clare's, is built at the CS while the rest of the school becomes St Therese and the annexe, St Agnes. The St Clare's new matron is a disaster and soon leaves. Joey's schooldays end.

"No, but the rule says no talkin' after silence-bell," rejoined Biddy dismally. "It's throuble's before me, gerrils! Oi can fale it in me bones!"

12. JO RETURNS TO THE CHALET SCHOOL (1936). Ostensibly just to say hallo, Jo pops back, but a surge of illness and the appearance of Polly Heriot prolong her stay and add her temporarily to the teaching staff. Her first book is accepted for publication.

"Even when I'm an old lady with white hair, telling all my great-great nieces and nephews all about my wicked deeds, I'll never count myself as anything but a Chalet School girl."

13. THE NEW CHALET SCHOOL (1938). Mlle Lepattre's illness forces her to hand the headship to Miss Annersley. St Scholastikas closes and becomes a summer residence for the Russells. The pupils there join the Chalet School and integrate well. Jo's book appears in print.

"Gone home to bed," said Miss Stewart. "Not the King of England, the Pope and Hitler all combined would get her out of it again before tomorrow morning."

(N.B. The paperback edition was split into two volumes, the second being entitled 'A United Chalet School')

14. THE CHALET SCHOOL IN EXILE (1940). An action-packed story. The arrival of the evil Nazis and their threats of vengeance on the girls after they have helped a local Jew, forces the school to move to Guernsey. Joey marries Jack Maynard and produces triplets. Gertrud Becker appears at the school as a Nazi spy to check up on Germans and is nearly blown up by a U-Boat. Mademoiselle Lepattre dies.

"It isn't the Germans who are doing it," said Robin. "It's the Nazis. Joey says she thinks Hitler is anti-Christ - from the Bible, you know. If he is, well, he'll come to a sticky end."

15. THE CHALET SCHOOL GOES TO IT (1941). The Nazi menace to the Channel Islands forces another move on the School, this time at Plas Howell in the vicinity of Armiford in Armishire, England. Joey makes it across the Channel but only after being attacked by an enemy warplane. The triplets are named Margot, Helena and Constance.

16. THE HIGHLAND TWINS AT THE CHALET SCHOOL (1942). Joey takes in Flora and Fiona (inevitably known to all as Flora and Fauna) who start at the Chalet School. A document in their possession is of more than passing interest to the Germans, but Fiona's gift of "second sight" helps to comfort Jo when she believes that Jack, serving in the Navy, is dead. He returns in time for the Nativity play.

"Joey-Joey!" sobbed Madge. "Oh, my darling, don't look like that! Don't, Joey! Cry, darling, but, oh, DON'T look like that!"

17. LAVENDER LAUGHS IN THE CHALET SCHOOL (1943). Lavender Leigh arrives and her conceited, ignorant and empty-headed demeanour causes her to be ostracized from school life until friendship with Liamani and an accident in the snow mellows her. Joey bears a son, Stephen, with accompanying demands that his middle name be "Green" following a concurrent accident with some dye of that colour.

18. GAY FROM CHINA AT THE CHALET SCHOOL (1944). Miss Annersley is involved in an accident. A Miss Bubb becomes acting head and succeeds in being disliked by everybody and forced to leave. Most notably, she alienates Gay who, thanks chiefly to her assistance to Jacynth, wins a special prize donated by Joey.

19. JO TO THE RESCUE (1945). A story of a summer holiday with no school happenings at all. Joey takes her family to a holiday cottage and there meets Phoebe, helping her towards her engagement to - yes, another doctor.

19A.* TOM TACKLES THE CHALET SCHOOL. Tom Gay, despite being a girl, finds it hard to adjust to the female atmosphere of the Chalet School, but helps to make a Sale of Work a resounding success.

(* This is number 31 in the series, but properly fits in here. It was included in the Second and Third Chalet Book For Girls and was published separately in 1955)

20. THREE GO TO THE CHALET SCHOOL (1949). Mary-Lou Trelawny arrives at the Chalet School at the same time as her friend Clemand also Verity-Ann. Mary-Lou works hard to achieve the same class as Clem. The fathers of ML and VA go exploring the Amazon; ML's father fails to return.

21. THE CHALET SCHOOL AND THE ISLAND (1950). Because the drains need overhauling, the Chalet School moves to the fictional island of St Briavels off the South Wales coast and proceeds to be enthralled by a birdman.

22. PEGGY OF THE CHALET SCHOOL (1950). Peggy Bettany, Jo's niece, unexpectedly becomes Head Girl of the Chalet School as the school continues its island stay. We are introduced to two boisterous girls, Polly and Lala Winterton. Joey re-appears as a "visiting mistress."

23. CAROLA STORMS THE CHALET SCHOOL (1951). Having had her appetite for the Chalet School whetted by Biddy O'Ryan, Carola succeeds in being different and running away to school rather than soak up the Jamaican sun.

24. THE WRONG CHALET SCHOOL (1952). Katharine Gordon is sent by her guardian aunt to the wrong Chalet School. Coincidentally, another girl of the same name was expected but never appeared. The "wrong" Katharine stays on and ultimately hears that her missing parents have escaped from Communist China.

25. SHOCKS FOR THE CHALET SCHOOL (1952). In the second Christmas term spent at St Briavels, an Australian firebrand and incendiary is sent on Miss Maynard's recommendation to the Chalet School and succeeds in getting on everybody's nerves. Felicity and Felix increase Joey's children to eight.

Then Madge's sweet mezzo sounded in the French carol 'Dans cette etable' and was followed by Verity Anne in the quaint old Cuckoo Carol. Both sang behind the curtains and this added to the unearthliness of it.

26. THE CHALET SCHOOL IN THE OBERLAND (1952). While Miss Annersley remains in Armishire, Miss Wilson takes the sixth formers to start a fresh branch of the Chalet School in Switzerland - effectively a finishing school. Sixth formers come from far and wide and have to get used to Kaffee und Kuchen - back with a vengeance - and remembering to speak the right language on the right day. Edna Conroy, one of the fresh intake, finds conformity particularly tough. Miss Wilson is not amused.

27. BRIDE LEADS THE CHALET SCHOOL (1953). Bride Bettany, Joey's niece, becomes head girl of the Chalet School. Unfortunately, the school has taken a number of pupils from another school whose headmistress has just died. They resent the move to St Briavels, but Diana Skelton resents it in particular and makes life hard for Bride.

28. CHANGES FOR THE CHALET SCHOOL (1953). Arrangements are made for the transfer of more of the Chalet School - not just sixth formers - to the mountain air of Switzerland, whilst the junior branch stays at Carnbach in Wales. In the heat of the summer term, a regatta is mounted, a chocolate factory is visited, and an outdoor midnight feast in the Old Orchard is ruined by squealing pigs.

"The courts are cracking," Bride said. "As for the pitch, I'm thankful that the Cwyst High match had to be scratched. What the fast bowler's balls of theirs would have been like on it, I shudder to think!"

29. JOEY GOES TO THE OBERLAND (1954). If the Chalet School goes, so must Joey. Under the helpful pretext of Jack's sanatorium shift, our heroine sallies forth with her massive collection of offspring, and meets some old friends on the way. The story, which ends in their new home, might be subtitled the Mobile Old Girls' Reunion.

(N.B. By now the dustjackets contained an invitation to readers to join the Chalet Club, privileges of membership including "miniature Edelweiss badge of attractive design.")

30. THE CHALET SCHOOL AND BARBARA (1954). Barbara Chester, who has been a source of anxiety throughout her early years, comes to the Chalet School. However, Joey takes her in hand and Barbara is soon integrated fully into Chalet School life.

31. TOM TACKLES THE CHALET SCHOOL. See 19a above.

32. THE CHALET SCHOOL DOES IT AGAIN (1955). Adventures on Lake Luzern include a near drowning for Margot Maynard. Margot's saviour is Prunella, who is something of a problem child before she arrives at the Chalet School but by the end is a true Chaletian.

33. A CHALET GIRL FROM KENYA (1955). Jo Scott, Joey's unofficial god-daughter, arrives at the Chalet School. Although she is unlike Joey in many ways, she is extremely plucky and unselfish, and having saved the life of Emerence Hope she succeeds in winning the Margot Venables Prize, a high honour indeed.

34. MARY-LOU AT THE CHALET SCHOOL (1956). What could be described as the definitive "later" CS title, with all the ingredients - a difficult, highly strung new pupil in Jessica Wayne who thanks to the influence of Joey and Mary-Lou comes good; a trip to Zurich and lots of history to go with it; Mary-Lou's tobogganing which results in a near fatal accident; and as Christmas draws near, some seasonal entertainment.

"The rest seem to think you're the cat's bathmat."

35. A GENIUS AT THE CHALET SCHOOL (1956). Nina Rutherford wants to be a concert pianist and it is only at the end that she realises that trivial things like work need to be fitted round ivory-tinkling. Despite making herself unpopular with her constant practising, she comes to love the Chalet School, particularly when some of her music appears in the Chaletian.

"Oh, Miss Dene, please let me go on! Just for half-an-hour! I promise to give up after that!"

(N.B. The paperback edition was split, the second title being 'The Chalet School Fete')

36. A PROBLEM FOR THE CHALET SCHOOL (1956). Rosamund Lilley wins a scholarship to the Chalet School but thinking it will be a snob school is not keen to go. Joan Baker, from the same school as Rosamund, joins as a paying pupil after her father had a big pools win. Both cause problems for the Chalet School.

"You've given way to the demon of pride for a long time now, and you can't expect to slay him when you've only just put on your uniform."

37. THE NEW MISTRESS AT THE CHALET SCHOOL (1957). Kathie Ferrars' first teaching post is at the Chalet School. She joins it shortly after the birth of Joey's ninth child. In an effort to assert her authority she is initially brusque but eventually establishes a rapport and is told that she has come through with flying colours.

38. EXCITEMENTS AT THE CHALET SCHOOL (1957). The School celebrates its Silver Jubilee, there is a feud between V and Va, Karen the cook develops a passion for fancy cleaning materials, there is an encounter with a raging goat, and the unpopular Miss Bubb reappears.

39. THE COMING OF AGE OF THE CHALET SCHOOL (1958). Miss Annersley takes her pupils back to the Tirol to get a taste of the good old days of Briesau and the Tiern See. A group of girls from Carnbach joins the Oberland branch.

40. THE CHALET SCHOOL AND RICHENDA (1958). Richenda - or Ricky - has a father who is a Chinese porcelain expert. Ricky is sent to the school so that her grubby hands can be diverted away from the china.

41. TRIALS FOR THE CHALET SCHOOL (1959). Naomi, disabled due to a fire, and angry and bitter as a result, is taken under the wing of Mary-Lou, now Head Girl. An accident involving Naomi proves to be a blessing in disguise, and she turns from her agnosticism to faith in God and acceptance among her peers. Other adventures include a scarlet fever epidemic, a flood, an avalanche and a pantomime with temperamental lights.

"How could anyone bearing the disabilities she did go through life without some help, and who could give it but God?"

42. THEODORA AND THE CHALET SCHOOL (1959). Problems for Mary-Lou when Theodora, or Ted, is packed off by a grumpy mother to the school having already been expelled from three schools. She makes good in the end, however, and Mary-Lou leaves the Chalet School in a blaze of glory, winning a prize for her leadership skills.

43. JOEY & CO IN TIROL (1960). Unable to keep away from the Tirol, Joey buys a chalet there. A "holiday" story.

44. RUEY RICHARDSON - CHALETIAN (1960). Ruey, who with her brothers Roger and Roddy, was a ward of Joey and Jack Maynard, joins the Chalet School, and plays a large part in introducing lacrosse to the school. Despite finding a ready-made enemy in Francie Wilford who is jealous of her, she integrates fully into school life. She has a mad dad whose ambition is to go into space.

45. A LEADER IN THE CHALET SCHOOL (1961). Jack Lambert, niece of Gay from China, arrives at the Chalet School. Unfortunately she has a penchant for pranks, and gets into some difficulties as a result. Len, one of the triplets heading the Maynard clan, takes her in hand and shows resourcefulness herself when the school heating breaks down.

46. THE CHALET SCHOOL WINS THE TRICK (1961). Five outside girls named Audrey, Solange, Val, Celia and Win, with a mysterious vendetta against the Chalet School, succeed in lighting a camp fire on the school cricket pitch. At length they come to their senses and look forward to becoming Chalet girls themselves.

47. A FUTURE CHALET SCHOOL GIRL (1962). The story of Melanie Lucas, an English day school girl who is forced to leave her native land because her uncle/guardian is being transferred to Geneva. She spends a summer holiday with the Maynards but is jealous of Ruey and Len. All ends happily when she learns she is to join the Chalet School.

48. THE FEUD IN THE CHALET SCHOOL (1962). Another Alpine school named St Hilda's is to be started but burns down before it is opened, and as a consequence the Head is injured. The Chalet School is forced to accommodate the staff and pupils, but in an atmosphere of hostility, largely because the acting head of St Hilda's wishes the schools to be housed separately. The plot is similar to that of *Rivals of The Chalet School*.

"What is the meaning of all this noise?" she demanded in her fluent German. "And why are you not speaking in German? Have you forgotten what day this is? Pay your fines into the box."

49. THE CHALET SCHOOL TRIPLETS (1963). A skiing expedition nearly ends in disaster for Jo's children Len and Con. Len finds herself under suspicion of shoplifting, and Cecil is kidnapped by a confused widow but rescued by her sisters. Betty Landon is knocked unconscious by a bookend.

50. THE CHALET SCHOOL REUNION (1963). The special Gold title, being the fiftieth Chalet School book. Jo organises a reunion of some of the first Chalet School pupils and they go on various expeditions. Grizel, having been out in New Zealand, returns because of the death of her stepmother. She falls in love with Dr Neil Sheppard and marries him.

She flung out her hand towards the window through which the sun was streaming in. "You've walked long enough in the shadows. Now you're going to walk along sunlit ways."

51. JANE AND THE CHALET SCHOOL (1964). Inspired no doubt by Elinor's early theatrical contacts, this story is about a new Chaletian with thespian parents. The pupil's name is Jane Carew. She becomes a bitter enemy of Jack Lambert when Jack is ousted from Len's dorm to make room for her. In the end Jack and Jane are on their way to becoming real friends.

52. REDHEADS AT THE CHALET SCHOOL (1964). A superabundance of redheaded girls lead to a case of mistaken identity as vengeance is sought on Flavia Letton (alias Ansell, also known as Copper), the copper's daughter with copper hair, whose father has brought some evildoers to justice.

"I think," Len said seriously, "that in the hereafter we are judged according to our chances here and what we've made of them."

53. ADRIENNE AND THE CHALET SCHOOL (1965). Adrienne is offered a scholarship to the Chalet School by Jo. She is a hard worker, and makes an enemy of Janet Henderson who hitherto had always been top of the class. Adrienne helps put out a fire but loses her hair. This makes her resemble Robin, one of Jo's best school friends, and it transpires that she is a second cousin to Robin.

54. SUMMER TERM AT THE CHALET SCHOOL (1965). A serious railway accident results in the unofficial adoption, by Joey and Jack, of a baby they call Marie-Claire - as if they did not have enough children of their own.

The school settled down to Mittagessen which today consisted of Karen the cook's famous vegetable sausages, the recipe for which she refused to everyone.

55. CHALLENGE FOR THE CHALET SCHOOL (1966). Miss Annersley leaves on business for most of the Christmas term. Difficulties caused by her absence are compounded by the arrival of two difficult pupils, Evelyn Ross and Jocelyn Marvell. Whereas Evelyn Ross reforms quickly, Jocelyn takes rather longer.

"Some day," she told herself as she snuggled down under her plumes, "I'll be a really decent Chalet girl."

56. TWO SAMS AT THE CHALET SCHOOL (1967). Samantha van der Byl, from America, and Samaris Davies, a Welsh girl, become firm friends when they arrive at the Chalet School together. It is after a mountain accident - yes, another one - that they discover that they are long-lost cousins.

"Methuselah in the Bible lived to be nine hundred," Samantha reminded her. "I'll bet he didn't enjoy the last part of it much," Samaris told her.

57. ALTHEA JOINS THE CHALET SCHOOL (1969). Althea is sent to the Chalet School when her parents go on a cruise for her mother's ill-health. She falls out with Val Pertwee after, among other things, tripping over Val's workbox in Needlework, and in the end Miss Annersley is forced to intervene. A group of girls foil a thief on a half-term outing.

58. PREFECTS OF THE CHALET SCHOOL (1970). The very last Chalet School title, published posthumously, sees Len getting engaged to Reg, who has saved her following an avalanche, and who himself gets lost in a thunderstorm. More criminal activity, in the form of hooligans coming up to the school, is foiled by the police shooting at them.

"If I live to be a great-grandmother I'll be a Chalet girl to the end."

Other titles:
CHALET BOOK FOR GIRLS;
SECOND CHALET BOOK FOR GIRLS;
THIRD CHALET BOOK FOR GIRLS;
CHALET GIRLS' COOKBOOK;
THE CHALET SCHOOL AND ROSALIE.

LA ROCHELLE SERIES
(All published by Chambers)

1. **GERRY GOES TO SCHOOL (1922)**
2. **A HEAD GIRL'S DIFFICULTIES (1923)**
3. **THE MAIDS OF LA ROCHELLE (1924)**
4. **SEVEN SCAMPS (1927)**
5. **HEATHER LEAVES SCHOOL (1929)**
6. **JANIE OF LA ROCHELLE (1932)**
7. **JANIE STEPS IN (1953)**

CHUDLEIGH HOLD SERIES
(All published by Chambers)

1. **CHUDLEIGH HOLD (1954)**
2. **CONDOR GRAGS ADVENTURE (1954)**
3. **TOP SECRET (1955)**

OTHER STORIES
(Mostly with a "schools" background):

A Thrilling Term at Janeways (1927, Thomas Nelson), Judy The Guide (1928, Thomas Nelson), The New Housemistress (1928, Thomas Nelson), The School by the River (1930, Burns Oats & Washbourne), The Feud in the Fifth Remove (1931, Girls Own Paper office), The Little Marie Jose (1932, Burns Oats & Washbourne), Carnation of the Upper Fourth (1934, Girls Own Paper office), Elizabeth the Gallant (1935, Thornton Butterworth), Monica Turns Up Trumps (1936, Girls Own Paper office), Caroline the Second (1937, Girls Own Paper office), They Both Liked Dogs (1938, Girls Own Paper office), The Little Missus (1942, Chambers), The Lost Staircase (1946, Chambers), Lorna at Wynyards (1947, Lutterworth), Stepsisters for Lorna (1948, C & J Temple), Fardingales (1950, Latimer House), The Susannah Adventure (1953, Chambers), Nesta Steps Out (1954, Oliphants), Kennelmaid Nan (1954, Lutterworth), Beechy of the Harbour School (1955, Oliphants), Leader In Spite of Herself (1956, Oliphants), The School at Skelton Hall (1962, Max Parrish), Trouble at Skelton Hall (1963, Max Parrish).

CRYSTALLISED CHEESECAKES

"It was the first afternoon of the Christmas term and Mr Carter was enjoying the peace and stillness, so soon to be shattered by the arrival of sixty-seven boys on the school train."

(Jennings Goes to School)

So begins the first book of the series of Jennings stories. By 1993 they had achieved world-wide sales of six million copies, had been translated into twelve languages, and had led to two television productions, a stage musical, and over one hundred radio plays and readings. The most recent readings, by Stephen Fry on Radio 5 in 1990, achieved the distinction of being issued on a BBC Audio Cassette as part of the BBC's prestigious Radio Collection.

By the time the Second World War broke out, the boys' school story had clearly lost the immense popularity that it had enjoyed over the preceding decades. The reasons for this are well documented elsewhere in this book, but it is as well to reiterate them here in order to recognise the magnitude of the achievement of Jennings' creator, Anthony Buckeridge. The patriotic story, emphasising the virtues of King and Country, now had an almost tasteless ring to it following the carnage of the First World War and the cynical outlook this had produced amongst the younger generations. Attitudes and morals had changed to a point whereby the traditional boys' school story seemed somewhat strait-laced and oriented towards the establishment. The colourful, action-packed Amalgamated Press papers, which appeared regularly throughout the inter-war years, together with the vast Pocket Library series and other periodicals, provided a more attractive pacy form of reading than the huge tomes of spongy paper with only sporadic illustrations which symbolised the work of such writers as Avery, Hadath and Cleaver. Indeed magazines and comics were destined to establish an even greater foothold after the war. The cinema, and the advent of talkies, had begun to compete fiercely with book publishers for money available for leisure. Radio was now well established and television was just around the corner; both at once provided a vibrant, exciting alternative to the written word in the comfort of one's own home. It was clear that it would take a writer of very considerable talent to compete in this new environment. The writer of the Jennings stories, set in a private preparatory school for boys, was one of the few who succeeded. What was remarkable was that at a time when the traditional school story was on the retreat and the only way forward seemed to be by a more modern approach to the subject

Anthony Buckeridge achieved success with an approach which was far from revolutionary. He succeeded, above all, because of his immense skills as a writer. Anthony Malcolm Buckeridge was born in London in June 1912, and himself attended a private school, namely Seaford College in West Sussex. He went on to study at London University. Having left university in the early Thirties he worked as a prep school master for many years, although his teaching was interrupted by a five-year stint in the fire service during the war. Buckeridge said of his own time as a pupil: "During my first term at school, the boys of my form were told to write a story during an English lesson. Mine was tragic and the writing of it moved me deeply. Unfortunately, when the master read it aloud the whole form rocked with laughter; and I was so taken aback that I decided that my next literary effort should be a comedy. Then if people still wanted to laugh, they might do so with perfect freedom."

This may explain Buckeridge's origins as a humorous writer. He stated that he always wanted to write humour, and whilst he was in the fire service the many hours of idleness between air raids allowed him plenty of time to develop his writing skills. Interestingly, his early writings consisted mainly of adult radio plays intended for such programmes as the *Wednesday Matinee*. It was hardly surprising, with his teaching and play-writing experience and his preference for humorous subjects, that he began to write humorous plays about school life. Initially his pupils at his Ramsgate school were his only audience. He would tell them stories about a boy called Jennings both during and after lessons. The boys in his charge used to clamour for "another Jennings story, please sir," at bedtime before lights out. Buckeridge would reply: "If you're in bed in thirty seconds, I'll tell you a story."

So great was Buckeridge's charges' enthusiasm for stories of this boy called Jennings, that the story-teller was moved to submit a script to the BBC Drama Department in 1948. It was passed on to the producer of *Children's Hour* who was so impressed that he not only accepted the script but commissioned five more on the spot, and commissions for a further half-dozen arrived a year later. The first Jennings play went out on the air on 16th October 1948. The name Jennings was taken from a boy Buckeridge knew - Buckeridge described him as "a bit of an oddball" - and some of the Jennings stories were based on incidents from the life of this real boy called Jennings. The authentic touch of much of the writing suggests that other characters were also based on pupils known by Buckeridge during his teaching days. The first words of the first story were spoken by the teacher Mr Carter:

"Ration book, clothing book, identity card, sweet coupons, health certificate..."
The first words spoken by Jennings were:
"Me sir, please sir."
Originally Jennings was played by David Page, his friend Darbishire by Loris

Summerville, Mr Carter by Geoffrey Wincott, and the bane of their young lives, Mr Wilkins, by Wilfred Babbage. The part of Jennings was later taken by both John Charlesworth and a child actor Glyn Dearman, who became a BBC Radio drama producer responsible, among other things, for a revival of *Dan Dare!* The voices of Jennings and his friends in *Children's Hour* were described by a Norfolk vicar in 1962, in a letter to *Radio Times*, as "refreshingly natural" and considerably preferable to "painfully over-acting females." On a number of occasions Jennings reached the distinction of an appearance in *Children's Hour* Request Week, and from September 1954 the plays were promoted to adult listening time.

It was inevitable that the success of these plays would lead to a demand for Jennings' adventures to be reduced to written form. Some of the stories appeared in *Childrens Hour Annuals*. However, Buckeridge also submitted a number of radio scripts to the publisher William Collins, and encouraged by the success of the radio plays, Collins accepted them. In 1950 they published *Jennings Goes to School* which was an amalgam, in written form, of work that had already gone out over the air. In the Foreword to this first book David Davis, the producer of *Children's Hour*, wrote of the plays: "I hope that as many of them as have found their way into this story version of Jennings' adventures will prove as acceptable in print as they certainly have on the air." Davis' hopes were more than realised. Between 1950 and 1994 twenty-five Jennings books, including a compilation volume, were to appear in print. Buckeridge's first few books were all written versions of his radio plays. The radio play scripts were never published for general distribution, although the typewritten originals still survive and it is a fascinating exercise to compare the play scripts and the books. Because the play scripts did not rely on linking narrative, Buckeridge's distinctive dialogue - about which more later - was allowed to shine through even more than it does in the books.

There were over 100 radio broadcasts, all under the general title *Jennings At School*, with most being broadcast on Saturdays. When the radio plays finished on 24th March 1963, Buckeridge continued to write new material. The commissions which he had received had long since forced him to give up teaching and take up writing on a full-time basis. It took him between three and four months to complete each book - he wrote in longhand - and a Jennings book continued to appear roughly annually until 1973 when after *Speaking of Jennings!* the series was discontinued; this despite the fact that merely five years previously they had been identified in *Who's Who in Children's Literature* as being among the most popular juvenile fiction then on the market. Just three further titles were to follow in succeeding years; *Jennings at Large* in 1977, in paperback form only, *Jennings Again!* in 1991, and *That's Jennings!* in 1994. Apparently it was felt that the popularity of the books had suffered by the proliferation of television! Even in 1993, he occupied several lines of Debrett's *People of Today*. The reviews of his

oks were gushing; Buckeridge was applauded for his humorous appreciation of
e juvenile mind, his inventive skill, and his unobtrusive good style, which meant
at the books were enjoyed by adults as well as children. A Swiss literary critic
d this to say: "Not since the *Pickwick Papers* do we remember laughing and
eing children and grown-ups laughing with so much joy and so many tears of
irth, as at a classroom reading of(his) adventures." David Quantick, writing in
e *Independent* newspaper in 1993, remarked: "Jennings survives in these cynical
mes because he is funny." The only discordant note appears to have been sounded
y Paul Donovan, who in his 1991 *BBC Radio Companion* wrote: "For critics the
oys were always insufferable prigs."

Priggish or not, the exploits of Jennings could not have travelled better, with
anslations of the works of Buckeridge into French, German, Norwegian, Spanish,
utch, Welsh, Swedish, Finnish and even Modern Hebrew. This was all the more

markable con-
dering the quintes-
entially English
oarding-school at-
osphere of the
oks. Bravely the
anslators sur-
ounted the prob-
m of the very
nglish name borne
y the hero of the
ories, renaming
im Bennett in
rance, Fredy in
ermany and Stom-
a in Norway.

In the search for
atures which link
e stories together,
omparison with the
ork of Charles Ha-

ilton is useful. There are a number of similarities with the latter's Billy Bunter
ooks. Firstly, the Jennings books, like the Bunter books, are stories of boarding
hool life with limited forays into the evils of the outside world. Secondly, the
ennings books, again like the Bunter books, evolved out of a different type of
edium, although the Jennings stories were never published in a boys' paper.
hirdly, the Jennings stories like the Bunter stories are rich in catchphrases that

are unique to the series. Fourthly, the audience for the Jennings stories has grown thanks to television as it did with Bunter; Jennings appeared on television in the 1960s. Fifthly, attempts at updating or expurgating the stories for modern audiences have not been an unqualified success. The sixth similarity is that neither writer resorted to sermonising in his work. And finally, to enjoy the Jennings books to the full, a certain suspension of disbelief is essential in the same sense as for the Bunter books. Between 1948 and 1994 - a period of nearly half a century - Jennings remained a member of Form Three at Linbury Court Preparatory School. In 1948 members of Form Three could pay 2d to travel by bus from the station to the hospital; in 1991 they were worrying about saving the rainforests and protecting the ozone layer. The adventures of the boys as related in the books could not conceivably have taken place over a period of one school year. Why does Jennings start his life as a third former? Why, if he is 10 years and 2 months at the start, is Venables, one of his colleagues in Form Three, "an untidy looking boy of twelve? The nit-picking could continue almost indefinitely. We are however invited to put this to one side and to place Jennings and his friends into the classrooms, tuck boxes rooms and bootlockers of the time of the reader's choice, making allowances for such small matters as, for instance, the conversion to decimal currency and th advent of direct-dial telephoning. Rather than the transitory characters of *Grange Hill* who are there for a season and then graduate to the adult world, there is therefore a reassuring permanence and constancy about the world of Linbury Court.

The essential difference between the work of Buckeridge and Charles Hamilton is that the Jennings stories are more credible. Although the adventures of Bunter and his chums are somewhat less exotic than those featured in the Penny Dreadfuls they are sometimes far-fetched, particularly when the stories have a foreign setting. Not only did Buckeridge keep his characters firmly in this country; his great skill was writing highly amusingly about *believable* events. Indeed it was the quality and individuality of his writing, rather than any gimmickry, that was the chief factor in ensuring his success. The authentic ring of the stories, and the ability of readers to relate to the fictional characters, were important selling points. Buckeridge certainly had no wish to extol a particular code of values or morals, and there could be no complaints of a right-wing bias as there was by George Orwell against Charles Hamilton's work.

Having briefly examined the ethos of the stories, it is now appropriate to consider the content. All the Jennings books are based at Linbury Court Preparatory School, an establishment for 79 boys in a South Downs setting half a mile from the village of Linbury which is in turn five miles from the town of Dunhambury. Keen Buckeridge buffs searching for the "real-life" location of the stories have few clues to go on, although rather more clues than Bunter fans get. The county is indisput ably Sussex. However, although we are told that the sea is within walking distance of the school, none of the adventures involve the sea, apart from an altercation with some French fishermen in Linbury Cove in *Jennings and Darbishire*. Buckeridge himself has stated that Dunhambury is modelled on a number of locations, none of which is necessarily by the sea!

For adventures that have spanned over forty years, Buckeridge relied on a remarkably small number of characters in the stories. After Jennings the most ubiquitous character is his Form Three colleague Darbishire, followed by Venables, Temple, Atkinson and Bromwich Major, with rather more occasional appearances by Nuttall, Thompson, Rumbelow, Paterson, Parslow and Martin-Jones, and the day boys Marshall and Pettigrew. There are only exceptional instances of a Linburian who appears in one title and then never appears again - the relay runners in *Jennings Follows A Clue* are examples. Outside Jennings' form the most regular visitors to the pages are the impish Binns and Blotwell. The only teachers to make regular appearances are Messrs Carter, Wilkins, Hind and Topliss, as well as the headmaster Martin Winthrop Barlow Pemberton-Oakes - one wonders if he developed writer's cramp filling in his driving licence application form. We learn almost as an aside of one other teacher in *Thanks to Jennings*, Mr Goddard, who is not mentioned in any other book. Tantalisingly we are told in *Jennings Goes to School* that there are women on the staff too, and we learn that:
"...they only taught Form Three for occasional lessons, for which they were thankful."

Does that mean that Form Three were thankful for the infrequency of their presence? Or that the women were thankful for the occasions on which they did teach Form Three? Perhaps it does not matter, since the only woman whom we see regularly appearing on the school premises is Matron. There is a change of Matron in the third title, *Jennings' Little Hut*, and the new incumbent apparently remains in post for the rest of the series. With her sympathetic nature and fierce sense of independence, she is a cross between Florence Nightingale and Joan of Arc. Other women appear less frequently; these include Mary, Ivy and Mrs Caffey in *Jennings Follows a Clue*, Mrs Hackett, the slapdash washer-upper and cook in *Jennings, of Course!*, and Margaret, Mr Wilkins' sister. Margaret assists the boys out of a difficult situation in *Jennings and Darbishire* and gains their eternal gratitude. On the subject of ancillary staff, one should not overlook Robinson, the odd job man, and Hawkins, the night porter, nicknamed Old Pyjams and Old Nightie respectively, although the former nickname and the latter character appear little apart from early on in the sequence.

Only two other schools are mentioned, and one of those, Bretherton House, is mentioned in *Jennings Goes to School* only and does not appear again. The other, Bracebridge School, is mentioned copiously, largely through the football and

cricket matches played - and not infrequently cancelled - between the two side
Only three of the stories contain protracted scenes within the confines of Brace
bridge. In *Take Jennings For Instance* Jennings pretends he and Darbishire ar
Bracebridge pupils to avoid an awkward confrontation between their Headmaste
and an unofficial chauffeuse; in *Jennings and Darbishire* we hear that Darbishir
becomes imprisoned in a detention class being presided over by Mr Fox, alias Fox
Type; and in *Trust Jennings!* it is related how Jennings interferes with the schoc
plumbing because he wants a hot shower. Even then, however, we are onl
introduced to two other personalities at Bracebridge, namely Mr Parkinson th
headmaster, and Hodges, alias Fliplugs, who claims Jennings has succeeded i
emptying Bracebridge's swimming pool. Archer, another Bracebridge pupil, i
mentioned in *Take Jennings For Instance* but only in the context of a cricke
statistic!

Jennings' parents feature only in *Jennings Goes to School* and *Jennings at Large*
a far more frequent visitor to Linbury is Jennings' Aunt Angela, whose prim
function, it appears, is to provide generous gifts and cash subsidies to top up th
contents of her nephew's tuckbox. She does however assist her nephew to aler
the police to Mr Wilkins' garage mechanic stealing his car in *Especially Jennings*
and goes round Dunhambury one Saturday afternoon counting TV aerials in *Th*
Jennings Report. It is thus to our considerable surprise that in *Jennings at Larg*
she is found to live not in a neat suburban detached house but a flat in a Londor
tower block! The only other relative of Jennings to appear is Uncle Arthur in *Ou*
Friend Jennings - his benevolence extends to a meal with baked beans on toas
served between courses, a ten-shilling note, and a couple of seats in the (verboten
cinema. As for Darbishire, it appears that the life of a pastor is too busy for hi
clergyman father and mother to pay their son more than an occasional visit.

Linbury, however, abounds in characters. There is no stronger character in the
village than Miss Thorpe, the village do-gooder who one moment is supervising
the village bazaar (*Jennings, of Course!*), the next is extolling the virtues of environ
mental friendliness (*Jennings Again!*). The Linbury Stores, with its part-time
fortune teller Miss Tubbs, contains what every one-stop convenience store shoulc
have; and the village even has its own teashop. This shop also offers bicycle repairs
although what a latter day environmental health officer would make of the myriac
cats kept by the joint owner Mrs Lumley and their effect on the cleanliness of the
surroundings, is left to the imagination. The neighbouring farming couple, Mr anc
Mrs Arrowsmith, have only brief moments of glory, principally in *Our Frienc*
Jennings when the presentation by Mrs A. to Jennings of some apples anc
chestnuts leads to an unlikely and disastrous attempt at a dormitory feast. Lav
and order in Linbury is maintained by PC Honeyball, and some of the finest pieces
of dialogue in the stories are reserved for confrontations between himself anc

Jennings and Darbishire as they present to him tales of stray cats, stolen bicycles and lost diaries; the ensuing wrath would put him well out of the running for Community Policeman of the Year. There are few regular visitors from outside the area, but one notable personage who puts in an appearance from time to time is General Sir Melville Merridew, Linbury's most distinguished Old Boy. Early on we read of his grandson Roger joining Linbury, but never hear another word about the boy. Perhaps while Jennings remained in the third form Roger was busy progressing through his schooling and on to the SAS.

"What on earth's the matter with your legs, boy?"

The action of each story, although based at Linbury, very often travels outside it, although it does not often go beyond Dunhambury. Although there are exceptions to this rule, it is the later stories which see larger proportions of the action taking place in outside locations. *Jennings at Large* sees no action inside the classroom at all, and there is precious little of it in *Speaking of Jennings!* or *Typically Jennings!*; all three of these stories were written late in the series. Ironically, *Jennings*

Again! contains a whole chapter set in the classroom - the subject is the destruction of rainforests - but not many pages later, Jennings is battling with the London Underground and helping to foil a robbery. What a contrast to his tearful, vulnerable demeanour in *Jennings Goes to School! Jennings at Large* is quite unlike any of the other stories, taking us to a London housing estate and introducing us to a number of girls of Jennings' age. It was a brave experiment but in retrospect Buckeridge might perhaps have agreed that he was safer in the rarefied air of Sussex.

The format of each Jennings book - other than the compilation, of course - tends to be the same; a pot-pourri of incidents, sometimes but not always bound up in one linking theme, with the action of each book spread over a single term. Keen followers of the chronology of Jennings books will discern a cycle - *Jennings Goes to School* is clearly set in the Christmas term, the next book in the spring term, the third book in the summer term and so on. There are some books where the linking theme is stronger than others. *Jennings Goes to School* is really no more than a series of short stories, whilst by contrast *Jennings Follows A Clue* has one continuous plot with little room for digression. *Jennings Again!*, written over 40 years later, has no plot as such but through each separate story-line there is a very strong accent on green issues, reflecting the national and global concern for the future of the planet.

Turning now to the personalities of the central characters, Jennings himself is the obvious person with whom to begin. Throughout the narrative Jennings is simply referred to by his surname, and at no time whilst on school premises is he addressed by his Christian name - John - other than by his Aunt Angela. Buckeridge's insistence on referring to him as Jennings creates a problem in *Jennings at Large* where for the only time in the series, a multiplicity of girls of Jennings' age group are introduced to the narrative, all referred to by their first names. Although we learn that Darbishire's first names are Charles Edwin Jeremy, there is only grudging and passing reference to the Christian names of any of the other characters. We hear Jennings lives in Haywards Heath, about fifteen miles away, and Darbishire lives in Hertfordshire, but the place of residence of all other characters remains a mystery. Indeed Buckeridge's achievement in creating such endearing characters without providing more than mere morsels of information about their backgrounds, was remarkable. Jennings remains the central figure in all the stories, and on the occasions on which we are allowed into the more formal atmosphere of the staff room or staff supper Jennings is not infrequently the chief topic of conversation. He is curious, inquisitive, impetuous, bold and often stupid, but essentially he is not disrespectful. He never answers back without good reason, and he faces philosophically up to the punishments he regularly receives. Buckeridge's skill lies in painting a picture of Jennings as an extremely likeable boy, frequently very well-meaning, often unselfish and considerate, and yet always managing to disrupt the smooth running of the school. Ian Ousby put it even more succinctly: "the amiable adventures... usually centre on the chaos created by Jennings' well-intentioned efforts to help." In *Jennings Goes to School* we read of the headmaster being kicked just below the kneecap, the fire brigade being called to a non-existent fire, and an assistant master being attacked by what he believes to be a poisonous spider. In each case Jennings is the culprit, yet in each case the motives are entirely innocent. Instances of deliberate breaches of school rules do occur, of course, but in each case Jennings rationalises them by saying that no harm will result or the course of action is justified; nowhere are his actions prompted by malice or anger. Jennings never goes out to cause chaos, disruption and hurt; it somehow happens. We see Jennings at his most caring in *Trust Jennings!*, the story being devoted to his fund-raising efforts for famine relief, and in *Jennings at Large* where his concern spreads to the welfare of animals in a London tower block. By the time we get to *Jennings Again!* he is positively green as matters environmental take priority in his life. In other books he saves life and limb (*Jennings Abounding*), catches criminals (*Jennings Follows a Clue* and *According to Jennings*) and saves his teacher from the wrath of school inspectors (*Thanks to Jennings*). With this combination of characteristics which would put him in line for chairmanship of the Metropolitan Police, the Green Party and Oxfam, it is a shame that his efforts are so often treated with disdain by his tutors. Often Jennings' problem is that he is so immersed by his next plan of campaign that his attention wanders in class - particularly, it seems, Mr Carter's English lesson - and many of the gems in the series spring from his failure to listen properly to what is being asked. Academically he is far from gifted, apart from one flash of genius in French in *Especially Jennings!*

The owlish, bespectacled Charles Edwin Jeremy Darbishire is the often unwilling accomplice of Jennings. Safety first is his motto. Where Jennings will swim through shark-infested waters, Darbishire will dip his toe anxiously into the shallow end and will only swim for his life when someone pushes him. One suspects that while Jennings was gaining his knighthood for services to the community, Darbishire would be sitting in an accountants' office poring over income tax returns and hefty audits. In *Jennings Goes to School*, while Jennings is plotting an escape route, Darbishire is blinking back the tears of homesickness. In times of crisis he will refer to the wise words of his father, The Reverend Percival Darbishire, whose erudition and wisdom know no bounds; these wise words are never more necessary than when Darbishire finds himself acting yet again as an unwilling backup to Jennings' rash schemes.

The other boys are stock characters and have few individual characteristics. The only exceptions are Binns and Blotwell, whose juvenile impertinence and First

Form brand of wit find little sympathy among their elders. Temple emerges
Jennings Goes to School as rather more dominant than the others, putting the fe
of God into the new recruit by promising him a bashing-up before tea next da
but before long he merges in with the others who throughout act merely as fo
for Jennings and Darbishire without the individuality and colour of Charl
Hamilton's Famous Five.

The two teachers who feature most often are Mr Carter and Mr Wilkins. Ous
summed them up well when he wrote: "Mr Carter always manages to restore order just at the moment when his irritable colleague Mr Wilkins has reached the end of his tether." If Jennings is now in line for an OBE, Mr Carter has already got his and is working as a missionary in darkest Africa. Throughout the stories Mr Carter comes over as a benign, generous, caring man with limitless tolerance, patience and understanding of the workings of the juvenile mind. Mr Wilkins, however, rejoicing in the

"Here I am, sir!" he shouted. "It's me, sir, Jennings, sir."

- 144 -

nickname Old Wilkie, comes across as brusque, extremely noisy, and intolerant of the foibles of preparatory school boys. He does however, as Buckeridge is at pains to point out, possess a kind heart beneath his explosive exterior. His readiness to act first and think afterwards, for which he so often castigates Jennings, lands him in more than the occasional dilemma. Indeed it is a source of considerable satisfaction to readers when they hear of the master's comeuppance after one of his more heavy-handed pronouncements or actions, no more so than in *Jennings Goes to School* where he takes it upon himself to cancel a football match with another school and then finds he has to reinstate it. He is at heart a likeable, humane man, and mere mortal that he is, his failure to live up to Mr Carter's saintly bearing is perhaps excusable. Mr Hind slips intermittently in and just as quickly out of the action. His heavily ironical drawled comments suggest many years' experience of dealing with errant juveniles, and his oft-lit cherrywood pipe causes much angst to unwilling passive smokers. The Headmaster, Mr Pemberton-Oakes, or the "Archbeako" as he is nicknamed, is a combination of Carter and Wilkins. He is an avuncular figure who is only occasionally constrained to enforce school rules by means of his corner cupboard cane. Although this implement is discreetly abandoned in more recent tomes, it is certainly present at the start. Despite that, only one beating is officially recorded - in *Jennings Follows A Clue* - and Buckeridge's recording of it is so circumspect that the reader might be forgiven for missing it altogether. Buckeridge certainly did not give it the treatment accorded to it by Charles Hamilton!

Buckeridge has been immortalised in the expression "fossilised fish-hooks." Indeed the back-cover blurb on recent Macmillan reprints of the Jennings stories begins with the words: "Fossilised fish-hooks! It's Jennings again." Anthony Buckeridge would have been well aware of the phenomenal appeal of the concurrent Greyfriars books, where catchphrases littered every page. His skill was in being able to carve his own niche in the catchphrase market, rendering himself immune from any suspicion of plagiarism, and creating a fresh, rich stock of language by which everybody could identify the Jennings stories. By so doing he not only ensured the uniqueness of his work; as Ousby pointed out, it was in any event preferable to the "contemporary argot that would soon seem dated."

Buckeridge freely admitted that schoolboys in real life did not talk as they did in his books. He did hope, however, to create the impression of schoolboys talking. Whether or not he succeeded with his readership is perhaps open to debate. What is beyond question is the fact that the Jennings books derived their individuality and immortality from passages such as these:

"Well, I like your cheek. You're a gruesome specimen, Bromo."
(Typically Jennings!)

"Oh, fish hooks. The beastly thing's stopped again."

(Just Like Jennings,

"Wow! Oh, help, this is frantic!"

(Thanks to Jennings,

"Coo! Mouldy chizz!" said Darbishire staunchly. "Atki's batting is chronic, and he's about as much use at square leg as a flat-footed hedgehog, if you ask me."

(Take Jennings For Instance,

"Honestly, Jen, I reckon you win the booby prize for shrimp-witted ideas against all-comers. The next time you get one of your bat-brained ideas you can wizard well leave me out of it."

(Take Jennings For Instance,

"Crystallised cheese-cakes!"

(Take Jennings For Instance,

"Wow! Fully-fledged frogs! What a gruesome bish! There'll be a frantic hoo-hah if Sir gets to hear about it."

(Take Jennings For Instance,

"Don't be such a dehydrated clodpoll, Darbi."

(Take Jennings For Instance,

"Huh! We'd only just got started when the Archbeako came stonking up and ticked me off for tearing my pullover."

(Take Jennings For Instance)

"Petrified paintpots! Look what I've done!" he moaned feebly.

(According to Jennings)

"Fossilised fish-hooks! What a gruesome mess!" cried Atkinson.

(According to Jennings)

"You great addle-pated clodpoll, Darbishire! Where have you been?"

(According to Jennings)

"What? Golly, how super-wacko-sonic!"

(According to Jennings)

"Oh, how supersonic! This is going to be lobsterous fun."

(According to Jennings)

"We did just look in, as it happened," said Temple, "but we beetled out again at supersonic m.p.h. when we found the old geezer was in there."

(According to Jennings)

"Wacko! Super beefy swipe, Jen," approved Bromwich major.

(According to Jennings)

"Oh, gosh, this is ozard!" cried Darbishire in despair. "Why do these frantic hoo-hahs always have to pick on us to happen to?"

(Jennings' Little Hut)

Such expressions are not just confined to the older works. This is a quotation from *Jennings Again!*, published in 1991:

"Nobody but a clodpoll would stick his dirty great paw out like that when the waiter had started pouring."

The irony is that the word "geezer" is still very much in vogue, and the word "stonk" was popularised by its use in an early-1990's television fund-raising extravaganza! The word "clodpoll" remains firmly confined to the Jennings pages; the second syllable is technically superfluous, since the whole means "blockhead-head." The word "pate" also means "head" so the expression "addle-pated clod-poll" could be translated into "muddle-headed blockhead-head." The object of the insult would certainly have got the message!

One of the loveliest moments in the Jennings series is when Jennings' parents share with Grandma what they think they have learnt of Linburyspeak:

"He said a lot of things," replied Mr Jennings. "I didn't follow it all, but I gathered that the most important event of the term was when some ozard oik's frog came down to breakfast in his pyjama jacket."

"No dear, that's wrong," corrected his wife. "The frog was the property of a bogus ruin and it ate stale cake crumbs out of an ink-well behind the bootlockers."

Grandma's face wore question marks.

"Is that so very important?" she asked.

"Important?" echoed Mr Jennings in tones of mock incredulity. "My dear Grandma, it's more than that. It's - it's super-wizzo-sonic!"

(Jennings Goes to School)

One master has his own stock of unique catchphrases. As one might guess, that master is Mr Wilkins:

"Of all the trumpery moonshine!" Mr Wilkins exploded.

(According to Jennings)

Mr Wilkins emitted a sound like a medieval fowling piece being discharged at the Battle of Agincourt. "Cor-wumph," he barked.

(Jennings Goes to School)

"I-I-I-Doh! Don't ask such stupid questions, you silly little boy!"

(Jennings as Usual)

"What in the name of thunder are you doing?"

(Jennings Again!)

It is noticeable that although the more recent titles contain flashes of "traditional" Buckeridge, they are rather more restrained in the use of Linburyspeak. *Jennings Goes to School*, by contrast, is far more generous in its use of schoolboy slang than any of the subsequent stories, and has a distinctive style all of its own. Interestingly, Buckeridge admitted that he made a mistake by using what was then current slang in that book; he felt that even two years later it rendered the book "embarrassing to read!" After that he tried to use his own slang or words which could not date. In early chapters of *Jennings Goes to School* boys and masters have nicknames; Temple becomes Bod, Mr Carter becomes Benedick and Mr Wilkins becomes Old Wilkie. The latter nickname sticks; the other two last only a short while longer. A new word is imported:

He emptied the container on to the burning contents.

"What did you say you wanted?" he asked, helplessly.

"The ozard," repeated Atkinson, marvelling that new boys could be so stupid.

"I don't know what - oh, d'you mean the jam?" asked Jennings.

"Of course I do," said Atkinson.

The word "ozard" recurs on only a handful of occasions in the subsequent stories! Incidentally, Buckeridge was not entirely successful in trying to use words which could not date; in the original edition of *Jennings' Little Hut*, which was written soon after the war, use was made of the word "spivish" which of course had wartime connotations. This was in fact dropped in the Armada paperback issue of this title.

Buckeridge's prose owed much to the style of P.G.Wodehouse; he was described by Humphrey Carpenter and Mari Prichard as "a slick farceur with a command of verbal wit." The writing is never patronising, and remains robust and vigorous despite the juvenile readership. Quantick commented on the "extraordinary humour" of the books, and a "kind-heartedness which is lacking in the work of some of (his) contemporaries." The combination of often complex vocabulary and phraseology, and the unique utterances of his characters, creates some memorable sections of writing, no more so than in *Jennings Goes to School*:

> *The master's desk was close to the classroom door. One entered the room; one turned sharp left; and there one was. And there now, the overturned ink-bottle was, with the ink flowing north and south over the desk, and gushing soddenly into tributaries and estuaries towards all the other points of the compass. Small lakes appeared at the lower contour levels, and shallow creeks to the north-west filled up as the work of irrigation spread.*
> *"You clumsy goof," Bromwich shouted at his would-be benefactor.*

It had sounded simple enough when Darbishire had worked it out, but in practice snags arose which he had not foreseen. For instance, Temple had been placed on the list for lending Darbishire a piece of blotting paper, but when on the following day he had called Darbishire a "radio-active suet pudding," he was informed that his name had been expunged from the roll. Temple's answer to this was that unless he was re-admitted to the ranks of the chosen, Darbishire would be bashed up forthwith.

Much of the humour in dialogue stems from misunderstanding and nit-picking:

> *"Gosh! You lucky bazookas. I wish I was in the team."*
> *"That's what I was going to tell you. Mr Carter says scorers can count."*
> *Darbishire looked up from his drawing. "Of course they can count," he retorted. "They wouldn't be much use for adding up the scores if they couldn't."*
> *"No, you clodpoll! He means they count as being in the team. In other words, you're coming to Dunhambury with us."*
> *"What!" Golly, how super-wacko-sonic!"*
>
> (According to Jennings)
>
> *"He's in a kettle in the woodshed."*
> *"Who - Mr Wilkins?"*
> *"No - Elmer. Mr Carter said they found him when they let the water out and he got stopped by the strainer."*
> *"Who - Mr Carter?"*
> *"No, you ancient monument, I'm still talking about the fish."*
>
> (Jennings' Little Hut)
>
> *"Wilkie's a mean cad," said Jennings. "He's as ozard as a coot."*
> *"You can't say that," objected the knowledgeable Darbishire. "You can only be as bald as a coot."*
> *"Who can?"*
> *"Anybody; it's a simile," the pedant explained. "What you meant was, either Wilkie*

is as bald as a coot..."

"I never said he was bald," Jennings objected.

"No, but if you wanted to."

"Why should I want to say he was bald if he isn't? I said he was ozard, that's all."

"Of course," said Darbishire. "I s'pose you could make up a simile and say he was as ozard as a buzzard."

(Jennings Goes to School)

"My father was making a piece of toast on the gas stove in the kitchen," Darbishire recounted in dramatic tones, "and suddenly it caught alight, and before he knew where he was, there was a mighty 'swoosh' and..."

"Why didn't he know where he was?" demanded Jennings.

"He did. He was making a piece of toast in the kitchen."

"But you said it went 'swoosh' before he knew where he was," objected Jennings. "And if he was in the kitchen all the time, he must have known, unless he was suffering from loss of memory."

(Jennings Goes to School)

"My father says you're right as ninepence," Darbishire chimed in.

"Then your father must be crazy! How can Jennings be as right as ninepence, if he's been in bed all day with a temperature?" said Atkinson.

"No, he doesn't mean JENNINGS is as right as ninepence..." Darbishire began.

"You just said he did."

"I mean, my father would be able to say so tomorrow, when Jennings is better."

"How's he going to know that? He lives a hundred miles away."

(Jennings' Diary)

Reading one of the old play scripts is particularly rewarding in this respect, as demonstrated by a perusal of Number 3 of the third series of *Jennings At School*. This was entitled *Jennings Buries the Hatchet* and first broadcast on Saturday 30th December 1950 between 5.00pm and 5.35pm as part of *Children's Hour*. Rehearsals were not scheduled to finish until 4.30pm the same day! The play was later worked into *Jennings Goes To School* in the chapter entitled *The Literary Masterpiece* and is all about Darbishire's attempt to write a detective story for the school magazine. One piece of dialogue which did not make it to the book is Darbishire's first approach to Mr Carter:

Darbishire (approaching) Please sir, Mr Carter, sir?

Mr Carter: Oh, come in, Darbishire. What can I do for you?

Darbishire: I've got a contribution for the school magazine, sir. It's a report of tomorrow's match against Bracebridge.

Mr Carter: Tomorrow's match? If we could all foresee the future like that, Darbi-

shire, it would save us making a lot of mitakes (sic).

Darbishire: Yes sir - it's all ready except for the final score, sir. You see, as it's the first time Jennings has been picked for the first eleven. I thought I'd give him a helping hand, sir, just to encourage him. Here it is, sir!

Mr Carter: Right. (He reads the report. Fade) H'm. Oh, no, Darbishire, I'm afraid I can't possibly accept this as it stands! All these things you've said about Jennings - 'Outstanding player' - 'Brilliant footwork' - 'Excellent ball control' - 'Unrivalled skill' - 'Supersonic speed' - 'Remarkable performance' - tut, tut, tut! This won't do at all, Darbishire.

Mr Wilkins bent to his task of freeing the unhappy prisoner.

Darbishire (dashed) Won't it, sir? I went to an awful lot of trouble and used dictionaries and things. I did hope you'd like it, sir, because you see I've planned to be a great writer, sir.

Mr Carter: Well! I don't want to discourage you, Darbishire, far from it; and if you'd like to write something else for the magazine - say a poem, or a story even - I'll be only too pleased to have a look at it. But this football report is very one-sided. You can't ignore everyone in the team except your best friend, and in any case it's quite impossible to describe the match until it's over.

As the series continues, there are subtle changes in style as well as in terminology. A reader of *Jennings Again!* will note that the paragraphs are generally briefer, with the story and the storylines more concise, than in *Jennings Goes to School*. As has been mentioned, inflation and decimal currency are taken into account. *According to Jennings*, where much of the early part of the book is devoted to space exploration, is an example of how quickly a particular story-line can date. It relates how Linbury's most distinguished Old Boy, crusty General Merridew, returns to see how life has changed since he was an inky-fingered third-former back in 1897!

Despite the Englishness of the stories - the concept of a boys' preparatory boarding school is curious enough to foreigners - the translations have been both widespread and successful. Without exception the noble translators have found "Fossilised fish-hooks" or "petrified paintpots" somewhat hard to put into a foreign tongue, but with Mr Wilkins' outbursts the French translator Olivier Sechan has done his best:

"L'un de vous a-t-il vu Bennett et Mortimer?" demanda-t-il. "Ils auraient du monter depuis deja cinq minutes. Je n'imagine pas ou ces petits sacripants ont pu encore..."

Les lumieres s'eteignirent.

"Brrrloum brrrloumpff! Qui a eteint?" rugit le professeur.

(Bennett entre en scene, a translation of Our Friend Jennings)

Nils-Reinhardt Christensen was entrusted with the responsibility of Norwegian translation and brings further variety to Mr Wilkins' invective:

"Det hores jo ut som om det er en elefant som har glemt a ta av se skoytene! Du store alpakka! Hor pat det der! Nei, dette skal jeg fa satt en stopper for for de river ned hele huset! Jeg-jeg-jeg skal... umph!

(Stompa skriver dagbok, a translation of Jennings Diary, this edition 1992)

The assiduous collector of the Jennings books will, if he is missing any volumes, only be satisfied by the colourful dust-jacket and reassuring red, later grey, hardcovers of the Collins editions. To the purist the Jennings books should be read as they were written originally, with outdated terminology and currency being an enhancement rather than obstruction to enjoyment of the stories. The paperback reissues undertaken by Armada during the 1960's remained largely faithful to the originals with certainly no distortion of the definitive text. However, firstly John Goodchild and then Macmillan began issuing new and completely revised editions of the stories to a modern audience. By 1994, sixteen titles were on offer in this modern edition. A certain amount of updating has been undertaken with a view to making the stories more acceptable to a modern readership. A prohibition on parking on one side of the road on odd dates in *Thanks to Jennings* in the original 1957 version becomes merely a yellow line in the 1988 version; the pound which Jennings had at the beginning of *Jennings Goes to School* becomes a fiver; and the schoolboy slang is somewhat modified. The stories do remain entertaining and absorbing in the new editions; *Thanks to Jennings* preserves some "crystallised cheese straws" and even "petrified cheesecakes" so the new Jennings convert will not feel he has been missing out. It is however arguable that the totally unique style of certainly the earlier volumes should never be compromised by late-twentieth-century demand. It cannot be denied that the modern version of *Jennings Goes to*

School, one of the few early titles available in updated form, is but a pale imitation of its original. Joseph Connolly, who deplored the revisions, asked "what has become of period charm?" Buckeridge himself was only too aware of the controversy which this updating would produce. He felt that there should be no changes, but the publishers argued that old terminology and expressions - not to mention the masters' pipe-smoking - would be off-putting. The Jennings stories that were issued in 1991 as part of the BBC Radio Collection - *Jennings Goes to School* and *Jennings Again!* - had to fulfil the impossible task of compressing a full-length story into a single cassette. It has to be said that the deliciously fruity voice of Stephen Fry, described by Buckeridge as "absolutely spot on," was the only thing that really made the purchase worthwhile. The tapes consisted of nothing more than anonymous, very emasculated paraphrases of the original texts with none of the Buckeridge magic allowed to blossom. One is left wondering if the substitution of the original by modern versions deters rather than attracts potential Jennings enthusiasts, and whether diluted translations do more harm than good to the Jennings cause. It would be grand to think that one day, when collectors had emptied the second-hand bookshelves of all Collins' original titles, a publisher of Hawk Books' enterprise could reproduce faithful facsimiles of the original versions as has been done for the Billy Bunter books, and so present Jennings as it was originally written and should be read.

Besides the *Children's Hour* plays and the BBC Radio Collection tapes, Jennings has made other appearances both in sound and vision. There have been two television productions of Jennings' adventures, one in 1956 and one in 1966; Buckeridge himself recorded versions of some of the stories on to cassette, although these have not been available for many years; and in 1971, Radio 4's short-lived Saturday afternoon radio programme for children called *4th Dimension* included some Jennings plays with Mark Hadfield playing the part of Jennings. In addition, there is a musical based on the Jennings stories, called *Jennings Abounding*. The idea came from two writers named Hector Cortes and William Gomez. They submitted a completed work to Buckeridge - words and music - for his approval. Buckeridge enjoyed the tunes, but felt the lyrics could be improved and rewrote them himself. The musical received its premiere on July 7th 1978, at New College School, Oxford, and a further performance was given in Buckeridge's home town of Lewes in December of the same year. It was directed by Buckeridge's wife Eileen, and Buckeridge himself played Mr Wilkins. Jennings was played by Danny Marshall and Darbishire by Nicholas Cory-Wright. Linbury became a co-educational school, including characters such as Rowena Binns and Christine Archer. The plot was a combination of two major incidents in the Jennings stories, one from *According to Jennings* (Mr Wilkins' "leaving") and one from *Our Friend Jennings* (the school revue). There are however snatches from other Jennings stories which the avid reader will instantly recognise, most notably from *Just Like Jennings* and *The Trouble with Jennings*. The musical, containing such numbers as "I never knew Matrons had birthdays", "Three boos for Sir" and "Crossing Off the Days" captured much of the fun and enjoyment evident in the books, and the acting edition was still in print nearly fifteen years later.

The Jennings books were not Buckeridge's only school stories. He also created the schoolboy Rex Milligan who far from being educated in a tranquil countryside prep school environment, attended an outer London grammar school for day-boys, Sheldrake. Buckeridge was himself a Londoner by birth, although he found that he preferred to live in the country, and this may explain why he wrote more about Jennings than about Milligan. Only four

"What in the name of thunder is going on up there?"
Mr Wilkins spluttered.

Rex Milligan titles appeared, although, as with Jennings, Milligan won himself a television series. Originally, the Milligan stories were published in *Eagle* and *Eagle Annual*. The first of the four books, *Rex Milligan's Busy Term*, was published by Lutterworth Press in 1953, some years after *Jennings Goes to School*. Milligan was televised in 1955.

There are in the Milligan stories many reminders of the Jennings books. Some of the Linbury catchphrases appear at Sheldrake too, with plenty of clodpolls (some addle-pated), petrified paintpots, crystallised cheesecakes and the occasional "Doh!". As with the Jennings books, the stories centre around one character with good intentions but also seemingly endless ability to disrupt the smooth running of his school, duly aided, abetted and occasionally scorned by a supporting cast of fellow schoolboys.

As with the Jennings stories, Buckeridge is very economical with his use of other characters. The only colleagues who regularly appear in the Milligan stories are Milligan's best friend J.I.G.Johnson, inevitably referred to as Jig, and who has none of Darbishire's wimpish characteristics; Alfie Cutforth, who fancies himself as a cross between James Bond and Arthur Daley; J.O.Stagg who with his gadgetry and flair is a cross between Professor Branestawm and Heath Robinson; and Boko Phipps, described in *Rex Milligan Holds Forth* as:

"...a worthy character with high fidelity brain cells; but somehow I couldn't see him as the central figure of my tale."

The teacher who appears most often is Mr Birkinshaw, Mr Wilkins' Sheldrake equivalent in every department (to the extent of being nicknamed Old Birkie); there is no Mr Carter at Sheldrake, but Messrs Stanton and Frisby (alias The Frizzer) possess sufficiently endearing characteristics to compensate. We hear little of the headmaster, whose name is Hunter and who therefore becomes the Head-Hunter. The inter-school rivalry, which Bracebridge provided in the Jennings stories, is here provided by the neighbouring technical college which provides a first class venue for much of the excitement in *Rex Milligan Holds Forth*. Indeed in *Rex Milligan Raises the Roof* we spend rather more time with the Tech and its characters Spikey Andrews and Bubblegum Tucker. It is Tucker to whom Milligan becomes chained and is forced into a consequent and most unwelcome confrontation with Snorker, Birkinshaw's opposite number at the Tech. In *Rex Milligan Reporting*, the whole book is taken up with a feud between the schools, exacerbated by a piece of umpiring incompetence on the part of Stagg.

There are a number of differences from the Jennings stories. Firstly, and most obviously, Sheldrake is a day-school and not a boarding-school as Linbury is. As a result, far more of the action takes place off the school premises, and indeed far less time is proportionately devoted to classroom capers than to outside antics and heroics. On occasions we are permitted a glimpse inside Milligan's home; such a privilege is never accorded to us with respect to the Jennings household. Secondly, the hero is referred to as "Rex" by his best friend Johnson, and there is not the rigid adherence to surnames that characterises the Jennings books. Thirdly, the Milligan stories are related in the first person, with the corresponding informality in style that this inevitably brings. Fourthly, Buckeridge was here writing about older boys. Milligan is almost 14 when we meet him, and therefore has rather more canniness and less youthfulness than Master J.C.T.Jennings. In some stories he displays an ingenuity that would be the envy of most real-life fourteen-year-olds. Indeed the most obvious criticism of the Milligan books, which could never be said of Jennings, is that the stories really are very far-fetched. *Rex Milligan's Busy Term* (1953, Lutterworth Press) sees the boys encompassing the downfall of a local motor vehicle fraudster who is trying to use a fake lease to deprive the school of its playing fields. His doom is only assured when he slips on some conveniently-placed vehicle oil, and his deception is found out when Milligan just happens to be set an imposition on the Gregorian Calendar which in turn proves the falseness of the lease. *Rex Milligan Raises the Roof* (1955, Lutterworth Press) sees the police alerted to an unexploded bomb that turns out to be a bathroom geyser. There are problems with a top-secret scientific formula that turns out to be just another of Stagg's flights of fancy. We also meet a foreign agent who turns out to be a refugee fearful of repatriation. *Rex Milligan Holds Forth* (1957, Lutterworth Press) sees the boys in pursuit of a dangerous drugs thief, stowing away on a pigswill lorry to recover the school flag, and interrupting a rugby match to apprehend a jewel thief. Just as alarming for our heroes, if not more so, is being threatened by a youngster with a loaded shotgun whilst out for the day with a newly-acquired pet monkey. *Rex Milligan Reporting* (1961, Lutterworth Press) does not have this degree of unreality, but some of the scenarios are very odd indeed. These include a full-blown trial to enable justice to be done to Stagg after messing up a cricket match, with tree-trunk and car tyres replacing the oak panelling of the courtroom; attempts to prevent Mr Birkinshaw watching a news item about disruption caused to a civic procession; and Alfie Cutforth striking the fear of God into an unsuspecting archaeologist.

It is, however, Jennings for which Anthony Buckeridge - 38 when the first Jennings book was published, and producing *That's Jennings* when he was over 80 - will be most fondly remembered. It is perhaps symbolic that long after the last Jennings book appeared he was still living happily in the East Sussex countryside which provided the inspiration for so many of the stories, having brought up two sons and a daughter there. He succeeded because of his elegant, readable prose totally devoid of clichés and banalities; his entertaining highly individual dialogue full of catchphrases and memorable moments; his avoidance of the somewhat outdated emphasis on what Quantick called "duty, pulling together and supporting

King and Country;" and his ability to write about incidents that were very funny yet totally believable. Such skill has never, in this writer's opinion, been equalled in the realms of schools fiction in book form. Indeed one wonders if it will ever be equalled again, particularly when one considers recent trends in children's literature. These will be examined in more detail in the next chapter. It is paradoxical in the extreme that Buckeridge should once have admitted: "I've never been that much in favour of boarding schools, unless there's a very good reason for them." A brave admission to make from a man who has done so well through their existence! Perhaps the last word should be with Connolly, who described Buckeridge as "creator of the funniest and best-written schoolboy books, bar none."

THE JENNINGS STORIES

All titles were published by William Collins except *Jennings Again!* and
That's Jennings published by Macmillan. *Jennings at Large* was published
by Armada, Collins' paperback imprint.

Included in the bibliography is a summary of the action of each book,
and as all Jennings stories are such a delight, a quotation from each.

1. JENNINGS GOES TO SCHOOL (1950)

Our introduction to Linbury Court, and Anthony Buckeridge's masterpiece.
Initially forced to run away when his father's advice to stand up for himself becomes
impossible to follow, Jennings soon gains a reputation for impetuosity and resi-
lience. His idea of dealing with school fire practice is to call out the fire brigade
and get his colleagues to crawl around the floor on their stomachs with their faces
swathed in dripping towels. He is desperate to represent his school at football,
but his ambition is foiled firstly by illness then by misconduct; he is reprieved when
he lifts from Mr Wilkins' neck a spider the master erroneously believes to be
poisonous. He scores an extremely fluky goal on his debut against Bracebridge
School.

The Headmaster's face fell like a barometer. Dark rainclouds appeared on the
horizon of his countenance, accompanied by a deep drop in temperature. A deep
depression was approaching; thunderstorms seemed imminent, and the future out-
look was anything but settled.

2. JENNINGS FOLLOWS A CLUE (1951)

The only Jennings book which constitutes a complete story in itself rather than
a collection of stories out of one or more linking themes. Jennings, inspired by the
reading to him of a Sherlock Holmes story, sets up the Linbury Court Detective
Agency with Darbishire. After initial bunglings, including the attempted citizens
arrest of the Linbury sports cup engraver for burglary of the cup, the amateur
sleuths play a major though largely fortuitous part in the apprehension of a real
burglar in the form of the school laundry van driver.

"Then perhaps," said Mr Wilkins in persuasive tones, "you'll be good enough to
explain it to me."

"But you know it already, sir."

"Of course I know it already," barked Mr Wilkins. "I wouldn't be asking you if I
didn't know, would I?"

"You mean the other way round, sir," suggested Darbishire. "You would ask him
if you did want to know, wouldn't you, sir. But you don't really want to know, sir -
you just want to know if he knows." ·

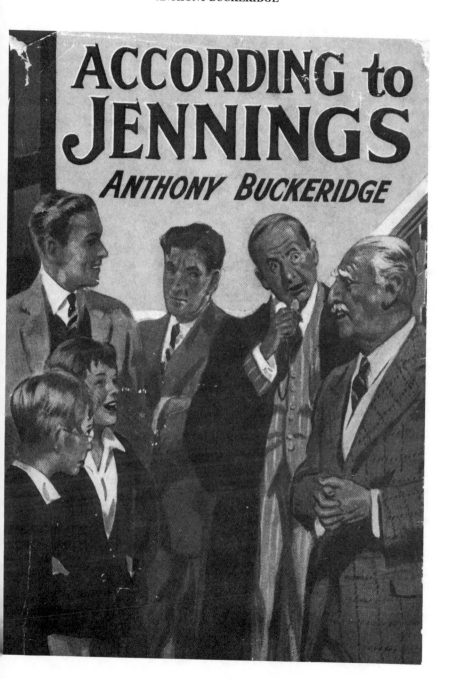

3. JENNINGS' LITTLE HUT (1951)

The first summer term we witness at Linbury brings a craze for hut building which is cut rudely short when the Headmaster becomes almost inextricably wedged inside Jennings' creation. The ban, however, is lifted following the timely intervention of a parent of a potential pupil who happens to be the grandson of General Merridew, Linbury's most distinguished Old Boy. On the way Jennings releases a carp into the swimming pool, falls fully clothed into a pond and smashes the Headmaster's cucumber frame.

He rolled the paper from the machine and passed it to his assistant.

"NOT ICE," it read. "In fiyutre no buys will be preMnitted to bluild nuts ub the neiHghbourhoof uf the pond? & the a#5rea will be plAvced ou98t of hounds@%.'

"You're quite right, sir," Mr Carter agreed. "I think I know what you mean, but it's a little obscure in parts."

4. JENNINGS AND DARBISHIRE (1952)

The gift to Jennings of a printing outfit by his Aunt Angela inspires him to set up the Form Three Times. Copy for the FTT during the term includes a confrontation with French fishermen in Linbury Cove, a poetry competition with a Latin text book as first prize, a football match followed by a hazardous journey home and boyhood memories of Mr Wilkins as provided by his more than obliging sister

"A camera! Gosh, how super-wacko sonic! It's the one thing I was hoping he wouldn't give me anything else except!" he crowed delightedly, and turned the small object over and over in his hands. "We can do all sorts of things with a camera, can't we, Darbi?"

"We'll bust it, if we do," his friend warned him solemnly. "Much better just to use it for taking photos with."

5. JENNINGS' DIARY (1953)

When Aunt Angela's generosity extends to a diary for her nephew to record the outstanding events of the Easter term, she had little idea that the entries would refer to the bowling of an old Dunhambury Borough Council refuse cart wheel through the school premises, the displaying of said wheel amongst the exhibits of the town's museum, or Mr Wilkins' being threatened with having to spend all night adding up 10,000 marks.

"Twelve and fifteen are twenty-seven and eighteen makes forty-five and three makes forty-eight and twenty seven are seventy-five..."

From the next room came a sudden thump, followed by a discordant clash of notes as though some bulky object had been spread-eagled over the keyboard of the piano.

"Doh!...What on earth's the silly little boy playing at now!" fumed Mr Wilkins, losing count of his marks for the eighth time.

6. ACCORDING TO JENNINGS (1954)

The space craze sweeps Linbury; the school's most famous Old Boy plays a practical joke on Mr Wilkins; Jennings is a guest of R.J.Findlater the famous cricketer and helps apprehend a thief of Findlater's belongings; and Darbishire learns to swim.

"Fit? *See if it would fit? You must be off your head, boy,"* fumed Mr Wilkins. *"Civilised people don't do things like that. You never see Mr Carter or me going round sticking our heads into glass cases to see if they fit, do you?"*

"No, sir. I was just pretending it was a space-helmet, sir."

7. OUR FRIEND JENNINGS (1955)

Jennings erroneously believes he has come upon an original Penny Black; a chestnut-roasting escapade ends in tears; Jennings mounts a performance of part of Shakespeare's Henry V without anyone to play the title role; and Darbishire is punished for going to the cinema by being made to see the same film again.

"Doh!" A sound like an innertube exploding under pressure burst from the outraged Mr Wilkins' lips. "I-I-Corwumph! I've had enough of this trumpery moonshine!" he spluttered. "You came to me for a stamp this morning saying you'd got to pick it up with pliers and chase it with a butterfly net. And now you want another one for posting coals to Newcastle in a nutshell!"

8. THANKS TO JENNINGS (1957)

Jennings conducts an investigation into the masters' eating habits; he is freed from park railings with Jack Carr's car jack; chaos is caused by a cat named George the Third and a guinea pig named F J Saunders; and Jennings saves the good name of Linbury Court by reciting six pages of thirteenth century history.

"I will now proceed to give my famous demonstration of prune-stalking. I focus ye telescope on ye plate, like so... yes, I think I can see it wallowing in the shallows of the uncharted custard swamp - the smallest specimen of prune known to science."

9. TAKE JENNINGS, FOR INSTANCE (1958)

The establishment of the Natural History Club with Jennings as Chief Frog Spotter sees a nature trip nearly sabotaged by a handkerchief in Mr Wilkins' exhaust pipe. Other highlights of the Chief Frog Spotter's brief career include a highly illegal trip on the River Dun, and the invitation of a scientific frogman to the end-of-term prize-giving.

"I should say he's - well, fairly tall and dark, wouldn't you, Darbishire?"

"M'yes," his friend agreed solemnly. "Though if anything, I would describe him as somewhat on the short side and going a bit bald. And quite old, of course - well, about thirty at least."

10. JENNINGS, AS USUAL (1959)

Before a Christmas dinner reconciliation with Mr Wilkins in the guise of a junior Father Christmas, Jennings sets fire to his india rubber, sends Mr Wilkins in search of a non-existent intruder, comes into a class with a roller skate wedged to his foot, and reduces to Christmas decoration a whole term's geography notes.

"Please, sir, I've only got about two inches of my ruler left, sir."

"What about it?"

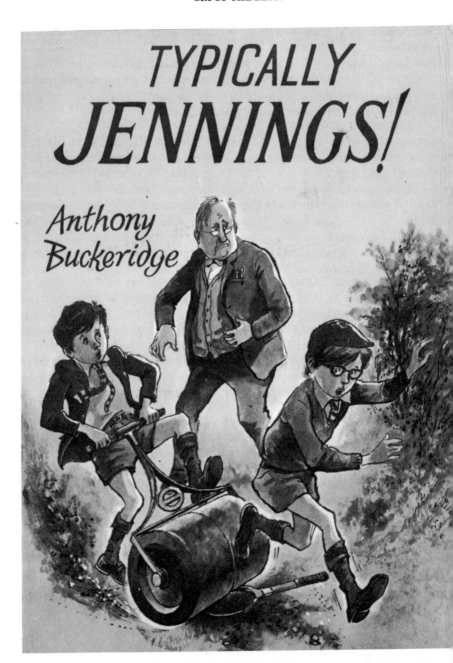

TYPICALLY
JENNINGS!

Anthony
Buckeridge

"Well, sir, my name's too long to go on all in one piece, sir, so will it be all right if I write 'Darbi' on one side and 'shire' on the other, sir?"

11. THE TROUBLE WITH JENNINGS (1960)

Jennings makes some New Year resolutions including one to be kind and helpful to old people, also hard-working and punctual. He subsequently sleepwalks his way into an unwanted night-time fire practice, brings the music room ceiling down after flooding the bathroom, and arranges a party for masters with a bill of fare consisting of bread, liquid butter and a foam rubber washing sponge.

"Ah yes, this is a very famous scene," Mr Wilkins observed as he scanned the page proffered for his inspection. "This is the passage where Lady Macbeth walks in her sleep."

Jennings looked puzzled. "It doesn't say she walks in the passage, sir," he objected. "Mr Carter said she comes down the stairs."

12. JUST LIKE JENNINGS (1961)

Summer term at Linbury sees Jennings and Darbishire arriving at Dunhambury by specially-chartered brake van; laying a trap for a bird-watcher they believe to be a villain; organising a mountaineering expedition on the school staircase; and winning for Mr Wilkins a vase he had taken great pains to get rid of.

"Right! Now first of all, is everybody here?"

"Yes, sir!" the whole party chorused in unison.

"Be quiet! If you all shout 'yes' together at the tops of your voices, I can't hear if anybody's saying 'no.'"

Bromwich I wrinkled his nose in puzzled query. "But if we weren't here, we couldn't say no, could we, sir?"

13. LEAVE IT TO JENNINGS (1963)

Having had his fortune told at the end of Just Like Jennings, our hero sees all the prophecies fulfilled, even though the seer turns out to be none other than Miss Tubbs of the Linbury Stores bacon counter. One of only two books which follow naturally on from where the previous one left off.

On the following page a physical map of the British Isles had been amended to include mountaineers tobogganing down Ben Nevis and half a dozen Channel swimmers battling with rough seas in the Straits of Dover.

14. JENNINGS, OF COURSE! (1964)

Jennings goes on an illicit laundry expedition; tries to impress his friends with his ventriloquial skills; and obtains for the school a new cook after inviting half of Linbury village to a school jumble sale.

An appreciation of Rumbelow and Atkinson's rendering of "The Fairies Lullaby" speaks of the performers' intense feeling and subtle variation of pace; a polite way of describing the groping for the right notes, and the five-second pauses while the piano was waiting for the violin to catch up.

15. ESPECIALLY JENNINGS! (1965)

Jennings forms a club imaginatively named the Jennings Membership Club, devoting itself in the first instance to crude wireless communication, then the acquisition of space guns and finally to the more sedentary swapping of matchbox labels; it is the promise of a new pen from his aunt which motivates Jennings to come top of the class in French this term.

Light dawned in Mr Wilkins' brain. "Doh! So that's the game, is it!" he exclaimed. "Passing off as his own work an essay in French written by a native."

"Oh, no, this boy isn't a native. He hasn't got a tom-tom or anything like that."

16. A BOOKFUL OF JENNINGS (1966)

The only compilation volume, with excerpts from all the stories in the series thus far and even a short chapter devoted to some of Buckeridge's more delightful similes. Each chapter ends with a choice quotation from the series. It was later reissued in 1972 as *The Best Of Jennings*.

17. JENNINGS ABOUNDING (1967)

Jennings' keenness on bird life and his care for a racing pigeon he names Swing Wing results in an eventful afternoon in the Dunhambury area including a ride on a fire engine; and ultimately the whole school is converted to bird-watching. Meanwhile, Henri Dufour, a French boy, becomes a pupil and Jennings' cricketing half-century is ruined by Darbishire's ice-cream feast.

The pupil was baffled. So far as he could understand the pitch meant wicket and the wicket meant the stumps. Surely then, the pitch and the stumps must be the same thing!

(Note: This was reissued by Macmillan in December 1993 as **Jennings Unlimited** ostensibly to avoid confusion with the musical play entitled Jennings Abounding. How many Jennings buffs thought a brand new Jennings book had appeared?)

18. JENNINGS IN PARTICULAR (1968)

Jennings' over-zealous cricket stroke loses a ball, which takes him to the roof, which leads to punishment, which leads to their doing a job at the village fete, which leads to his winning a pig, which leads to more punishment, the acquisition of a valuable stamp, and the discovery of many more balls for many more cricket matches...

"Ordinary human beings have to use their first names or their initials like, say, for instance, Yours truly, Obadiah Binns or X.Y.Z.Blotwell."

"But my name isn't Obadiah," Binns objected.

"And if my initials were really X.Y.Z. what on earth could they stand for?" Blotwell wanted to know.

19. TRUST JENNINGS! (1969)

A piece of pulp fiction written by Jennings for Mr Carter leads to a determined effort to raise money for famine relief, a round ten-pound target being achieved when Jennings "sells" an English essay to Mr Carter - for 10p. The fund-raising reaches a climax one Saturday afternoon in Dunhambury when an attempt to sell a honky-tonk piano to a snooty music shop owner turns into a street sing-along.

"Sir, please sir, if he was stone deaf he wouldn't have heard what he was saying to himself if he was muttering. He ought to have been shouting."

Jennings was annoyed at the interruption. "He didn't need to shout. He'd taught himself lip-reading," he explained.

This didn't satisfy his critic. "Well, in that case he'd have to stand in front of a mirror to find out what he was saying."

20. THE JENNINGS REPORT (1970)

On an afternoon walk Jennings discovers, and adopts, a hedgehog. The antics of the animal prove invaluable following Mr Wilkins' rude rejection of Jennings' and Darbishire's ill-fated research into the TV-watching habits of the local populace.

This report proves that people living in two houses, plus twenty-three hundredths of all people living in another house watch more television in the country than in town.

21. TYPICALLY JENNINGS! (1971)

Instead of seeking Mr Carter's help to replace a broken tennis racket, Jennings goes to Dunhambury to find one. He ends up in an auction sale and manages to come away with a cooking stove, consequently engaging in high adventure on the South Downs with mysterious cave paintings and a stranded sheep. Mr Wilkins' birthday is enlivened by the cooking stove exploding and the school minibus getting wedged against the side of a garage.

"Oh, no, it's quite safe," Jennings assured him. "Safer, actually, than it was in your locker, because Mr Wilkins is very kindly looking after it for you. The only snag is," he finished up uncertainly, "the only real problem is that he refuses to give it back."

22. SPEAKING OF JENNINGS! (1973)

Jennings is taken for a ride by Linbury's small-time con man Wally Pink, and loses for Linbury a prospective new boy by laying the remains of 79 burnt breakfasts on the path.

Briefly, he outlined the case for the prosecution. He agreed that most small boys were known to be clumsy, having about as much control over their limbs as a cow on a cattle grid. He went on to say that bulls in china shops were nimble in their movements compared with first formers asked to carry out some simple task such as moving a tray of paints from one table to another.

23. JENNINGS AT LARGE (1977)

Four years went by between *Speaking of Jennings* and this book, the longest gap between stories so far, with all the action out of the classroom; the story tells of Jennings' efforts to raise money for an animal rescue mission following a school camping expedition. Like *Jennings Follows a Clue*, the book is monopolised by this one story-line.

"What in the name of thunder did you want to do a stupid thing like that for?"

"You told me to, sir."

24. JENNINGS AGAIN! (1991)

Fourteen years after Jennings at Large, we find Jennings and his friends "going green." As well as causing chaos with a heap of leaflets in Marina Gardens, Linbury, Jennings helps a man on the London Underground who happens to be an ecologist.

Dear Miss Thorpe

We hope you are quite well. We are very sorry we did not do your leaflets very well owing to strong winds but we will try and do better next time. Darbishire has some new laces so we will give you your elastic band back when we come but it has got stretched a bit owing to Darbishire's shoe...

25. THAT'S JENNINGS (1994)

Mr Wilkins' sick leave is rendered even less pleasant by Jennings' well-meaning efforts to cheer him up. Jennings wreaks further havoc by the formation of a secret bird-watching society.

"Hey, shut up and listen, you cloth-eared lot," Jennings began. "Darbi and I have worked out a plan to soften up old Sir. We're going to send him a Get Well card and a plant in a pot."

The announcement was received with mixed feelings. Atkinson said "It'd need more than a flowerpot to soften up Old Wilkie - even if you biffed him over the head with it."

(Note: A number of the Childrens Hour episodes were reduced to written form in Childrens Hour annuals.)

OTHER SCHOOL BOOKS BY ANTHONY BUCKERIDGE (AS EDITOR)
(All published by Faber & Faber)

Stories For Boys (1957)
Stories For Boys 2 (1965)
In and Out of School (1958)

Anthony Buckeridge also wrote an adventure story
called *A Funny Thing Happened.*

PLEASE MISS?

Ten past five on 8th February 1978. Opening music and titles. Scene One begins. Iron school gates are unlocked to admit a coloured boy without uniform carrying a football. A scene change as, in the meantime, an anxious mother calls up the stairs:

"Judy? Are you up yet?"

These were the first scenes from the first programme in the first series of *Grange Hill* which since being introduced to the nation in 1978 has become the most popular fictional school in the country. It is hard to think of a starker contrast between the cloistered, rarefied world of Tom Brown and even Billy Bunter and the boys of Greyfriars and St Jim's, and the harsh modern world of which Grange Hill is so much a part.

Over one hundred years had passed between Thomas Hughes' masterpiece, which highlighted the demand for stories about school life, and that Wednesday tea-time in 1978. The school story had during that century-and-a-quarter seen more changes in style, emphasis and popularity than at any time in English juvenile literary history. Many such changes have already been highlighted in this book. The boys' story, as seen in the works of Harold Avery, had declined and fallen during the inter-war years as the hearty optimistic attitude it encouraged was replaced by cynicism and doubt, and the influence of the "pop" stories became greater. The "pop" story, pioneered by Charles Hamilton, had itself gone into decline by the time the Second World War broke out, and the influence of the comic strips and other media became more powerful. The girls' story was still going strong during the Twenties and Thirties, but Mary Cadogan and Patricia Craig wrote that in the 1940s "girls at an early age were tending to lose interest in their schooldays. They wanted to grow up and start work, which they felt would give them a greater sense of involvement in the war, with its indefinable energy and purposefulness." There was also growing competition from detective and pony stories and what Humphrey Carpenter and Mari Prichard described as the "career novel". These stories served to highlight the increasing independence of women, and thus provided a natural continuation of the process of emancipation which Angela Brazil had recognised in her own writing. As a result it diverted attention, and writers, away from the traditional girls' school story.

It would be entirely wrong to claim that schools fiction dried up entirely after the Second World War. Indeed three of the subjects of this book produced large amounts of their work in the post-war period. Elinor Brent-Dyer's Chalet School series was still going, although the quality of her later work was regarded by almost all the critics as markedly inferior to her earlier pre-war writing. Charles Hamilton, as Frank Richards, produced several Billy Bunter books, but he had the advantage of having already built up a formidable reputation, as well as having created, in Bunter, a cult figure with ageless appeal. Anthony Buckeridge might well not have achieved the popularity he did achieve had it not been for the broadcasting of his early work on radio, his realistic and sympathetic portrayal of prep-school life, the popularity and changelessness of his central characters, and the exceptionally high quality of his writing. Enid Blyton's St Clare's and Malory Towers series, both in the traditional girls' school mould, enjoyed great post-war success, but the author was already well-established and popular as a children's writer, and school stories constituted only a small percentage of her total output. A number of other writers continued to produce schools fiction in the pre-war mode, but the quality of their writing was mediocre and generally unremarkable. Some publishers resorted to desperate measures. In *Girls Will be Girls* by J.Radford-Evans, published in 1949, we are informed that Brenda Dickson is "Britain's 'most popular schoolgirl.'" The very fact that a publisher found it necessary to make such an exaggerated claim in order to sell more copies does itself suggest that the producers of new schools fiction were deeply worried about its future. It was clear that the creator of a popular latter-day school series would have to swim with the tide and adapt to change rather than fight it. The subject matter of this chapter represented the culmination of many of the post-war trends in storytelling for children. It is therefore necess-

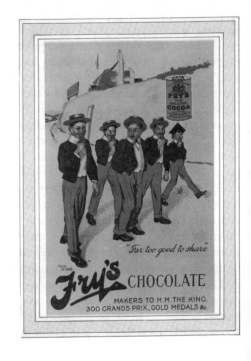

EVEN IN DAYS GONE BY, THE SWEET-TOOTHED PUBLIC SCHOOLBOY WAS RECOGNISED AS A FIGURE OF FUN. SUCH ADVERTISEMENTS NOW PROVIDE A WELCOME TOUCH OF NOSTALGIA AND A REASSURING REMINDER OF CHILDHOOD INNOCENCE

ary to study these trends in a little more detail.

The first trend was the narrowing of distinction between the "boys' story" and the "girls' story." All the writers covered so far were writing either for boys or for girls. Undoubtedly some girls might have enjoyed Billy Bunter's gluttonous excesses, and some boys might have thrilled at the Chalet girls' taking flight from Austria amid the gathering war clouds. None of the writers described so far, however, were aiming at a "mixed" market. The decades following the Second World War saw a growth in fiction that was acceptable to both boys and girls, and at the same time the 1950s saw a decline in the number of books written specifically for girls. With the concept of equal opportunities becoming more and more dynamic, and the demand for women to be treated as equals in all aspects of English life, the idea of "ownership" of a particular story, as in the *Boys' Own Paper* or the *Girls' Own Paper* suddenly seemed very dated. By the 1990s, the majority of good quality children's fiction would be as acceptable to one sex as the other.

The second trend was what Ian Ousby called "a new spirit of modern and social concern... writers slowly began to explore new areas of interest while also shifting the settings of their plots from the middle-class world to which their chiefly adult patrons had always previously belonged." Authors of children's books began to break into areas which nobody had previously dared to touch. Cadogan and Craig wrote: "children's books in recent years have become more open, more daring, episodic, highly charged; there has been a blurring of the rules which separate... adult literature from that intended for children. "They went on to say: "Children's writers have been helped, basically, by the ending of restrictions on what they are allowed to mention," remarking that only a few decades ago "sex could not be referred to, for example, even obliquely." Even death has not been considered too strong, as borne out by the work of Raymond Briggs. Cadogan and Craig recognised the development, in the 1960s, of a "social problem" genre of children's literature, addressing areas such as delinquency, child neglect, teenage pregnancies and juvenile vagrancy. The subject matter made the stories suddenly relevant and acceptable to both children and adults. A new market emerged; the "teenage fiction" or "young adult" market, dealing with serious emotional issues relevant to adolescence and early adulthood. With the permissive society promoting more casual and relaxed attitudes to sexual matters, and an even greater questioning of establishment views and principles, there was a growing demand for fictional stories about teenagers as they faced these issues.

Thirdly, the safe, comfortable world of the boarding-school or public school ceased to be the chief focus of the school story. During the Second World War a well-established adventure writer for children, Geoffrey Trease, gave many lectures to children in public libraries as a member of the Army Educational Corps. At one such talk, two girls asked him to write "true-to-life stories about real boys and girls, going to day-school as nearly everybody did." At the time, as Carpenter and Prichard said, this was regarded as "almost unthinkable" but in 1949 Trease wrote just such a book, *No Boats on Bannermere*, and this was followed by four sequels. The opening words in the series are:

People don't often put day schools into stories. I don't know why. Life there is just as interesting as it is at boarding schools.

From then on, many writers used day-schools and even secondary modern schools as the setting for their work. One example of a writer who moved with the times was Mary Kathleen Harris, whose *Gretel at St Brides* in 1941 was set in a conventional boarding-school. Her last work, however, entitled *Jessica On Her Own* and published in 1966, was set in a secondary modern school. As well as Geoffrey Trease and Mary Harris a number of authors which included Gene Kemp, Laurence Meynell and E.W.Hildick produced between them several novels set in state-run day schools. Hildick, with first-hand experience of such schools, was particularly effective. He recognised the need in post-war Britain for books written for, and about, working-class children. He set his Jim Starling series in Cement Street Secondary Modern, which provided some contrast to Greyfriars or the Chalet School! Gene Kemp wrote with what Carpenter and Prichard called "cheerful acceptance of the lawlessness of present-day schoolchildren." In one story, for instance, the pupils determine, in order to atone for earlier misdeeds, that there shall be no groping or snogging in public, and no shop-lifting! The opening paragraph of Gene Kemp's story *M13 in Form Once More* showed just how far away from the cosy boarding-school post-war authors had gone, featuring a fight between Slasher Ormeroyd and Mandy, complete with size 12 army boots, and the poker-playing Cat inspiring fear and trepidation amongst all his class-mates. Later in the story we read that M13 is a hotbed of lies, thefts, vandalism, dishonesty, cheating, bullying, greed and truancy!

The fourth trend, to which reference has already been made, was the enormous influence of other means of communication. In the 1920s and 1930s, writers of books for children had had to compete with periodicals which had become increasingly competitive and aggressive in their approach to marketing. The Second World War did nothing to halt the trend, and the comic paper was still maintaining its popularity in the final decade of the twentieth century. Although youngsters in the 1990s were enjoying the escapism contained in the cult science-fiction and fantasy stories that modern comics were providing, the *Beano*, first published in 1938, was still appearing weekly as was its sister paper, the *Dandy*, which first appeared in 1937. Just as a market for "teenage" books established itself, magazines for teenagers have been flourishing for many years, with photostories replacing cartoons. However, communications ceased long ago to be confined merely to the written word. The radio, which arrived between the wars, had an enormous influence during the 1930s and immediate post-war years; it has already been noted that the Jennings stories of Anthony Buckeridge were first introduced to the nation on *Children's Hour*. The cinema provided a further distraction from the world of books and another way of spending pocket money, although it could hardly be said to contribute to the development of the school story. Indeed most films about school life were knockabout comedies, of which the St Trinians films were the most obvious examples, although there were films of a more thought-provoking nature such as *To Sir With Love*. The most revolutionary means of communication, which would have a profound effect upon reading habits of the young, was of course the television. Few people boasted a set during the immediate post-war years, but even though it was still regarded as a luxury item in the Fifties it had by 1964 succeeded in killing off Children's Hour. The advent of cable and "sky" television in the late 1980s widened to a bewildering extent the choice of channels available to those who wished to subscribe.

It was clear, therefore, that to make maximum impact, a writer of schools fiction for children in the last quarter of this century would need to do a number of things. Firstly he would need to target an audience comprising both male and female; secondly to address key issues of concern to youngsters of all ages; thirdly to use a setting to which the majority of the audience would relate; and fourthly to reach out to the audience by means of the television, which had become accepted as the most stimulating and enthralling means of storytelling.

Before February 1978 there had been some school dramas on television that were aimed at children. These included a number of dramatisations of Jennings, Rex Milligan and Billy Bunter stories, a serialisation of *Tom Brown's Schooldays* and even a situation comedy for children called *Whacko!* The latter series was written by Frank Muir and Dennis Norden. Set in a school named Chiselbury, it starred Jimmy Edwards and Julian Orchard. Many children would also have tuned in to the ITV situation comedy with a school setting, *Please Sir!* Nothing, however, had been produced which gave youngsters a fictional yet *realistic* view of contemporary school life, observed from their angle. Nor had any dramas been set in a comprehensive school, even though such schools had become the chief centres of secondary education in Great Britain by the mid-1970s. The man who set out to fill this perceived gap in the market was Phil Redmond.

In the mid-1970s Redmond, who came from Liverpool, was struggling to make a living as a comedy writer. In 1975 he decided to turn his attention to real-life drama about children and for children, but set firmly in the hard modern world. This led him to the idea of a drama set in a school: "something we all have to face in one shape or form," as he put it. Another incentive for him to use a school as a setting for his work was provided by his social studies degree course at Liverpool University, a major part of which was the sociology of education. It was his own background which was to determine the type of school in which the drama should be set. Born in 1949, and one of the first products of the comprehensive school system, he wondered why children's television never reflected his own working-class life. "The real reason," he wrote, "(why) I wanted to write about a comprehensive school was simply because I thought television could do more for children than film series like 'Robin Hood' or the period drama I had watched as a child. It also needed to do more for people from my type of background. The working class, comprehensive school kids." Ironically, the school Redmond went to was single-sex and Catholic so although some of the incidents in the storylines were based on his schooldays, his school was not much like Grange Hill. At least one producer and one script editor of the programme went to schools at which corporal punishment was regularly used, and one director recalled that as a schoolboy, in definite contrast to the Grange Hill pupils, he had to go to church every morning!

Initially Redmond had some difficulty in persuading television companies of the value of a series set in a comprehensive school. He remembered that he "traipsed around all the ITV companies trying to sell a schools series, and they all turned it down." However, ITV's loss was the BBC's gain; his approach in 1976 to Anna Home, at that time executive producer of BBC children's drama, yielded a commission almost straight away. It was thus that *Grange Hill* came into being. As Anna Home herself said: "I was... looking for a series that would reflect contemporary school life rather than the traditional worlds of Bunter and Jennings. (*Grange Hill*) was not originally intended to be a long runner but it became obvious that it was filling a great need and could constantly be renewed." Redmond was helped in his development of *Grange Hill* by Monica Sims who as the head of Children's Programmes at that time was determined to expand the Children's Department and to give the series every encouragement. He was also helped by the man who was to direct the first series, Colin Cant. In Redmond's own words, Colin Cant "helped lay the foundation of *Grange Hill*'s continued success in that first series. From the beginning it was small but extremely important and innovative touches - like putting the camera at the kid's eye level, not that of the adult teachers, staff or parents - that indicated Colin had a real understanding of what the programme was all about." The production of the first series, including the hiring and training of actors, took most of 1977, and it was thus a full three years between the idea coming to Redmond and the transmission of the first programme.

The setting was to be a 1000-pupil comprehensive school in north London. (Curiously there was - and is - a north-east London suburb called Grange Hill, but there is no obvious connection between it and the stories.) The actual school used for filming was Kingsbury High School in the north-west of the capital. Originally it was going to be called Grange Park but the BBC were advised to change it because there were several real schools with that name. Such a school, fictional though it was, would provide unlimited opportunity for consideration of issues affecting schoolchildren everywhere in the country.

Redmond's aim was simple - to show contemporary school life as it really was, not as others might like it to be. In order to ensure authenticity, Anna Home and a BBC team paid regular visits to schools across the country and asked children what sort of issues they thought would be interesting. The rule was that a particular topic would only receive an airing if Redmond and his team came across it in a variety of schools. Despite his commendable vision and quest for accuracy, Redmond recalled that the first series was, by comparison with those that followed, fairly tame. Indeed his ambitious objectives were certainly hard to discern from the first programme, where the most exciting incidents involved a boy without a class allocated to him on his first day, and a girl being deliberately misled by some older girls. It was not until he wrote a second series that he got away from "'Boys' Own Paper' type stuff", as he put it, and began to tackle real moral and social issues as they affected children. These issues will be studied in greater depth later in this chapter. After the modest nine-episode introduction to Grange Hill life, sub-sequent series, like a good soap opera, went out twice weekly with up to 20 or more episodes at a time; the 1986 and 1987 series had 24 episodes. A clear pattern emerged, with a new series beginning in January or February and running into March or April; the whole series would then be repeated in the autumn of the same year. The whole time between the end of one new series and the start of the next, with the exception of a short summer break, would be devoted to making that next series. Some viewers asked why it was not possible for *Grange Hill* to be on every week of the year. The answer quite simply was that this would cost four times the amount of money, and require four times the number of children.

The televising of the stories meant that the lives of those involved could not stand still as helpfully seemed to happen at the schools of Charles Hamilton and Anthony Buckeridge. The stories have had to move with the times in a number of ways. A good example is that of corporal punishment; the first series in 1978 contained a scene in which, for trespassing, Tucker Jenkins and Benny Green were each sentenced to a caning. Such punishment was outlawed in state schools in 1987. It also stood to reason that a pupil who appeared in 1978 in the first form could not still be expected to occupy the first form fifteen or twenty years later. That having been said, Phil Redmond confined himself to writing about the first, third and fifth forms with characters moving up to a new year rather more quickly than would really happen. The turnover of characters has, quite apart from the distress it has caused to the fans, meant a lot of work for the production team, with many hundreds of auditions. Following recruitment of the cast members, there has been

Some of the cast of Grange Hill outside their fictional school.

the challenge of managing very young actors, mostly in their early teens, with rigorous licensing and performing laws governing their work. However, although the Grange Hill community is fluid and not static like other fictional school communities, certain characters linger on in the memory. Perhaps the most charismatic character, whose name springs most readily to mind when Grange Hill is mentioned, has been Tucker Jenkins (Todd Carty). His first name, Peter, was rarely heard. From the very first programme viewers were aware of a tough, streetwise character, hailing from a working-class background, living on a large inner-city council estate. Even before he was allocated a class on his very first day he was flicking objects in the direction of an innocent new recruit and being severely reprimanded for so doing. Tucker has been just one of many outstanding characters, and everybody who has watched Grange Hill will have his or her own particular favourite. It may be the entrepreneurial genius Pogo Patterson, the overweight Roland Browning, the sporty Benny Green or the loner Danny Kendall. It may even be a teacher such as the stand-no-nonsense Mr Baxter or the broad-minded tolerant Miss Booth. All these, and many more, have been used by Redmond and his team of writers to attempt to portray comprehensive school life as it really is.

Although a number of different writers have been used to write the scripts - indeed, continuity has been a problem for the producer - Redmond was from the beginning writing out all the story-lines, and continued to guide the story-line even when the writing was delegated to others. In response to the demand for realistic material targeted at an audience with an average age of 13, the issues that have been tackled are wide-ranging. As Anna Home said: "The programme's aim was always entertainment first, but entertainment with a hard core." In order to provide entertainment value, the programme had to go rather further than take a snapshot of ordinary everyday life in a comprehensive. The success of the programme has been in highlighting a vast range of subjects, both positive and negative, both happy and disturbing, both constructive and destructive. While the story-lines are inter-esting and often gripping, all the incidents are wholly believable and always very realistic. Some aspects of comprehensive school life recur constantly, such as the relationships and rivalries between students, the comings and goings of vast numbers of people, and the teaching itself. *Grange Hill* has, however, constantly sought to highlight certain specific concerns and issues in the context of each series, mingling light and serious, perennial and topical, disturbing and reassuring. Single episodes may deal with a whole variety of ongoing situations. Each series, as already intimated, sets out to reflect those issues which affect schoolchildren in real life. The constant popularity of the programme is an indication of the success of the writers in this area.

Perhaps the most important issue ever tackled on the programme has been that of drug-taking. The subject of smoking, and its harmful effects, had been dealt with in 1980 and 1981; the more serious matter of drugs was tackled in the 1986 series. Approved by education authorities, the series showed the character Zammo Maguire, played by Lee MacDonald, mixing with the "wrong" people and becoming a teenage heroin addict. Even those involved in the programmes had their doubts about the wisdom of introducing drugs to a young audience who might not otherwise have been aware of them. However, the production team was determined that the message should be put across both fearlessly and forcefully. The story-line was used as a catalyst to encourage a campaign called "Just Say No" which involved a collaboration between the BBC and the Standing Conference on Drug Abuse in an effort to stop children getting into hard drugs. A record, also called "Just Say No", was released, featuring twenty members of the *Grange Hill* cast. The impressive total of over £100,000 was raised through sales of the disc. Lee MacDonald featured in a special leaflet produced by the campaign, and straight after the final episode in the 1986 series, a special programme called *It's Not Just Zammo* highlighted the real extent of the drug abuse problem. Some MPs, many of whom had complained about *Grange Hill* in the past, tabled a motion congratulating the series. As a result of the campaign, the cast of *Grange Hill* were invited to the White House to meet Nancy Reagan, wife of the then President of the USA. The story was a fine example of how a serious message could be put across to children in an entertaining and non-patronising way. The tragic irony is that less than a decade later, drug abuse amongst schoolchildren once again appeared to be on the increase.

One issue which has been particularly fertile for *Grange Hill* writers has, perhaps inevitably, been young love and the consequences thereof. The subject has been taken at a number of different levels. Boy-meets-girl is common enough - for instance Freddie (Simon Vaughan) and Laura Reagan (Fiona Lee-Fraser). The straightforward "eternal triangle" has been witnessed, ironically once more involving Zammo with Jackie (played by Melissa Wilks) and Banksie (Tim Polley). Zammo and Jackie were engaged for a while during the 1987 series, and it was to be hoped that their good sense in breaking the engagement prevented many real-life couples from plunging into a commitment too early in their own lives. Romance between staff and pupil, and the inevitable heartbreak at the end of it, was featured in the relationship of Fay (Alison Bettles) and Mr King, again the 1986 series, after an earlier series in which Fay had had a "crush" on Miss Gordon. A touch of humour was injected in 1985 with a crush by the obese Roland Browning (Erkan Mustafa) on a fat French girl, Fabienne. However, these affairs of the heart were as nothing compared with the story of the fifteen-year-old Chrissie (Sonya Kearns) who became a mother in the 1992 series. Mary Whitehouse felt that discussion of teenage sex and related matters was inappropriate at so early an hour.

The journalist Polly Toynbee disagreed, and in the *Radio Times* she commended the producers on their bravery in running this story. Once again, *Grange Hill* had been seen to tackle a sensitive and difficult subject in a robust and unsentimental way.

Another issue which many millions of schoolchildren in real life have had to confront is that of bullying. *Grange Hill* has seen a number of bullies pass through its gates, and, perhaps reassuringly, expulsion has resulted for at least some of the perpetrators. The first programme of all saw Judy Preston (Abigail Brown) being tormented by three extremely unpleasant older girls. (It is ironic that Judy, one of the very first pupils to feature in *Grange Hill*, should be somewhat untypical of the characters as a whole, with her immaculate flowing golden hair and her precise, refined voice. She was perhaps deserving of a bigger following!) Three notable bullies during the 1980s were Mauler McCaul (Joshua Fenton), Imelda Davis (Fleur Taylor) and Gripper Stebson (Mark Savage). Mauler had a fixation for American Football and would use first-year pupils instead of a ball when it came to the touchdown. Imelda with her Terrorhawks graduated from terrorising first-years and mocking the Liverpudlian new recruit Ziggy Greaves (George Christopher) to helpfully attempting to set the school on fire. Gripper was perhaps the most vicious and sadistic of them all, extracting menaces money from Roland on a regular basis, and then forming a group of racially-motivated thugs. The victims were lucky in that Gripper and his henchmen were expelled. At many real-life schools the pupils would not have the advantage of a sympathetic script-writer! Assisted by a BBC campaign, school bullying would in due course become one of the major issues on the education agenda. Perhaps the greatest service the writers of *Grange Hill* did in this area was to reassure real-life victims of bullying and indeed racism that they were not alone. For many this reassurance on its own would represent a significant step forward. Torment of an equally ominous kind was highlighted in the racist attacks by Michael Doyle (Vincent Hall) on Benny Green (Terry Sue Patt) in 1978, and the 1988 story of Matthew Pearson (Paul Adams) who despite initial concealment, revealed that he had been abused by his father.

Grange Hill has throughout its life continued to portray non-conformism in all its aspects, including truancy, outbreaks of rebellion, lawlessness, or simply fits of individualism. However, the non-conformist will not be moulded comfortably into the shape of their conformist colleagues by the end of the story, as he or she might be in an Angela Brazil novel. Truancy was explored in the 1982-1984 series with the story of Suzanne Ross (Susan Tully). Initially fed up with having to wear uniform, she left school and started work, even though it was illegal. When she returned, she again became disinterested in school because she was not given the options she wanted; however she was eventually persuaded to return, wear the uniform and even help start a pupils' school magazine. As a fifth former in 1984 her social conscience had extended to her attending a mock UN conference. Once more, the writers had turned a negative experience into a positive one. School uniform, and dislike of it, was the cause of one of the best examples of pupil rebellion. Those responsible belonged to the Students' Action Group which was formed in the 1979 series to campaign for its abolition. Again, however, the establishment was too much for the SAG and its campaign of pickets and barricades. The headmistress in 1987, Bridget McClusky, had to deal with a sit-in following increased editorial control by the staff over the output of the school radio station, although this, too, was resolved peacefully. Other antisocial activity has not been so easy to eliminate. *Grange Hill* has, unfortunately, bred a number of vandals, arsonists, brawlers, thieves and shoplifters. Booga Benson and Imelda Davies are just two who have tried to destroy the school with the aid of fire and fibreglass, there have been numerous battles with pupils from the rival establishments of Brookdale and Rodney Bennett, and a few have fallen prey to the temptations of shoplifting. Suzanne Ross was one, but Cathy Hargreaves (Lyndy Brill) and Madelin Tanner were witnessed stealing clothes in 1979, and Veronica (Ronnie) Birtles (Tina Mahon) was cautioned by the police for similar behaviour in 1988. The school itself has not been immune from acts of dishonesty by its students. Thefts of bicycles, antique pistols, light bulbs, personal stereos, project work and even window putty have all caused upset to the pupils and staff, but the miscreants have virtually always been caught, and in some cases expulsion has resulted. Purely individual frolics have abounded. There have been acts of bravado, such as the exploration by Tucker and Benny of an old ammunition dump in 1978 (the only time that corporal punishment has been applied in the history of *Grange Hill*), a boat race in the school swimming pool using benches as boats (from the same series), clock tower climbing in 1979, high wall walking in 1980 (resulting in a fatality), and even exploration of service ducts underneath the school in 1982. Trisha Yates (Michelle Herbert) and Justine Dean (Rachel Roberts) respectively got into trouble in 1978 and 1988 for wearing jewellery, and the tattooing of Helen Kelly (Ruth Carraway) served as another cautionary tale. *Grange Hill* has always had its share of characters who stand out for their individual idiosyncrasies. One example was Danny Kendall (Jonathan Lambeth), who refused to acknowledge any authority at all, and succeeded in antagonising all the staff. He was placated only by the introduction of the Speaking Wall, but regained the sympathy of everyone, including the staff, when it was discovered he was ill and needed specialist treatment.

Grange Hill has always tried to highlight individual problems and conditions affecting teenagers, whether physical or psychological. The obese Roland Browning, for example, was one of the sadder characters in the history of the programme.

The 1983 story of Diane Cooney's skin problem, and the 1984 story of head-lice infestation, could hardly be said to have been riveting television but both stories would have comforted many youngsters suffering with the same complaints. One of the most touching stories, from 1979, concerned the dyslexic Simon Shaw, and the efforts of Trisha Yates to help him to read. A similar story-line was run in 1988, this time involving Tegs Ratcliffe (Sean Maguire) aided by Justine Dean. Troubled home lives have not been overlooked, and unlike with Angela Brazil, these were not easily resolved. Examples have included Cathy Hargreaves' shocked discovery of her father in 1979, the amorous adventures of Laura's mum in 1988, the discovery by Caroline (Calley) Donnington (Simone Hyams) in 1986 that she was an adopted child, the beatings given to Annette Firman (Nadia Chambers) as discovered in the 1984 series, and in 1993, the thorny problem of a pupil having to give up his own bedroom (because of the arrival of a new baby in the household) and thus having nowhere to entertain his friends. Susi McMahon's difficulties with her first bra, in 1980, must have raised a few wry smiles amongst those who had been through the same experience themselves!

It would be a mistake, however, to believe that *Grange Hill* only concentrates on the negative aspects of schooling, however much some of its critics may believe that to be the case. In between the harder-hitting storylines, there are numerous examples of creativity, outdoor adventure, good works and enterprise, even if the legality of some of that enterprise is questionable! Examples of creativity have included a school festival (1978); a production of *Joseph and his Amazing Technicolour Dreamcoat* (1979); a general knowledge quiz (1980); the formation of a rock band by Cathy Hargreaves and her friends (1981); the formation of a pupils' school magazine (1983); the writing of a musical by the school (1985); the formation of a school radio station (1987); the formation by Ronnie, and her friend Fiona, of a pop group which grew out of the hip-hop craze (1988); and the visit by a choral group from the school to the Eastern German town of Gorlitz (1994). Outdoor adventure of a legitimate kind has among other things consisted of sporting activity. Justin Bennett, played by Robert Morgan, was one pupil who, following in the Avery and Hamilton tradition, gained credibility after a good sporting performance, and the coloured Benny Green enhanced his popularity on the sports field. There have also been field trips, orienteering, a boating holiday, an Outward Bound course, and French exchanges. Concern for fellow beings, both human and animal, prompted the attempted establishment of an outdoor centre (1980), the formation of a Donkey Rescue Squad to help Harriet (1987), the holding of a Sponsored Walk in 1984 to raise funds for *Grange Hill's* own sports pavilion, a fund-raising effort to finance treatment for Danny Kendall (again in 1987), and a series of sponsored events to raise money for a school camcorder (1993). *Grange Hill* has always fostered a keen spirit of private enterprise, the definitive entrepreneur being Pogo Patterson (Peter Moran) whose schemes included the theft and resale of window putty, the use of the school computer for a chain letter system, the sale of the school magazine on a commission basis, the sale of cakes he had made in his cookery class, the devising of an ingenious system for cheating in exams, and the establishment of a black market for books removed from Brookdale. The tradition was carried on by Luke (Gonch) Gardner (John McMahon) and Paul (Hollo) Holloway (Bradley Sheppard); examples of their dubious skills included foraging on a rubbish dump for buried treasure, the sale of fresh toast during the closure of the school tuckshop, the formation of a company hiring out sportswear to those who had forgotten it, and the laying of bets on who would fail to complete the Fun Run! Private enterprise was taken to extremes in 1994 when Josh (Jamie Groves) in order to acquire an Iron Curtain border guard's cap on his visit to Germany, traded in a quantity of goods in a Polish market and found himself the proud owner of a live grenade! More legitimate and respectable forms of enterprise, which the fictional school adopted years ahead of many of its real-life counterparts, have included experimentation with continental school hours, the advocating of judo as a means of self-defence, and a book-sharing system to get round the shortage of textbooks. Academic achievement is recognised where it occurs, although it should be said that the bleak prospect of joblessness on leaving school had become one of the issues featured on the programme as it moved into the nineties.

Notwithstanding that the programme sets out to portray comprehensive school life from the pupils' angle, with the cameras positioned at the childrens' eye-level, teachers play an important part in the stories. It is fair to say, however, that no one teacher is or has been particularly dominant. It must also be accepted that no teacher has acquired the following achieved by some of the pupils, and none have gone on to bigger things after resigning from their posts. (Video buffs might recognise Michael Cronin, the actor who played Mr Baxter, in a delightful cameo role as an incompetent builder's mate in an episode of *Fawlty Towers*!) Head-teachers have perhaps been most notable, and most conspicuous, during the not infrequent outbreaks of pupil anarchy at Grange Hill, for instance Mr Llewellyn during the SAG rebellion concerning school uniform, and Mrs McClusky. She had to cope with a wave of vandalism right at the start of her tenure and later was confronted with the sit-in, more of Gripper Stebson's excesses, and Imelda's fibre-glass antics referred to above. It cannot be said that the head-teachers at Grange Hill have been manifestly lacking in the guts and determination to keep order in the school and punish offenders when necessary. However, the wealth of creative activity in Grange Hill, and the tolerance of such projects as the school magazine, school radio and school council, demonstrate that Grange Hill as an institution is commendably democratic and indeed possesses a far-sightedness which is the envy of many real-life schools.

The class teachers range from strictly disciplinarian to liberal and creative. Amongst the former, Mr Hicks, a sports master with the unpleasant habit of pushing boys about, had to be dismissed in 1981 for causing injury to "Stewpot" Stewart (Mark Burdis). Another sports master, Mr Baxter, stood no nonsense, and was instrumental in the failure of the SAG campaign. Perhaps the definitive teacher in the disciplinarian category has been Mr Bronson. Not only did he not want to understand Danny Kendall's problems but he also made life a misery for "Ant" Jones in 1986 and caused him to run away from home for a while. This particular story-line illustrated only too well the dangers of imposing too strict a regime on youngsters (or perhaps the scriptwriters were simply allowing Bronson to get his revenge after having his toupee taken by some mischievous pupils in the series before!) Some teachers have, by contrast, striven for an affinity with the pupils; Miss Mather, Miss Summers, Mr McGuffy and Miss Warrington have all assisted in the production of school musicals. Mr McGuffy was nicknamed "Scruffy" for his casual appearance and was so popular that when he was suspended for looking so scruffy the pupils successfully demonstrated for his return. Mr "Sooty" Sutcliffe assisted Cathy Hargreaves and two of her friends in their musical development by forming a band called Sooty and the Sootettes. Miss Gordon, Mr King and Mr Hopwood have all been the subject of "crushes" by pupils; indeed the crush by Claire Scott (Paula Ann Bland) on Mr Hopwood resulted in Claire's father hurrying down to the school to "sort out" the object of her affections, even though nothing had actually happened at all. Ironically one adult enthusiast of Grange Hill admitted that it was her passion for Mr Hopwood that made her watch it! One of the best examples of a teacher going out of her way to help a wayward pupil, and persevering when the cause seemed hopeless, was Miss Booth's assistance to Danny Kendall; this contrasted markedly with Mr Bronson's bullying approach to the problem. *Grange Hill* has highlighted the difficulties and embarrassment that could arise from having a parent on the staff or the board of governors; although Laura Reagan's mother, one of the teachers, was popular and well-liked, the father of Laura's friend Julia Glover was, as a school governor, certainly not. It would not be fair to say that the teachers' own problems were glossed over; the 1994 series ended with Mr Robson virtually in tears over the decision of Martha, a stunning young American, to leave him and return to her native land.

By the mid-1990s, *Grange Hill* had changed quite considerably from even its mid-80s appearance. The catchy but almost incongruously corny signature tune, and equally anaemic cartoon opening captions, had been replaced by more powerful, upbeat music with impressively artistic visual accompaniment. The filming on location in Gorlitz, close to the Polish border, made earlier school trips

and classroom activity seem parochial by comparison, even when that activity w
seen to be addressing issues of vital importance. The portrayal of disturbi
images of Eastern European life - the neo-Fascist subculture, the bleak housi
estates surrounding the football ground, and the constant reminders of earli
conflicts and ideologies, demonstrated a commitment to depicting much deep
social problems with which other students were confronted.

It is perhaps slightly paradoxical that whereas most pupils will claim to disli
school, and the programme paints hardly the rosiest picture of the rising gene
ation, it is pupils themselves who consistently vote *Grange Hill* their favouri
programme. It did not take long for the popularity of what Cadogan and Cra
described as an "innovatory and addictive" programme to spread. Five years aft
its inception, the viewing figures had climbed to twelve million, representing :
incredible 75% of all those between the ages of 5 and 15! (The truth is, of cours
that many viewers were adults.) A survey in 1981 showed it was the favouri
programme of six to fourteen-year-olds; in 1987, 36% of all children in the UK sa
they watched it; in 1993, twenty-five per cent of all four to eighteen-year-olds we
regularly watching it. Redmond claims that 75% of all 12-25 year olds in Brita
have watched *Grange Hill*, and it has been sold to a number of European countri
as well as Australia, New Zealand and Canada. In 1979, 1980 and 1987, th
programme won the BAFTA Childrens Entertainment award. For three yea
running it won the Multi-Coloured Swap Shop Award for Best Children's Pr
gramme; in 1981 it was voted Favourite Children's Programme in a *Sun* Reader
Poll; and in 1984 it won the Anna Scher Theatre Award for Favourite Televisio
Programme. All these facts and statistics suggest that the series is continuing t
succeed in doing what it set out to do. As well as being featured in the Guinnes
Book of Classic British Television, *Grange Hill* was also accorded the honour o
an entry in a *Book of Cult TV* which was published in 1994! The very coverage o
key issues affecting comprehensive school pupils can reassure viewers faced wit
similar issues that they are not alone in having to face them. Indeed man
youngsters have told the makers of the programme that the series had helped the
in showing some of the problems that might be faced at secondary school, and ho
to deal with them. As a fourteen-year-old girl said after the first series: "It wa
written for us, the children - the pupils at schools like *Grange Hill* who reall
understand what they are like."

It is not surprising that given the controversial subject matter, the series has ha
its critics. Parents saw it as anti-authority and anarchic, blaming the programm
for real-life bouts of bullying, truancy and disrespect, and some parents banne
their children from watching the programme. Mary Whitehouse said the serie
encouraged bad behaviour and undermined teachers' authority, and she criticise
the "pupil pregnancy" story-line on the basis that children's viewing time was a

inappropriate forum for the discussion of abortion. In 1979 the Womens Institute of Castle Cary went as far as to pass a motion demanding the abolition of the programme! Teachers said the programme encouraged hooliganism and bad language, "and how dare children call teachers by their first names!" An official of the National Union of Schoolmasters said in 1980: "The teachers come out as buffoons and all we see are strikes and sit-ins, larceny and violence." The episode referred to above involving the boat race in the swimming pool was not only criticised as "wildly unlikely" but the critics said that a teacher ought to have been present supervising the pool, and the offenders set a "bad example". The critics seemed to have overlooked the fact that the incident had happened in real life, the supervising teacher was attending to a badly injured foot at the time, and the offenders were seen to be punished! The creators of the programme, and many others, hurried to defend it, maintaining that its tales were cautionary. The BBC claimed that although it showed school and teachers "warts and all" the programme took a clear moral stance and explained the consequences of actions. Redmond defended his story-lines staunchly. He made no apology for the realism of the action, stating: "Adopting a head-in-the-sand attitude does no service to anyone." He pointed out that many of the problems featured in the series pre-existed *Grange Hill*, and claimed that "no-one seemed to remember that bullying existed before *Grange Hill*." He maintained, despite the accent on realism, that the influence of the programme was over-exaggerated, and that in any event there was nothing objectionable about the stance adopted by the programme; he cited an early incident of classroom rebellion, where the programme was criticised for having shown the problem to have been dealt with on a conciliatory rather than confrontational basis. Even a parent was moved to write to say that she did not find anything wrong with the programme and could not understand why so many people complained about it. She did go on to admit that the main reason she watched it was a crush on one of the teachers! Some pupils have even said that their own school is *worse* than *Grange Hill*, pointing out that the bad language for which the programme has been criticised is mild compared to that which is used in real-life comprehensives. It was pointed out that it was not so much the language, rather the accent, to which critics of "Gwane Jill" were really objecting. The scripts contain little language that is offensive, and on the one occasion when an unacceptable expletive was uttered, the word was cut out of the repeat programme. The irony was that the offender was merely an extra in a crowd scene, and Redmond thought that the word would have been considered totally inoffensive in the North! Others have defended the programme on the basis of the positive aspects of school life that it projects, and its pioneering of certain schemes as described above.

A number of people have very special reason to be grateful to *Grange Hill*. For several of the stars of the programme, leaving the comprehensive meant a graduation to the wider showbiz world. Two of the stars have since become household names; Susan Tully went on to play Michelle Fowler in the immensely popular BBC soap opera *EastEnders*, and Todd Carty, having had his own series as an adult Tucker Jenkins in *Tucker's Luck* joined Susan Tully in *EastEnders* by playing Michelle's brother Mark. This followed the suicide of the character originally playing that role. Nobody has fared quite as well as those two, but there have been some successes. Paula Ann Bland, who played Claire Scott, has since worked on the popular children's programme *Crackerjack* and with the well-known popgroup the Supremes in Africa; Lyndy Brill, who played Cathy Hargreaves, got a part in the West End musical *Evita*; Terry Sue Patt, who played Benny Green, has appeared on the *Lenny Henry Show*; and Melissa Wilks who appeared as Jackie has been seen in the Pink Floyd film *The Wall*. Several, including John Alford who played Robbie Wright, have been in demand for so-called Personal Appearances at clubs and other functions. Others have come and then quietly disappeared again, with no obvious leap to stardom. An example was Michelle Herbert, who played Trisha Yates in early series; in 1993 she was a jeweller in Dundee and confessed, rather to her disappointment, that nobody recognised her any more!

Although repeats of the early series were shown in the early 1990s, no *Grange Hill* videos have been produced. However, a number of novels about life at the comprehensive have been written, and diaries and annuals have also been prepared, thus ensuring a certain immortality for the school and its characters. Inevitably, the impact of the novels has not been as great as that of the programmes themselves, and their success has ridden exclusively and unashamedly on the back of the television series. Ironically the book trade may actually have been assisted by television in this case, in that the books have sold extremely well even amongst children who are not habitual readers.

The novels have used existing TV storylines as the bases for the plots, but have not simply set out the scripts of the television programmes in published form. Despite their limitations, they have striven to capture some of the spirit and atmosphere of the programmes, with some disturbing writing which would certainly have helped to etch some of the story-lines even more deeply into the memory. Cadogan and Craig wrote: "The books provide, for *Grange Hill*'s heroes and heroines, experiences rather more complex than the small-screen programmes can encompass. The... books offer a sufficient range of characters for almost every kind of child to find in them a focus of interest." All the extracts given below are from books written by Redmond himself. It should however be noted that Redmond did not write all the books based on the series, a significant number having been written by Jan Needle and the established children's author Robert Leeson.

Arguably the programme's most famous issue, Zammo's drug taking, was deal with in *Grange Hill on the Run:*

It was 11.00pm. Zammo was crying. Quietly. Tears rolling down his cheeks. Trying to suppress any sound but unable to stop the sobbing. Neither could he stop the sniffing nor the noise in the back of his throat as his body tried to gulp in the air his lungs needed between sobs. He was trying to keep as quiet as possible, although the noise seemed deafening in the echoing subway. Zammo was cold. Zammo was hungry. Zammo was still withdrawing from heroin. Zammo was desperately un-happy...

Zammo stood by the door, listening to all this. He had heard it all before, but each time it had made him think about what had happened to him. How the coffee mugs representing his life had soon become filled with heroin. He still didn't really know how. Or even why. He had spoken to the other addicts in the Unit. They couldn't explain it either. Everyone was right. It was stupid. Those posters the Government had stuck up everywhere. They were right too. Heroin screws you up. But he still couldn't explain why he had started. That's what made him feel so useless. So inadequate.

Zammo's drug problem is one of many issues the books have sought to tackle alongside the TV series. Another is bullying:

Zammo was actually on his feet when the shadow fell on them. Jonah looked up but couldn't make out who it was because the sun was immediately behind him. However, the worn and scuffed DM's gave him a clue and a quick look at Zammo's worried face confirmed the fact, even before one of the DM's whipped out and kicked him on the thigh.

"You first years?"

"Er... yes," Jonah replied.

"What's it got to do with you?" Zammo asked, then wished he hadn't, as Gripper's hand was suddenly gripped around Zammo's left ear. The pain was almost unbear-able; Zammo now appreciated the aptness of the nickname. It was almost impossible to believe that anyone could squeeze so hard with just one hand, but the agony down the left side of his head convinced him...

"Aaarrgghh... get off!"

"I never heard you say you were sorry."

"What for... aarrgghh!" Gripper tightened the hold.

"All right... I'm sorry."

"Sorry, what?"

"Er... very sorry...Owwww..."

"Use my full title."

"Sorry... er King Gripper," Zammo squealed. He was having difficulty in holding back the tears.

"Sorry, your Highness, King Gripper."

"Sorry... your... Highness, King Gripper."

"And you won't be disrespectful again?"

"No... honest... aarrgghh." Zammo squealed again as Gripper gave one last twist that forced a tear out of Zammo's eye.

(Tucker & Co

Roland's obesity, and indeed the problems of any "misfit" at school, seem somehow even more hideous when words are applied to them:

As he progressed through life so his physical appearance grew. By the time he reached Grange Hill he had gone from tubby to blubber, bubble, fatty, fatso and now to Roly Poly. What Roland couldn't figure out, was why people had to make an issue out of it. Still, in more confident moments, which were becoming fewer, he realised it wasn't just him they picked on, but anyone who was different in any way, shape or form. Four eyes; lanky; shorty; rake; stump (for a boy with only one leg); chinky; paki; wog and so on and so on. Once you were identified as a target that was it.

(Tucker & Co

Perhaps I should go on another diet, he mused, as he broke off the end of a chocolate cream bar and devoured half in one easy chomp. Never works, though, always get too hungry. Perhaps I'm naturally like this. Why should I change? Perhaps I've got a rare disease like people get when they're trying to stay thin. Wonder if I should get Mum to take me to the doctor's. Mind you, she reckons I'll grow out of it doesn't she? And Dad. He reckons it's puppy fat. He looked down at his stomach forcing its way out between the two sides of his blazer.

(Tucker & Co

The above extract shows that the innermost thoughts of the pupils could be communicated more intimately and compellingly in book form than through television. Another example of "thinking out loud" comes during Ant's darkest days as he copes with the tyrannical Mr Bronson:

He kicked at a discarded orange juice carton in frustration. All the trouble and worry. For what. Nothing. Nothing'll happen to Bronson will it? It never does. I'll be the one who'll get it in the neck. I'll be the one who'll get it for running off. For bunking school. For trespassing in that old house. For trying to steal from that fruit stall. Knowing my luck, that old drunk in the house probably had a heart attack when he saw me and I'll get it for that.

(Grange Hill On the Run)

All this because of him, Ant continued. Me. Mum. Dad. Georgina. The rest of the family. Probably a few at school. Everyone suffering because of one bloke. One bloke has it in for me, and everyone else has to suffer. I even nearly got run over. And for what? Nothing. I'll go back and get it off Mum and Dad. Georgina probably won't even speak to me again.

(Grange Hill on the Run)

And I'll have to leave Grange Hill. They wouldn't let me stay, even if I wanted to. And he gets away with it. Well he won't this time. Not this time, Bronson.

(Grange Hill on the Run)

It is worth remembering that unless videos are ever made, it is likely that the books will be the only readily available permanent record of life at Grange Hill, and those who in future decades read the following pieces of dialogue might wish to pause and consider the comparisons with Harold Avery, Charles Hamilton and Angela Brazil:

"Where've you been?" Robbie asked.

"Taking a pike at the Speaking Wall," Ziggy replied.

"A what?" Robbie asked, rather puzzled. He still wasn't used to Ziggy's Liverpool accent, or his slang.

"A pike," Ziggy repeated. Then added in response to Robbie's blank stare, "A blimp. A scan. Casting me bins over it? Flippin' 'eck, Robbie. Haven't you heard of nothing?"

(Grange Hill Graffiti)

"Well, we can stop giving him all the evidence he needs for a start," Georgina said in reply to Ant. "What good will it do staying off school?"

"What good will it do going to school?" Ant replied, with a touch of sarcasm in his voice. "He'll only pick on me again, won't he?"

"Not if you keep out of his way, he won't."

"How can I? He's my bloody Form Tutor, isn't he?"

(Grange Hill Graffiti)

What of the creator of *Grange Hill*, Phil Redmond himself? He soon graduated to writing for adults, going on to set up Mersey Productions and then creating the soap opera *Brookside* for Channel Four in 1982. Set in Liverpool, Redmond's own home city, it soon became Channel Four's most popular programme. Without the success of *Grange Hill* it is arguable that *Brookside* might never have been created. Although Phil Redmond does not script *Grange Hill* now, his name still rightly appears on the credits at the end of each programme, as a reminder to both new and established fans of the man who first brought the sometimes cruel, sometimes hilarious, always fascinating world of the big comprehensive into the lounges an front rooms of Great Britain.

Phil Redmond has been careful not to overestimate the effect of the series c the behaviour of schoolchildren in real life. However, it would be a shame if th very positive approach to such issues as drug taking did not have some benefici effect around the classrooms of Great Britain, just as it would be a shame if th pupils in those classrooms did not derive some positive benefit from seeing the own experiences, hopes and fears acted out in front of them. Numerous oth authors have both preceded and followed Phil Redmond in producing scho stories that address the social needs of youngsters and do not attempt to create fantasy or escapist world for the readers. The immediate success of *Grange H* would seem to suggest that there will always be a place for the realistic, real-li drama which its writers have brought to the homes of so many millions. As Ph Redmond said: "Its continued success is due to the fact that it deals with issu and topics of concern with which schoolchildren can identify... So long as th audience stays with the programme and keeps indicating that we are getting right... I will always want to continue."

The current school story scene is interesting. Cynics might argue that the golde years of schools fiction for children have disappeared; that the book market ha suffered and will continue to suffer through the proliferation of television, comp ters and other juvenile distractions. Publishers, fearful of becoming victims of th recession which had gripped Britain in the early 1990's, have become mor selective about the books they accept, which reduces the chances of a new, excitir author being recognised and adopted. Even if television were selected as a mea of introducing such an author to the youth of today, there is no guarantee he c she would become recognised or successful, bearing in mind the bewilderin choice of both terrestrial and satellite channels that are now available to su scribers. In an era where rapid - often terrifyingly rapid - change is a fact of lif nobody can predict the fate of the school story over the next decade, let alone th next century.

However, such views, apart from being unduly gloomy, are also somewh simplistic. A number of traditional school story writers have emerged in th post-war decades and enjoyed considerable success even in the 1970s and 1980 Ann Digby, with her Trebizon series, Antonia Forest, with her stories about th Marlow family, and Harriet Martyn, writing about Balcombe Hall, have shown th there is still a market for books about life in a traditional girls' school. A numbe of compilation volumes have been prepared and recently published, not for th nostalgia market but for a new generation of children. These have encompasse

a wide range of styles and traditions, and because they have included chapters from books of well-known authors which could not be regarded as "school stories" the quality of the writing has been very impressive. A compilation volume published by Kingfisher Books in 1989 contained material by M.R.James, Charlotte Brontë, William Golding, Mark Twain and Keith Waterhouse as well as children's authors such as Gene Kemp and Talbot Baines Reed, both of whom have been referred to above. Alison Prince, Gillian Gross, Jan Mark and, as we have seen, Gene Kemp, have bravely attempted to portray contemporary comprehensive school life in their books; Robert Westall, though not specifically a school story writer, was singled out by Carpenter and Prichard for the "chilling accuracy" of his treatment of boarding school life.

There are other reasons to be optimistic about the British school story. In the 1990's there has been an unprecedented revival of interest in the work of the earlier masters of this century, not only the five authors studied in the preceding chapters, but many of their contemporaries. The forces of change and uncertainty have inspired for many adults an interest in and nostalgia for the stories which they enjoyed as youngsters; stories which are so well written that they are as accessible and enjoyable now as they were when first published, if not even

more so. Reference has already been made to *Greyfriars For Grown-ups*, which examined the world of Billy Bunter and its characters from an adult viewpoint. Far from being a rather patronising critique, it was a glorious appreciation of Charles Hamilton's writing style. The publishers of that book, Howard Baker, are not the only publishers who have revived the work of the masters for present-day readers to enjoy. Facsimile reprints of some of the Elinor Brent-Dyer titles have become available in recent years; first editions of the works of even Anthony Buckeridge are in great demand; and a number of second hand booksellers regularly issue lengthy catalogues consisting exclusively of children's books. A West Sussex dealer was in 1994 asking £47.50 for a signed first edition of Anthony Buckeridge's *Thanks to Jennings*, and a children's second-hand bookshop in Cecil Court in the West End of London was in the same year asking £50 for first editions of Elinor Brent-Dyer's later works. Whole bookshops, not just in London, have been given over almost exclusively to the sale of second-hand children's books, with considerable shelf space devoted to school stories. There are a large number of private mail-order dealers too.

The fact is that the place and method of purchase are irrelevant. Whether one pays up to £50 or more for a rare edition bought perhaps as a little investment, or one pays a couple of pounds for a dog-eared reprint, one is delving into literary history and helping to keep a treasure house of children's literature in existence. It may be motivated by unashamed nostalgia and escapism, or it may be motivated by a hankering for an age which has long gone. Yet it is this author's humble opinion that all of the subjects of this book would be only too delighted to think that their work was still capable of providing enjoyment, happiness and pleasure to other people long after they themselves had laid down their pens for the last time.

THE END

SERIES OF GRANGE HILL
(With the exception of the first series which went out weekly on Wednesday afternoons, and the eighth series which appeared on Mondays, all series have consisted of 25-minute episodes on both Tuesday and Friday afternoons, usually at 5.10pm)

1st series: 9 episodes, 8.2.78 - 5.4.78
2nd series: 18 episodes, 2.1.79 - 2.3.79
3rd series: 16 episodes, 8.1.80 - 29.2.80
4th series: 18 episodes, 30.12.80 - 27.2.81
A Christmas Special appeared on 28.12.81
5th series: 18 episodes, 5.1.82 - 5.3.82
6th series: 18 episodes, 4.1.83 - 4.3.83
7th series: 18 episodes, 3.1.84 - 2.3.84
8th series: 16 episodes, 18.2.85 - 22.4.85
9th series: 24 episodes, 7.1.86 - 1.4.86
10th series: 24 episodes, 6.1.87 - 27.3.87
11th series: 20 episodes, 5.1.88 - 11.3.88
12th series: 20 episodes, 3.1.89 - 10.3.89
13th series: 20 episodes, 2.1.90 - 9.3.90
14th series: 20 episodes, 8.1.91 - 15.3.91
15th series: 20 episodes, 7.1.92 - 13.3.92
16th series: 20 episodes, 5.1.93 - 12.3.93
17th series: 20 episodes, 4.1.94 - 11.3.94

GRANGE HILL BOOKS BY PHIL REDMOND

Grange Hill Stories (BBC Publications, 1979)
Tucker & Co (BBC Publications, 1982)
Grange Hill On the Run (Magnet, 1986)
Grange Hill Graffiti (Magnet, 1986)
Grange Hill After Hours (Magnet, 1986)
Grange Hill Rebels (Magnet, 1987)*
Grange Hill Heroes (Hamish Hamilton, 1987)*
Grange Hill Partners (Magnet, 1988)*

* - denotes written with David Angus.

Phil Redmond also contributed to the *Grange Hill Annual* and helped to compile *Grange Hill - The Official Companion* in 1988.

ABOUT THE AUTHOR

David Bathurst is a solicitor and legal adviser to the Arundel and Chichester Magistrates in West Sussex. His first book was **The Selsey Tram**, published by Phillimore in 1992, and he has made some contributions to the **Justice of the Peace** magazine; he regularly scripts tapes for the Chichester Area Talking News For The Blind. Whilst not working or writing he enjoys singing, cycling and amateur dramatics. He lives just outside Chichester with his wife Lizzie.

BIBLIOGRAPHY

N.B. The bibliography lists commentaries and reference works, *not* the texts themselves. The sources of quotations from the texts are given in each chapter.

The Magnet Companion [Howard Baker, 1971]

*Frank Richards - the Chap Behind the Chums - Mary Cadogan [Viking, 1988]

*Chin Up Chest Out Jemima! - Mary Cadogan [Bonnington Books, 1989]

*You're A Brick Angela! - Mary Cadogan & Patricia Craig [Gollancz, 1976]

*The Oxford Companion to Children's Literature - Humphrey Carpenter & Mari Prichard
[Oxford University Press, 1984]

*Modern Children's First Editions - Joseph Connolly [Macdonald,1988]

The Guinness Book of Classic British Television - Paul Cornell, Martin Day & Keith Topping
[Guinness, 1993]

*Phil Redmond's Grange Hill - the Official Companion - compiled by Andrew Corrie and
John McCready [Weidenfeld, 1988]

Take a Cold Tub, Sir! - Jack Cox [Lutterworth, 1982]

*The Oxford Book of Schooldays - Patricia Craig [Oxford University Press, 1993]

*Daisy Pulls It Off - Denise Deegan [Samuel French, 1983]

Who's Who In Children's Literature - ed. Brian Doyle [Evelyn,1968]

The Schoolgirl Ethic - Gillian Freeman [Allen Lane, 1976]

Goodnight Children Everywhere - Ian Hartley [Midas, 1983]

*Into the Box of Delights - Anna Home [BBC Enterprises Limited, 1993]

*The Independent Newspaper

*Bullies, Beaks and Flannelled Fools - Robert Kirkpatrick [privately published, 1990]

Cult TV - Jon E. Lewis & Penny Stempel [Pavilion, 1993]

The Men Behind Boys Fiction - W.O.G.Lofts & D.J.Adley [Howard Baker, 1970]

*Behind The Chalet School - Helen McClelland [New Horizon, 1981]

*The Chalet School Companion - Helen McClelland [Armada, 1994]

School Stories - chosen by Jan Mark [Kingfisher, 1989]

Girls Will Be Girls - Arthur Marshall [Hamish Hamilton, 1974]

Life's Rich Pageant - Arthur Marshall [Hamish Hamilton, 1984]

*From Brown to Bunter - P.W.Musgrave [Routledge & Kegan Paul,1985]

*The Cambridge Guide to Literature in English - Ian Ousby [Cambridge University Press, 1993]

The Collectors' Book of Boys' Stories - Eric Quayle [Studio Vista, 1973]

The Heirs of Tom Brown - Isabel Quigly [Chatto & Windus, 1982]

Buckeridge at 80 - David Schutte [Book and Magazine Collector, May 1993]

Greyfriars For Grown-Ups - Lawrence Sutton [Howard Baker, 1980]

*The Box of Delights - Geoff Tibballs & Hilary Kingsley [Macmillan, London Ltd., 1989]

*Written For Children - John Rowe Townsend [Bodley Head, 1990]

Boys Will Be Boys - E.S.Turner [Michael Joseph, 1948]